Howard Sounes is the author of eleven previous books, including biographies of Bob Dylan, Charles Bukowski and Paul McCartney, and three true crime books. Working as a reporter for the *Mirror* in 1994, he broke stories in the Fred and Rosemary West murder case, which he worked on for two years, giving the case its name – the House of Horrors – leading to publication of his first book, *Fred & Rose*, a true crime classic.

Howard also presents the podcast series, *Unheard: The Fred & Rose West Tapes*. The series went to number one in the podcast charts in the UK and was top 20 in the US and Australia, with over three million downloads. Most recently, he acted as Senior Producer on *Fred & Rose West: A British Horror Story*, the number one Netflix series in the UK and a global top ten hit.

THE FRED WEST TAPES

Secrets of the Fred & Rose West Murder Investigation

HOWARD SOUNES

First published in the UK in 2025 by Blink Publishing
An imprint of Bonnier Books UK
5th Floor, HYLO, 105 Bunhill Row,
London, EC1Y 8LZ

Copyright © Howard Sounes, 2025

All rights reserved.

No part of this publication may be reproduced, stored or transmitted in any form or by any means, electronic, mechanical, photocopying or otherwise, without the prior written permission of the publisher.

The right of author to be identified as Author of this work has been asserted by him/her/them in accordance with the Copyright, Designs and Patents Act, 1988.

A CIP catalogue record for this book is available from the British Library.

Hardback ISBN: 9781789468618
Trade Paperback ISBN: 9781789468625

Also available as an ebook and an audiobook

1 3 5 7 9 10 8 6 4 2

Design and Typeset by Envy Design Ltd
Printed and bound in Great Britain by Clays Ltd, Elcograf S.p.A.

Every reasonable effort has been made to trace copyright holders of material reproduced in this book, but if any have been inadvertently overlooked the publishers would be glad to hear from them.

The authorised representative in the EEA is
Bonnier Books UK (Ireland) Limited.
Registered office address: Floor 3, Block 3, Miesian Plaza,
Dublin 2, D02 Y754, Ireland
compliance@bonnierbooks.ie

www.bonnierbooks.co.uk

Also by Howard Sounes:

CRIME

Fred & Rose: The Full Story of Fred and Rose West and the Gloucester House of Horrors
Heist: The True Story of the World's Biggest Cash Robbery
This Woman: Myra Hindley's Prison Love Affair and Escape Attempt

BIOGRAPHY

Down the Highway: The Life of Bob Dylan
Charles Bukowski: Locked in the Arms of a Crazy Life
Bukowski in Pictures
Notes from the Velvet Underground: The Life of Lou Reed
Fab: An Intimate Life of Paul McCartney

HISTORY

Seventies: The Sights, Sounds and Ideas of a Brilliant Decade
Amy, 27: Amy Winehouse and the 27 Club

SPORT

The Wicked Game: Arnold Palmer, Jack Nicklaus, Tiger Woods, and the Story of Modern Golf

CONTENTS

INTRODUCTION	IX
HEATHER UNDER THE PATIO	1
SHIRLEY AND 'SHIRLEY'S MATE'	21
A PASSION FOR BONDAGE	37
FRED'S EARLY LIFE	53
NINE MORE (APPROX.)	71
EVIDENCE OF TORTURE	101
SEARCHING EVERYWHERE	119
OUR FAMILY OF LOVE	143
THE CODE OF SILENCE	171
THE DEVIL AND HIS WIFE	189
PLAN B	209
TOUGH COPS WANT ANSWERS	223
ROSE DON'T WANT ME	241
THE DEPTHS OF HUMAN DEPRAVITY	261
ACKNOWLEDGEMENTS	285
SOURCE NOTES	289
INDEX	319

DC Hazel Savage: You're enjoying it, aren't you?
Fred West: Yeah, why not?
DC Savage: I don't know. I don't understand it.
Fred West: You will in the end.

INTRODUCTION

Over thirty years ago, when I was a twenty-nine-year-old reporter, working for a national newspaper, I broke one of the first big stories about the Fred and Rose West murder case. Between 1967 and 1987, Fred West murdered twelve young women and children in and around the city of Gloucester, a little more than 100 miles west of London, most of the crimes committed with his wife, Rose. As rare as serial murderers are, married serial killers are exceptionally unusual. That made the story a sensation.

A news reporter gets used to covering a lot of different stories, most of which are here today, gone tomorrow. When inside information about the West case was first leaked to me, in 1994, I knew at once that this story was special. It was profoundly weird with a mysterious quality that intrigued me to find out more. In revealing that the Wests' home at 25 Cromwell Street in Gloucester was filled with human remains, a colleague and I gave the case its newspaper name, the House of Horrors.

THE FRED WEST TAPES

I am not especially proud of that; it wasn't primarily my idea. Frankly, there was little skill involved in my breaking the story – it was luck, as I explain later – and much of the subsequent reporting I did for my paper was unexceptional. However, I seized the opportunity to write a book about the case, alongside my day job, and in writing what became *Fred & Rose* I gave all my energy to the story, telling it as well as I could, without newspaper hyperbole. I wanted to write a quality book that would still be read after my newspaper clippings had turned to dust. I wanted to capture the essence of the case.

Fred & Rose was a bestseller on publication in 1995, and it has remained in print. I left newspapers to write books full time a couple of years later, when I had a second book in hand. As I made a new career for myself as an author, I moved away from crime to concentrate on writing carefully researched biographies of exceptional people whose life and work inspired me, including Bob Dylan and the writer Charles Bukowski. However, the ongoing success of *Fred & Rose* kept pulling me back. When twenty-five years passed, and the book continued to sell, I decided to update it. I also made a podcast series that went to number one in the podcast charts; and I made the first of several television documentaries about the Wests, which was the start of a third interlinked career as a TV producer.

From the beginning, explaining the Wests to myself was my primary motivation. Understanding Fred and Rose and their relationship was an investigative challenge and an intellectual stretch. The subject was so fascinating that I would have written that first book for nothing. What sort of people kill together as part of their marriage? What was going on in their heads to drive them to commit such awful acts? The crimes were so extreme that I had never imagined such things possible. This takes a lot of thinking about, and research, to understand. It is

INTRODUCTION

the nub of the thing that gets a person sufficiently interested in a subject to write a book about it. The back story and psychology was, and remains, as fascinating to me as what the Wests actually did. That is true of all my books, which now include three crime stories: the Wests, of course; *Heist*, which is a story about a robbery gang; and *This Woman*, a book about Myra Hindley in prison.

Uncovering the truth about Fred and Rose has been a long quest. Crime is secretive. Criminals hide their actions and motivations, and all the facts were not available in the 1990s. I couldn't speak to everybody I wanted to while the case was unfolding. As the years have passed, however, I have met many more people, and I have found missing pieces of the jigsaw puzzle, fitting the whole picture together in my mind. Recently, I had a breakthrough when I was able to listen to recordings of over 100 hours of Fred West's police interviews. I had heard some of these interviews before, but suddenly I was able to hear them all. Criminals often say little or nothing in custody, replying 'no comment' to police questions. Unusually, Fred talked almost endlessly. He gave detectives his life story, from his childhood up to the time of his arrest, including the story of his two marriages, and his many crimes. He told lies but he also admitted to the murders, and he led the police to the graves of his victims, so his interviews cannot be dismissed. Importantly, even when he lied he revealed himself, as people do, in every word that he spoke, by the way in which he spoke.

Tape recordings of these remarkable interviews feature in a new Netflix documentary series, *Fred & Rose West: A British Horror Story*, a project I initiated and helped to produce, and that I also appear in. Transcripts of the interviews are part of this new book, more than are featured in the series, complemented by all the knowledge I have accumulated. As well as Fred's interviews, I quote from Rose West's police interviews, and I draw on witness evidence. I have met and interviewed most of the key people in the story over the years, including members of the West family and the victims' families, who have helped me to understand the human cost of these crimes. I bring all this information together in this new book, which focuses on Fred West in the interview room, reporting his words verbatim, with a few light corrections for clarity, from his arrest until his death. As he was questioned, a serial murder story was revealed.

As I listened to Fred talk to the police, I felt that I got to know the man as never before. His rough country voice, his quaint turns of phrase, the twisted obsessions that formed his character all became as familiar to me as someone I knew personally. I felt that I had got inside his mind at last, as you will. Much of what Fred said is disturbing and it can be shocking. Where he lied, or evaded the truth, I have interjected to explain and help guide you through the labyrinth of the interviews to what I hope is a final complete understanding of Fred and Rose West.

1
HEATHER UNDER THE PATIO

Thursday, 24 February 1994 • Day One of the Investigation
Gloucester Central Police Station

'You're digging me place up, so carry on doing it.'
FRED WEST

A scruffy middle-aged man in working clothes, short with curly brown hair, bushy sideburns and bushy eyebrows, a broken, misshapen nose and dull blue eyes, walked out of the rain into Gloucester Central Police Station at 7:50 PM and asked to see Detective Constable Hazel Savage. The police station was within a large office building in the centre of Gloucester, one of Britain's smallest cities, containing divisional headquarters. The visitor wanted to know why the police were at his house, upsetting his wife. DC Savage took him to an interview room on the first floor, where they were joined by a second officer. A cassette tape recorder was switched on.

DC Hazel Savage: First of all ... can you give us your full name?
Fred West: Frederick Walter Stephen West.
DC Savage: And your age?

THE FRED WEST TAPES

Fred West: Fifty-two.
DC Savage: Thank you. And your address?
Fred West: 25 Cromwell Street, Gloucester …
DC Savage: I don't think you mind if we call you Fred. Is that right?

Fred had no problem with that. He was Fred to everyone. Three years Fred's junior, Hazel Savage had been a CID officer since 1968, and she had known Fred for virtually her entire career. He had been in a lot of trouble with the police over the years, though nothing like this. 'Things are happening at your house at the moment,' she told Fred. 'The police have been there this afternoon and they are, in fact, digging up your back patio. You'll remember that when we last spoke [we] were concerned about Heather?' Heather was the eldest daughter of Fred and his wife, Rose West. She hadn't been seen since she was sixteen – nearly seven years ago. 'Let's go back to the beginning, Fred, and talk about how and when Heather disappeared.'

'Heather wanted to disappear. Right?' Fred spoke as a Herefordshire countryman, dropping the H on his daughter's name so she became 'eather. He appeared relaxed, even friendly, but it soon became apparent that he was a crude man. He told DC Savage that his daughter left home after a family row to do with an older female friend of hers who, he said, wore a very short skirt. 'Just about to the bottom of her knickers. You know, if she bent or lifted that, you could see everything.'

'Hmm,' said DC Savage, who was used to Fred's smutty talk.

He said that this woman was his daughter's 'lezzy friend'. Fred was sex mad and far from politically correct in how he spoke about women. He said that Heather and her friend planned to run off together.

DC Savage told Fred that she had made extensive inquiries

and there was no trace of Heather since 1987 – no medical records, bank or social security paper trail – most unusual for a young woman who would now be in her twenties. The detective had a direct manner. 'So, do you think she's dead or alive?' she asked Fred bluntly.

Fred West: Alive as far as I know. Why do you think anything else?

Suddenly, Fred added something which he thought might be of interest. He said he had seen Heather recently in Birmingham. She was dealing drugs. Before she left home, he said Heather had given drugs to some of his other children, including his youngest son, Barry. Heather had also been disrespectful to her mother, which caused trouble at home. 'Every time Rose spoke to her, she just bloody insulted her and walked away.' So they gave Heather money and she left with her friend in the mini-skirt, who drove a Mini car. He had kept in touch with his daughter, however, assuring the police that 'me and Heather was very close'.

DC Savage had heard another story. The police had spoken to some of the West children – it was a large family – and they said that their dad may have killed Heather and buried her under the back garden patio at 25 Cromwell Street. 'They say that it was a family talk, when they used to ask [you] about Heather, that she was under the patio,' Savage told Fred. 'Now, if that is true ... and you're laughing.'

'Oh, for God's sake. I mean, do you believe it?' he chuckled. 'I mean, you're digging me place up, so carry on doing it ...'

DC Hazel Savage: That's right. And obviously, if there's anybody under there, Fred, we will find them ... But if there is nobody under there ...

THE FRED WEST TAPES

Fred West: You would have dug that up for nothing. But you'll put my patio back.

Fred didn't seem at all worried. He gave the impression of being a carefree fellow who knew his rights and would be quick to demand compensation if, as he suggested, the police were making a big mistake.

The police had been at 25 Cromwell Street all afternoon. Rose was at home with her twenty-one-year-old second daughter May when five plain-clothes police officers, including DC Savage, arrived at 1:25 PM. May answered the door to them. There were more officers sitting outside in a van. The detectives asked to see Rose, who was watching the soap opera *Neighbours* on TV. They told her that they had a warrant to search the house and garden for Heather.

'This is stupid,' said Rose.

As Hazel Savage tried to talk to Rose, search team officers wearing blue overalls and Wellington boots started to troop through the house with shovels, heading for the back garden. The Wests' eldest son, Steve, who was twenty, arrived home and told the police that they couldn't start digging in the garden until his dad got back from work. He tried to call his father on his mobile telephone, but he couldn't get through to him. Rose, becoming more and more agitated, called Fred's boss, Derek Thomson, who employed Fred as a maintenance man: 'Rose rang me, "Where's Fred? I need Fred! The police are here. They are going to dig the garden up!" I thought it sounded serious.' Derek said that Fred was in Frampton Mansell in the Cotswolds spraying a roof. There was no signal there, so Derek rang the landline and spoke to the homeowner who got Fred to the phone. Derek told him that the police were at his house and Rose wanted him back urgently.

HEATHER UNDER THE PATIO

'I only spoke a couple of words and he was gone. That was the last I ever spoke to him.' But Fred didn't go straight home.

The house, 25 Cromwell Street, was an old semi-detached property, on a dingy inner-city street, where many of the Edwardian houses had been converted into cheap bedsits. The Wests' house was three storeys with two rooms on each floor. The ground floor had been extended, and there was a cellar. A tiny front area facing the street was enclosed within a low brick wall with railings. Unusually there were two gates, a regular garden gate and a larger pair of double gates that protected the front door. This was on the side of the house, part of the extension which joined the property to the Seventh-day Adventist Church next door. A lucky horseshoe was fixed over the front door, and to the side of this was an ornate house sign, the address *25 Cromwell St.* picked out in scrolled iron. The Wests were proud of their home.

Inside, the house was a warren of shabby little rooms decorated in mismatching scraps of carpet and wallpaper, with bodged home improvements by Fred, whose work tools were strewn about the place. A portrait of Rose hung on one of the walls, a silhouette against a blood red sunset. Fred painted the picture when he was in prison years ago. He also made the miniature model gypsy caravan in prison. He made it out of matchsticks. It was a prized ornament. A pin-up poster of a woman in a negligée was stuck to a door, the model beckoning visitors with her crooked finger to come upstairs, where there were surprises.

It was almost four hours before Fred returned home, though he was only twenty miles away when his boss told him that the police were there. What he did in that time remains a mystery. Meanwhile, the police photographed and videoed 25 Cromwell Street inside and out. Then the searchers started to clear the narrow back yard, a row of conifers on one side, the wall of the church on the other. At the bottom of the garden was a gate that gave access to St. Michael's Square. Against the church wall was a barbecue area and a shed which the younger West children had used as a Wendy (play) House. The police took down the washing line and shifted the dustbin out of their way, also moving a concrete lion. They started levering up the patio slabs.

'Here's the first slab being removed,' said the officer videotaping the operation.

The team knocked off about 5:30 PM, and departed, leaving a constable on duty to make sure nothing was tampered with overnight. Fred walked in the door shortly afterwards, as if he had been waiting for the police search team to go, acting as though nothing was wrong. He spoke to Rose in a whisper, then went to the police station nearby.

While Fred gave his interview, other officers came back to the house to interview Rose upstairs on the first floor, in what the Wests called their Black Magic Bar, the old front bedroom which Fred had converted into his idea of a Hawaiian-style bar, one wall of which was decorated with a mural of an exotic holiday destination. It was here that Rose entertained her visitors, including men who paid her for sex. Fred watched or listened to their lovemaking on a speaker attached to hidden microphones in the bedroom on the floor above (top floor) where Rose had a four-poster bed with the word 'cunt' on the pelmet.

Rose West was forty, small, dark and plump, with short brown hair and spectacles. Born in Barnstaple in 1953, she had a slight Devonshire accent, though she had lived in Gloucestershire since she was a child. In contrast to her husband, she was belligerent and defensive with the police, sitting on the sofa smoking Silk Cut as the officers tried to question her.

HEATHER UNDER THE PATIO

DS Terry Onions: Right then, Mrs West, this interview is being tape-recorded. We are in your own house, and we are upstairs in the bar room, whatever you want to call it, at 25 Cromwell Street ... Can you tell me your name, please, for the benefit of the tape ...?
Rose West: You don't know who I am?

Reminded that she was not under arrest, she retorted in her shrill voice, 'If I'm not under arrest, why are you here?' She was asked about Heather. Rather than show motherly concern for her missing firstborn child, she described a stubborn, awkward girl. 'I'm afraid we didn't hit it off that well,' she said. 'I had a problem with her because I knew what she was.'

DS Terry Onions: And what was that then?
Rose West: She was a lesbian, as far as I knew.

It was the same odd story Fred was telling the police. Rose argued that Heather's lesbianism was a bad influence on her other children, who she wanted to lead 'normal lives'. When Rose told Heather that boys might want to get to know her, Heather had made it clear that she wasn't interested in boys. '[She] said, "If a boy touched me, I would put a brick over his fucking head."' So Rose gave Heather £600 to leave home. She was asked what bank account she drew this money from, to verify her story.

Rose West: I cannot fucking remember. It's a bloody long time ago ...
DS Terry Onions: Well, yeah, but I'm just saying.
Rose West: What do you think I am ... a bloody computer?
DS Onions: No, I'm just asking you ...

> **Rose West**: If you had any brains at all you could find her ... It can't be that difficult.

Rose sounded angry at the police, and angry at a daughter who she suggested had abandoned the family. Asked if she had tried to find Heather, Rose complained further.

> **Rose West**: Look, when you've brought up a girl like that, and you've done everything you can – I mean this is sixteen years of a child you're talking about, you imagine the flipping work I put [in] – then they turn around and just turn their back on you, and say, 'I don't want to talk to you anymore, don't want to see you anymore ...' She has always been an obstinate child ...
> **DS Terry Onions**: Has Fred seen her lately, do you know?
> **Rose West**: No, I know he had several phone calls off her, but she didn't want to speak to me.

As he questioned Rose, Detective Sergeant Onions referred to a recent police investigation into child abuse allegations against the Wests. 'Look, just drop that one,' Rose snapped. 'I've had all those charges put to me, and they've all been flaming dropped.' Her five youngest children had been taken into care as a result of the investigation.

> **DS Terry Onions**: What about the family, have you heard ... what the children have been saying [in care], that she's under the patio ... have you heard that? Have you?

It had become a family 'joke', the kids saying that their missing sister was buried under the patio, three paving stones up and nine across. Rose muttered that her stepdaughter Anna Marie[1], Fred's daughter from his first marriage, had said something but she didn't know where the story originated.

> **DS Terry Onions**: [We] are going to dig up the patio ...
> **Rose West**: I ain't got nothing to worry about ...
> **DS Onions**: At the end of the day, we've got to find out where Heather is, haven't we? Because we've got a bit of mystery on, haven't we?
> **Rose West**: I'm sure it's only a mystery because you want it to be a mystery.

Onions said that he had a terrible feeling that Heather was dead, and she had been 'dust and bones' for years.

'Oh, you're lovely, aren't you?' said Rose.

* * *

Having attended the police station voluntarily, Fred was free to return home that evening, arriving back around 9:30. By 1994, Fred and Rose had been together for almost twenty-five years, man and wife at 25 Cromwell Street since 1972, having married shortly after they moved in. They were a close couple with a complicated family. There were children they'd had together, children from Fred's first marriage, and Rose's children by other men, ten children in total. Some had left home, five had been taken into care. Some were missing, one was feared dead. Only May and Steve were at home in 1994. They watched in surprise as Mum and Dad took the dogs out for a walk that evening, which was unheard of, but a late

---

1   Several of the children changed their names to distance themselves from their past, including Anna Marie West who altered her first name to Anne-Marie. I have kept to her original, registered name, which she was known by as a child.

night dog walk around the park at the end of the street gave Fred and Rose an opportunity to talk in private. When they returned, Fred stripped to his underpants and watched the evening news on TV, as he always did. Then the Wests spoke together in whispers as they looked out over their garden. The patio slabs were up and the police had hired a mechanical digger. They would start excavating with this machine first thing tomorrow morning. It wouldn't take them long to find Heather, if Heather was under the patio.

★ ★ ★

The next morning, at 11:15, DC Savage returned with some colleagues and asked Rose – who was again watching television – for her mother Daisy Letts' address, so they could ask Mrs Letts if she knew where her granddaughter was. Rose went off like a rocket, saying that she would 'kill that bitch Hazel Savage' if she upset her mum. Fred took his wife into the hall to calm her down. 'He told me to go upstairs and stay out of the way,' Rose later explained to the police, 'that he'd sort something out.' With Rose out of the room, Fred came back into the lounge, where the police were wondering what was going on.

'Can we go to the police station?' he asked Savage.

When they got into the police car, Fred made an unexpected and dramatic admission. He had killed Heather. His daughter was buried in the garden, but the police were looking in the wrong place.

An urgent message was sent to Fred's solicitor, Howard Ogden, who worked on his own out of a small office in Cheltenham, nine miles from Gloucester, specialising in small legal aid cases. He advertised for clients on local radio with the slogan, 'If you are nicked, call Oggie'. A large, heavyset man with a sardonic sense of humour, who had just turned forty, Ogden was an expert on Griffon dogs and a familiar face at Crufts dog show. He knew Fred, having represented him in the child abuse case. However, he was very surprised to be told that his client was now under arrest for murder.

'Keep your gob shut, Fred, until I get there,' he told him when he got him on the phone.

'Oh, I've already told them I did it!'

Meanwhile, Rose had been arrested on suspicion of murder and taken to Cheltenham Police Station. She was represented by another local solicitor, Leo Goatley, who was a couple of years younger than Ogden. Like the Wests, Goatley had a large family, though he was the opposite of his client in all other respects: a gentle, arty intellectual who painted in his spare time.

In addition to their solicitors, Fred and Rose had the support of volunteers known as 'appropriate adults'. Fred had poor literacy skills and could appear slow-witted, so the police called upon a volunteer to sit in on his interviews to make sure that he was OK and understood what was going on. His appropriate adult was Janet Leach, a mother of five in her thirties studying to be a social worker. She had no experience of a murder case.

Janet Leach and Howard Ogden were both present at Gloucester Central Police Station when Fred was interviewed just before 5:00 PM, by DC Savage and DC Darren Law, a lanky detective in his twenties. Leach and Ogden sat with Fred at the Formica table in the soundproof room facing the police officers, who sat with their backs to the door. An NEC analogue tape deck was switched on, its microphone picking up everything that was said in the room after the warning beep. The spools of two cassette tapes started to turn, creating a working copy and a duplicate which was sealed and could be referred to if the master tape was ever challenged. They had forty-five minutes before the tapes ran out, at which point they would have to stop the interview and re-start with a new set of tapes. At the start of each session the officers stated the time and date and asked everybody in the room to identify themselves for the record. Then they began.

Fred seemed almost bursting to tell the story of how Heather had decided to leave home, with the help of the woman in the mini-skirt who drove a Mini. 'Right, what happened was ...' he began, as he would begin many of his speeches in custody when he had prepared what he wanted to say.

> **Fred West**: Heather was going to leave home, the day before, and we stopped her and said, 'Give it the night to talk it over with us, because you're too young to leave home anyway and we'll talk it over.' Right? Well, we talked it over most of the night. Heather went down to bed, because she slept with May, in the same room as May, [and] Heather cried all night. She wanted to leave home. So the next morning May come up and told Mam, and told me, that Heather had cried all night, and Heather looked as though her had a rough night. So Rose said, 'Let her go ...'

Fred didn't give the police his daughter's biography clearly and concisely. He was almost incapable of telling a straight story, and was a selfish man who never remembered his kids' birthdays, even mixed up their names, but the facts were these: Heather West was born in 1970, when Rose was sixteen and Fred was twenty-nine, two years before Fred and Rose married. She was their eldest child, though Fred had a daughter and a stepdaughter by his previous marriage. By 1987, there were also seven younger siblings. Heather lived her whole life in Gloucester, attending St. Paul's Primary

HEATHER UNDER THE PATIO

School and Hucclecote Secondary School, which she left in 1987. She was an independent-minded, sometimes naughty girl who was caught shoplifting when she was eleven. However, she was also studious. Her ambition was to do well enough at school so she could leave home as soon as possible. Her dream, unusually, was to live as a hermit in the Forest of Dean, a secluded and beautiful place not far from Gloucester where the Wests sometimes took their kids for a day out. Heather wrote 'Forest of Dean I Will Live' in her school books. In the summer of 1987, having passed eight GSCEs, Heather applied for a cleaning job on a holiday camp in Devon. Her siblings recall that the job fell through at the last minute, which was why she cried all night. She was last seen alive the following morning, Friday, 19 June, at 8:00 AM just before Steve and May left for school. Rose would normally take the little ones to primary school at 8:30, before returning home. It was raining hard that morning – 'tipping down' Fred told the police – too wet even for Fred to work. Fred had worked like a Trojan all his life, manual work: labourer, driver, factory worker, currently a maintenance man for Carson Contractors. Heather had packed her bags. By Fred's account, she intended to go against her parents' wishes.

> **Fred West**: Rose said, 'I want to go shopping' or something [and I said] 'Don't hurry back, give me a chance to talk to Heather.' Right? So, anyway ... Heather had her stuff in the hallway. Now, whether this girl [with] this red Mini was going to pick her up, I don't know ...

Father and daughter argued. 'And she's standing there against the dryer with her hands on her hips, like that, against the washing machine, you know the big lady business ...' Fred then veered off topic, saying that Heather threatened to give drugs to her siblings unless he let her go. 'I'd already known that she'd give [drugs] to Barry ...'

Barry, then aged seven, had a totally different memory of Heather. He recalled a kind older sister who disappeared one day from a house in which they all lived in terror of their parents. 'My first memories – I know it sounds really sad – but my first memories have got to be being beaten by my mum,' he said.

Fred West: So that was it. [Heather] stood there and she had a smile, and a sort of smirk on her face, like 'You try me, I'll do it' business. I lunged at her, like that, and grabbed her round the throat ... she didn't bring her arms up to stop me, and I grabbed her round the throat like that, and I held her for a minute, how long I held her for I don't know, I can't remember ... I can just remember lunging for her throat and the next minute she's gone blue. I looked at her, and I mean I was shaking from head to foot. I mean, what the heck had gone wrong?

He claimed that he had tried to revive his daughter.

Fred West: I put her on the floor, blowed air into her mouth and that, and pumped on her chest, and she just kept going bluer ... I didn't know what to do. I mean, Rose was due back. I never intended to hurt her ... I mean, I just went to grab her to shake her and say, 'Take that stupid smirk off your face,' you know, because I was going to smack her across the face [but] she was just flat out, so I thought, 'Jeez, I've got to do something.'

HEATHER UNDER THE PATIO

He tried to put his daughter in the dustbin, but she wouldn't fit. So he took her body into the downstairs bathroom and fetched a serrated Iceland knife from the kitchen.

> **Fred West**: One of those big ice saws for cutting big blocks of ice. So I cut her legs off with that, and I'm telling you I have lived that a million times, doing that, since then. And then I cut her head off …

He started to cry. Through this tempest of tears he continued his story, as if what he was saying was almost reasonable.

> **Fred West**: Then I put her in the bin and rolled it down to the bottom of the garden behind the Wendy House and covered it up and left it there.

He wore Wellingtons for the dismemberment, and used the garden hose to wash the blood off his boots after. He then gathered up his daughter's belongings, including her books and the bags she had packed to go away, and put her things out in St. Michael's Square for the dustman, who happened to be his brother. 'Then Rose come back – must have been [an] hour or more later – and she said, "Oh, didn't you persuade Heather to stay?" Or something like that. And I said no. I said, "She decided to go."'

As graphic as this confession was, there were gaps in Fred's story, while his daughter wanting to leave home to take up a job didn't look like a motive to commit homicide. Fred had not admitted to *murder*, only to killing his daughter. By his account it was a dreadful accident. This didn't ring true. Barry argued that his parents had secrets they were frightened Heather might share with outsiders. 'He was always threatening if we told anybody anything he would kill us, but Heather wanted to leave,' said Barry. 'He couldn't risk it, so he murdered her.'

Continuing his confession, Fred told the police that he sent Rose out to sleep with another man that evening, which was a peculiar aspect of their marriage. While Rose was out with this man (Fred didn't name him), he dug a hole in the garden, took Heather out of the bin, which he sluiced out with the hose, like a labourer cleaning up on a building site, then buried her remains by the conifers. Later, he extended the patio from the back door to the fence at the bottom of the garden, so Heather was now under the pink and yellow paving slabs of the patio. DC Savage showed Fred a photograph of his garden, asking him to identify the exact spot.

> **Fred West**: Hmm, that's just a blur.
> **DC Hazel Savage**: I'll go and get your specs.

Detective and killer spoke with the familiarity of old adversaries, almost friendliness, but in the next moment the conversation reverted to horror as Fred showed Savage where on the photo he dug the hole.

> **DC Hazel Savage**: And what's going to be in this hole in the ground?
> **Fred West**: Heather.
> **DC Savage**: In how many pieces?
> **Fred West**: Three.
> **DC Savage**: What?
> **Fred West**: Two legs, and a head and a body ... But I mean, the thing I'd like to stress, I mean, Rose knew nothing at all ... Once Rose finds out about this, I'm finished.

HEATHER UNDER THE PATIO

He described how he removed Heather's head and legs, twisting the legs round and 'cracking' them off like drumsticks. 'I mean, I can still hear that in my sleep. I wake up very often screaming. I can hear it going *crack*.'

Having listened to this appalling confession, Fred's solicitor, Howard Ogden; the appropriate adult, Janet Leach; and the two police officers, Hazel Savage and Darren Law, were all in shock. A cup of tea was suggested. They went upstairs to the canteen on the top floor of police headquarters, the windows of which had a view across the city rooftops to the nearby cathedral. '[As] we were just gathering in the little tea room we had this silent group hug,' says Ogden. 'Complete strangers: the two police officers, the appropriate adult and me ... It was the matter-of-factness when he was giving this horrendous account. So that was one way in which we coped. This silent group hug.'

In contrast to her husband, Rose West was not admitting anything in Cheltenham, where she was accompanied by her solicitor, Leo Goatley, and her appropriate adult. Sullen and resentful, Rose kept her answers short, and when pressed she said that she couldn't remember.

DS Terry Onions: I'm telling you – and we're on tape, Mr Goatley's here – I'm telling you Fred has confessed to murdering Heather.
Rose West: What?
DS Onions: That automatically implicates you.
Rose West: Why does it automatically implicate me?
DS Onions: I'm just saying, our suspicions are aroused that you are implicated ... that you are involved in it.
Rose West: It's a lie!

At 6:34 that evening, when it was dark, Fred was taken back to 25 Cromwell Street by detectives Savage and Law. It was raining again and the ground was sodden. A small man of five feet five and a half inches, weighing eleven stone, Fred cut a sinister little figure in the light of the police lamps, handcuffed to DC Law, a filicide returning to the scene of his crime. The searchers stopped work to watch as Fred indicated where he had buried his daughter by stepping on a patch of mud with his boot, then turning to grin at the police and Janet Leach as if to reassure them that he was a good bloke really.

That evening Rose was interviewed again. DS Onions suggested to her that it was implausible that she could have lived in a small house with Fred all these years and not know that he had killed their daughter, cut her up and buried her in their garden. 'Either you're blind, extremely naïve, or totally trusting of your husband. Or you're a liar,' he said.

Rose West: Or I was sent out.
DS Terry Onions: Sorry?
Rose West: Or I was sent out.

Her alibi was that Fred sent her out to stay the night with other men, who paid her for sex. Fred controlled her, and now that Rose knew the truth about her husband she felt very foolish. She used another expression.

Rose West: I feel a bit of a cunt, to be blunt with it.
DS Terry Onions: What's your feelings now towards Fred, then ... What are you feeling now?
Rose West: Put it this way, he's a dead man if I ever get my hands on him ... He's finished.

HEATHER UNDER THE PATIO

The relationship between Fred and Rose West was at the heart of this murder case. As the investigation moved into its third day, the police tried to work the couple out. Rose wasn't being at all co-operative, so that made their relationship with Fred vitally important. He was an unusually affable suspect, who talked a lot but didn't necessarily tell the truth. They would have to figure out how his mind worked. It was the start of a journey into almost unimaginable depravity and horror.

2
SHIRLEY AND 'SHIRLEY'S MATE'

Saturday, 26 February 1994 • Day Three
Gloucester Central Police Station

> 'Anyone can say what they like about Rose,
> but she is the perfect mother.'
> FRED WEST

The next day the police got a better idea of what a complicated man they were dealing with when Fred changed his story. He now told them that he hadn't killed Heather. His daughter was alive and well, living in Bahrain, where she worked for a drug gang. 'She contacts me whenever she's in this country. Now, whether you believe it or not is entirely up to you.' This statement came the day after he had confessed to Heather's murder in detail, and guided the searchers to her grave. Was the man stupid, was he mad, or was he playing a game with detectives? He certainly seemed to be over-excited. A police doctor prescribed diazepam to calm him down.

It was hard to know what was going on in Fred's mind. He presented as an uneducated person, who was perhaps lacking in intelligence. He played up to this image, telling the police that he was considered to be as 'thick as two short planks' when he was at school. Yet he was a trickster who successfully deceived people for years, including the police, which took a kind of intelligence. One of his nicknames, he said with pride, was Freddy the Fox. His solicitor thought that this was closer to the truth. '[Fred] sought to play everybody off against each other, including [the] detectives,' says Howard Ogden. 'This notion that Fred was thick wasn't true in my experience.' However, there were also signs that Fred was mentally unstable.

In contrast to her husband, Rose played a straight bat with the police. She denied any knowledge of any crimes, and remained resolutely hostile to detectives in her interviews, which resumed on Saturday morning.

> **DS Terry Onions**: You've been in custody overnight ... The questions we put to you yesterday, is there anything [you wish to say] that may be relevant to this inquiry?
> **Rose West**: Just can't get my head around what's even happening.
> **DS Onions**: Is there anything you want to admit to as regards Heather's disappearance?
> **Rose West**: No.
> **DS Onions**: Because as you know you are still under arrest on suspicion of her murder, and the fact that [your husband] has confessed to that, a number of years ago, and you've been in that house ever since, suggests just by its mere basic ingredients that perhaps you have some knowledge of it. Is that the case, or is that not the case?
> **Rose West**: No, it isn't.

Rose was asked about Heather's medical records. Like most mothers, she could reel off the names and addresses of her children's doctor and dentist, and she became weepy as she did so, as if this struck a chord, but she lacked normal motherly

SHIRLEY AND 'SHIRLEY'S MATE'

feelings and basic knowledge of her children in other areas of their lives. Although Heather had only just left school when she disappeared, Rose had no idea what exams Heather had taken, for instance. Moreover, Rose seemed to dislike her daughter. 'She was never a clean girl, never washed that much,' she sneered.

The police tried to get her to talk about the evening of the day Heather disappeared. Rose had previously suggested that Fred sent her out that night to have sex with a man, a type of recreational prostitution that was a facet of their marriage, 'money came into it, but not particularly paid for it'. It was important to establish where she had gone.

> **DS Terry Onions**: Right then, so you did sleep out that night, and you remember who you were with?
> **Rose West** (muttering): I can't remember his name, because it's a Jamaican name ...
> **DS Onions**: And where did you sleep then?
> **Rose West**: In his house.
> **DS Onions**: And where's his house?
> **Rose West**: Just down Midland Road [in Gloucester] ... It's not actually in Midland Road, it's one of the end streets ...

She said that this man was an ex-workmate of Fred's, who 'instructed' her to sleep with the fellow. 'I didn't want to go.' Rose couldn't recall his exact address, or other details that would allow the police to find him. The man's name was a 'really awkward name'.[2]

---

2 In court in 1995, Rose belatedly remembered the name, but the man, if he existed, did not appear in her defence.

THE FRED WEST TAPES

★ ★ ★

Back at 25 Cromwell Street, the search team continued to dig up the garden. They quickly discovered bones, which caused excitement before they realised that they were chicken bones. While some officers concentrated on the spot where Fred said that Heather was buried, removal of the patio slabs and early digging had opened up other excavations. In one of these holes, under the downstairs bathroom window, an officer noticed a bone sticking up from the earth – too big to be part of a chicken. Almost at the same time, officers digging further down the garden uncovered more bones. When the Senior Investigating Officer (SIO) leant over this second hole and sniffed, his nostrils filled with the unique stench of decomposing human flesh.

Detective Superintendent John Bennett was a Gloucestershire man, speaking in the soft accent of the area, not dissimilar to Fred. He had joined the police as a cadet in his teens, and had risen through the ranks to become a stiff-backed commanding figure. Impeccably dressed, tall and fair with prominent eyes and fleshy lips, he was a man who exuded authority and rectitude, though he admitted that he could appear to be 'a control freak'. Aged forty-eight, he had investigated several murders but nothing like the case before him. He did, however, have the services of a man with vast experience of sudden death in all its forms.

Home Office pathologist Professor Bernard Knight estimated that he'd examined thousands of bodies in his forty-year career. Based in Cardiff, the professor was on duty that weekend when he received a call from Bennett's team. 'I remember going to divisional headquarters in Gloucester, and being handed a bone.' It was the large bone found under the bathroom window at 25 Cromwell Street.

SHIRLEY AND 'SHIRLEY'S MATE'

'Well, what do you think of this, doc?' Bennett asked the pathologist, handing him a brown paper exhibit bag.

When he looked inside the bag, the professor knew at a glance that the bone was human. It was a femur, or thigh bone.

'It's female, and it's young,' he told Bennett.

He could tell that it was female because of the curve in the bone. The men decided to go back to the scene.

It was getting dark and still raining as the winter day drew to an end. The main excavation was next to the conifers on the side of the garden. It was two feet deep and filled with muddy rain water, sewage (Fred had broken a pipe) and a soapy substance that smelt of death. This was adipocere, the scientific name for decomposing human flesh mixed with water. Bones were visible in this stinking mire, along with hair. The surrounding soil was stained black, and it was sticky where body fat had impregnated the earth. Professor Knight crouched down and extracted pieces of a human skeleton, not a complete skeleton laid lengthways – the leg bone connected to the thigh bone, and so on – but a jumble of human remains crammed into a tight space. The victim had evidently been mutilated. Legs and head were separated from the body, though there was no body as such anymore. There was a skull but no face; no eyes, nose, ears or lips. The soft tissue had decomposed, but it looked as if the head had been hacked off. There were no clothes. There were two lengths of cord buried with the remains, and a black bin bag. The victim must have been tied up and cut up when nude, the body pieces carried in the bin bag to the garden and dropped in the hole.

As ghastly as the crime scene was, there was another surprise. As he groped in the muck, Professor Knight pulled out two thigh bones, both left and right legs, in addition to the femur found nearer the house. The implications were obvious but nonetheless startling. 'Either we've found the first three-legged woman,' the professor told Det. Supt. Bennett, 'or you've got more than one body.'

Informed that the police had discovered human remains, Fred was acting strangely back in the interview room. 'When I walked in here, and I sat down there, I could feel my head like lifting up. I was going sort of into space, and I could see diggers and everything all ploughing round, and ripping the house up, tearing the floorboards up and bulldozing the house down. It was all weird,' he told Hazel Savage, who asked if he felt OK. Fred said that thoughts were 'colliding' in his mind, but he felt well enough to continue.

> **DC Hazel Savage**: I understand you have been told by your solicitor ... that we have found something. Is that right?
> **Fred West**: Yeah. Bones.

Savage said cautiously that she wasn't sure yet what these bones were, whether animal or human, but Fred had no doubt. 'It's Heather,' he said, instantly abandoning the pretence that Heather was in Bahrain.

> **DC Hazel Savage**: Could there be anybody else's bones in any part of the garden?
> **Fred West** (after a pause): That's a peculiar question to ask, i'n't?
> **DC Savage**: I'll ask lots of peculiar questions ...
> **Fred West**: I can't make out what you're on about. Others? There's Heather.
> **DC Savage**: Is there anybody else there?
> **Fred West**: No.

SHIRLEY AND 'SHIRLEY'S MATE'

The detective asked Fred about another child, a stepdaughter from his first marriage to Catherine 'Rena' Costello, whom he married in 1962, when she was pregnant with another man's baby. This child was Charmaine West, born 22 March 1963. Charmaine had lived with Fred and Rose for a time, but Fred said that Rena had collected Charmaine years ago, and he hadn't seen either one of them since. She would be thirty now. 'The mother took her. That was it. Finished.' Savage tried to go through the family tree with Fred to establish how many children there should be in total, a simple matter with most fathers but not with Fred. 'I did try to draw a family tree, which would explain who is who,' she explained to him. 'I just need to make sure I got this right ...' The child after Charmaine was Anna Marie, Fred's daughter with Rena, now a married woman of twenty-nine known as Anne-Marie Davis. There were several changed names and nicknames in the family. Next came Heather, born 17 October 1970, the daughter Fred had killed. Then there was May June, so named because she was due in May but born 1 June 1972, making her twenty-one; she disliked her jokey name and styled herself Mae when she became a teenager. Her younger brother Stephen (aka Steve) was born 19 August 1973. Fred tended to call him Boy. Confusingly, Fred also fathered a son named Steven (with a v) in Scotland; his details were as yet unclear to the police. There were five much younger children in Gloucester, all of whom had been taken into care: Tara Jayne, whom Fred called Moses (or Mo), born 9 December 1977, making her sixteen at this time; Louise, born 17 November 1978, was fifteen; Barry, born 16 June 1980, was thirteen; Rosemary (Junior), born 13 April 1982, was eleven; and Lucy Anna, born 16 July 1983, was ten. Some of these children had been fathered by other men. Fred suggested that there were even more. Somewhere.

THE FRED WEST TAPES

DC Hazel Savage: You told me once you had twenty-two children.
Fred West: Thirty. They're all over the world. I don't know half of them.
DC Savage: *Thirty* now?

Savage knew Fred well enough to allow herself to sound slightly sarcastic when she didn't believe what he said, though the truth with Fred was often stranger than fiction. Conversation returned to Heather, his first child with Rose, the child he said he had killed. 'Anyone can say what they like about Rose, but she is the perfect mother,' said Fred. 'We both loved Heather.'

DC Hazel Savage: Why didn't you ever tell her that you killed your daughter?
Fred West: I don't want to destroy the love I have there, when I have destroyed one love already … Don't get Rose wrong. Rose lived by the law. She didn't like the law, but she will not have it broken.

Savage responded by telling Fred that Rose lived by *his* law. The detective had read obscene private notes and poems between the couple, found in the house, in which Rose – described in these writings as Fred's 'cow' and 'bitch' – promised to do whatever Fred wanted when he wanted. 'I, Rosemary West, known as Fred's cow, give my cunt to be fucked by any prick at any time he so desires without my ever saying no,' she had written. Fred was fascinated with the mating habits of animals and humans, including the mad idea of man and beast copulating. Cows were sexualised and a term of rough affection in his world. He often called Rose his 'old cow'. 'I give my mouth to be fucked by anyone … I must always dress

SHIRLEY AND 'SHIRLEY'S MATE'

and try to act like a cow for Fred, also to bathe and wash when I am told. Signed Mrs R. P. West.'

The woman who wrote this extraordinary note was born Rosemary Pauline Letts in Devon on 29 November 1953, the fourth of seven children. Her parents, Bill and Daisy Letts, both had mental health problems, and the marriage was unhappy. A former merchant seaman, Bill Letts was a violent schizophrenic who terrorised his family, subjecting them to cruel and bizarre treatment. He beat the kids and dragged his wife about like a rag doll. Daisy suffered from depression so badly that she was receiving electroconvulsive therapy (ECT) when she was pregnant with Rose, who was a slow-witted child showing early signs of being disturbed. She rocked herself manically back and forth as a kid, paraded about in the nude as a teenager, and molested her younger brother.

Rose's dad was in and out of work, leaving a bad reputation wherever he went. He worked as a TV repairman in a seaside village in Devon before moving the family to Plymouth where he had a job in a school. 'We were so hard up in Devon,' lamented Rose's mum, Daisy. 'It was dreadful to live there. We had an awful time really.' When Rose was ten, the family moved to Bishop's Cleeve, a village near Cheltenham where Bill found a factory job. Rose said that Cheltenham people looked down on them and it was years before some of the neighbours spoke to her mother. Rose struggled at Bishop's Cleeve Comprehensive, and made few friends. She developed into an unintelligent, cold and rude young woman. Like her father, she had a temper. Sexually, she lacked boundaries. She was, however, soppy about children.

There was more to this family. Fred later said that Rose was sexually abused by her father, an incestuous relationship that extended into her adult life. 'Her father was making love to her,' he told his solicitor, in a taped interview broadcast by Channel 5 as part of the 2001 documentary *Fred & Rose: The West Murders*. 'I caught 'em at least half a dozen times.' This may have been how Rose managed to avoid being beaten as a child, unlike some of her siblings. When she was ultimately asked about this in court, Rose denied that she was sexually abused at home. She said that her first sexual experience was when she was raped by an unnamed older man at a park when she was about fifteen, but her daughter May says that Rose told her that her father had abused her sexually, and most people close to the case believe that this is true.

When Rose was fifteen, her parents separated and her mother took Rose and the younger children to live with her married daughter, Glenys, and her husband, Jim Tyler. Jim said that Rose made a pass at him and that she went off with his customers when she worked in his snack bar. As a result she soon had to find somewhere else to live, so was briefly homeless. She then moved back in with her father and took a succession of little jobs: in Dad's factory, at Sketchley the dry cleaner, and then in a Cheltenham baker's shop, which is where she was working when she met Fred in 1969.

Rose was fifteen at the time. Fred was a twenty-seven-year-old bread delivery man, living in a caravan at the Lake House site outside Bishop's Cleeve. In the interview room in 1994, Fred boasted that he slept with many of the women on his bread round. One customer who asked him to bring her a small brown loaf was waiting for him naked on a rug. 'And she said, "How about it then?" Well, I couldn't refuse …' She got pregnant, so he quit the bread round. 'These women ruin my jobs.' A lot of Fred's conversation was in this smutty, sub-comic vein.

Fred may have first seen Rose in the bread shop, but he chatted her up on a bus. 'This man started talking to me on the bus and just sat next to me without asking any permission,' Rose later said. 'Within a few minutes he had asked me out.' Rose's parents were appalled to discover that she was dating an older married man with children. 'I never liked him from the day I set my eyes on him, mainly because he said lies,' said Daisy later. 'Dad's opinion was that he was a gypsy.' (Fred said that he had gypsy blood.) 'He gave you the impression that he was a devoted father. He was always telling you that he took the children to see the daffodils, always talking about the children. It's quite mad, when you think about it.' Rose's parents forbade her from seeing Fred. Her father threatened them with violence, according to Rose. 'He said you can either stay at home, do as you are told, go to work, earn money, bring it back home [or] I could go off with this Fred West and never see my family again, and he said if he sees us in the street he would knife us.' This only served to drive Rose into Fred's arms. Fred told the police that Rose would 'creep down across the field to meet me' when he was living in the caravan, so her parents contacted the police and social services, who put Rose into a home. When she turned sixteen, in November 1969, she went straight back to Fred and soon discovered that she was pregnant with his child.

> **Fred West**: She said her father had gone up to her room and tried to talk with her. And said, 'Either you forget Fred and have the abortion ... live at home and be part of the family, or you keep your baby, go with Fred and you are bombed out forever, out of the family and forgotten about.' And she said, 'I'll take Fred.'

To put some distance between themselves and Rose's parents, the lovers moved to a flat in Cheltenham, then to Gloucester – where there was more work for Fred – firstly to a flat in

Midland Road, which is where they were living when Heather was born in 1970. Fred and Rose had been together in Gloucester ever since.

> **DS Terry Onions**: Who's the controller in your house, who's the dominant partner?
> **Rose West**: I'd say Fred was, really, in lots of ways …
> **DS Onions**: Has he ever hit you?
> **Rose West**: Used to, when he was younger … Not serious.
> **DS Onions**: Not serious … what do you call not serious?
> **Rose West**: Well, no broken bones … He hit me in the jaw once … twisted it.

The West children said that domestic violence went beyond this, that if Fred thought Rose was having too much fun with the men she slept with (at his instigation) he punched her. But Rose was like clay in Fred's hands. 'I mean, that is why our marriage worked out so well, for a simple reason. Rose had had no wild life, and she just blended into my way of life,' Fred told Hazel Savage. As she matured, however, Rose developed into a volatile woman with a temper that matched or even surpassed that of her husband. 'That's what people don't know,' said her son Barry. 'She was a complete psycho.' The police who dealt with the Wests over the years learned to be wary of Rose's hot temper. She once hit an officer with an ashtray when he tried to ask her questions. 'Rose wasn't very nice,' says the officer, '[but] I always got on alright with Fred. Her husband told her off.'

★ ★ ★

Back in the interview room, Fred was given more news. There had been a further development.

SHIRLEY AND 'SHIRLEY'S MATE'

DC Hazel Savage: In another part of your garden, Fred, the police have found another human bone ... a second [victim].
Fred West: What?

This was the third thigh bone Professor Knight had referred to. Fred fell silent, caught by surprise, wondering what to say. After a few moments his solicitor's clerk prompted him to speak.

Scott Canavan: Have you any knowledge where this other bone might have come from?
Fred West: Yes. Shirley ... Robinson, the girl who caused the problem.

He said that Shirley Robinson came to 25 Cromwell Street as a lodger years ago when the Wests took in tenants. Despite being 'a pure lesbian', as he put it, Shirley wanted a baby and she persuaded Fred to make her pregnant. Rose was pregnant at the same time, and when Shirley threatened to tell Rose about them he strangled her, killing her in the house when Rose was in hospital, giving birth, then buried her body in the garden. 'That was me on me own, sort[ing] out problems because she was threatening [to] tell Rose.' He insisted that Rose knew nothing about this. 'I don't think Rose even knew Shirley,' he said. 'Rose had nothing to do with them upstairs.' The police asked Fred whether this was all, that he had no more secrets he wanted to share? No, he insisted that he had now told them everything.

When the interview was over, however, Fred told Howard Ogden that there was a third body.

At 8:30 that evening Fred was brought before the magistrates' court across the road from the police station, where the presiding magistrate gave the officers another thirty-six hours to question their suspect. After this short hearing, the police sat down with Fred again. Although it was past nine at night, everybody was eager to hear what else he had to say.

> **DC Hazel Savage**: I understand that after the conclusion of our last interview [you] said to Mr Ogden [that] you wanted to tell him about further matters?
> **Fred West**: Yeah…
> **DC Savage**: What do you want to tell us, Fred?
> **Fred West**: Just where the three are.
> **DC Savage**: Now, when you say 'three', can you remind me of what we're talking about?
> **Fred West**: Well, Heather, Shirley and the one [whose name] I don't know … I said [to Shirley], 'Now, if I give you a baby, and you come back and threaten to tell Rose, or anything, I'll take your head off,' I said, 'because Rose is my wife, and I don't want her to know that I've touched anybody, certainly you …'

He spoke about the Shirley Robinson murder first. He killed her on a 'bright moonlit night'. 'And I'm thinking, where is this gonna end?' He didn't explain himself fully at once, but he said he buried Shirley in the garden near Heather. 'By this time there is three, sorry, two. That's right. Two,' he said, getting himself muddled. 'I have got to tell Rose, so she can get somebody to help me … I knew I should have got help with it.' Fred was shy of saying at first whether he had dismembered Shirley, but after a bit he admitted that he probably had. The awful implication dawned on his solicitor.

> **Howard Ogden**: Can I just clarify … am I right in thinking that at the time Shirley died she was carrying your child?

SHIRLEY AND 'SHIRLEY'S MATE'

Fred West: Yeah …
Howard Ogden: Did the baby stay in her tummy?
Fred West: Yes.

So that was Shirley. Fred then said that another woman came to Cromwell Street looking for Shirley, so he had to kill her, too. This was the third victim. 'She was going to get the police, and all this lot. So we had an argument, a row, and I punched her on the jaw first, and knocked her on the floor, and then strangled her.'

DC Darren Law: With what?
Fred West: Whatever I got hold of. I don't remember. A piece of [electrical] flex, or summat.

Although he had shown some emotion when confessing to murdering Heather, Fred spoke about these other two women without feeling, other than irritation at them for making his life complicated. Asked who the third woman was by name, he said he had no idea.

DC Hazel Savage: What can we refer to her as now?
Fred West: Shirley's mate.

He buried Shirley by the back of the extension, and her 'mate' against the bathroom wall. At the time there was a child's paddling pool in the garden, made of concrete, and he buried 'Shirley's mate' under the concrete paddling pool. He levered it up and just shoved her under. The pool had since been removed, the area covered over by the patio stones. It would turn out that the first thigh bone the police found belonged to this woman. As Fred described what happened, he seemed oblivious to how dreadful his confession sounded. 'This is horrific,' DC Law muttered to Hazel Savage who continued firing questions at Fred in the manner of a more experienced detective who was surprised at nothing she was told, and believed half of what she heard.

> **DC Hazel Savage**: How did she [Shirley's mate] get into bits then?
> **Fred West**: Well, I think I done it out there by the side [of the pool].
> **DC Savage**: How many bits would she be in?
> **Fred West**: Three. Four.
> **DC Darren Law**: And those are?
> **Fred West**: Head and legs.
> **DC Law**: Head! What, you cut the head off?
> **Fred West**: Yeah.

He cut her up with his sheath knife, 'an actual dagger'. He would show the police where to dig for her remains. With Heather, they would then have three victims. That was right. Three. 'There is no more,' he reassured the officers, as if this concluded matters and they could all go home. 'That's it.'

3
A PASSION FOR BONDAGE

Sunday, 27 February 1994 • Day Four
Gloucester Central Police Station

'We weren't living a straight sex life.'
FRED WEST

The following morning Fred told the police more about the death of Heather, now claiming that he tried to revive his daughter under a tap after he strangled her. When he realised that she was dead he cut her up in the bath in order to fit her in the dustbin while he worked out where to bury her. Forensic evidence indicated that Fred probably chopped his daughter's body up with an axe or a cleaver. Her upper left thigh bone (the largest and strongest bone in the body) had been broken clean in two by a blow with a heavy, sharp implement such as an axe. Professor Bernard Knight told the police that a knife couldn't cut such a big bone in two. Fred denied using a chopper or axe, however, on the basis that an axe would have damaged the bath enamel. He insisted that he used a bread knife on his daughter, now saying that the knife from Iceland proved too flexible and had 'ripped' her skin. He sniffed as he spoke, as if he was a little bit upset. Reading the transcripts of the interviews – which he didn't take part in personally – Detective Superintendent John Bennett concluded that Fred was a psychopath.

The interviewing officers then moved on to the other two murder victims, whose background was slowly coming to light. Born in Leicestershire on 8 October 1959, Shirley Ann Robinson was the first child of RAF corporal Royal Baden Robinson, and his wife, Christa Lewezki. Two more children followed. The family moved around as Royal Robinson was posted to various RAF bases. Christa left Royal in 1962, when Shirley was about three, moving to a homeless hostel. 'I took ill and had problems coping with three small children,' Christa told the police when they located her in Hartlepool. Royal took the children back, and the couple fought over custody. 'I did not see or hear from the children for about ten years,' she said. In 1974, when she was fourteen or fifteen, Shirley was taken into the care of social services and placed in the Extra Care Unit of Crescent School, a secure unit for troubled girls in Bristol, where a staff member told the police – not very sympathetically – that Shirley was 'extremely withdrawn and sullen'. She remained there until she was sixteen, when she moved to accommodation for older girls. She worked briefly in a boot factory, then as a chambermaid in Chipping Sodbury, Gloucestershire. Social workers were concerned that she was consorting with older women and getting into trouble. She soon acquired a criminal record. By the time she was seventeen, Shirley had found her way into Gloucester. Some of the cheapest accommodation in the city at the time was at 25 Cromwell Street where Fred and Rose rented bedsits on the first and second floors of their house for as little as £7 a week (roughly £50 in today's money) to help cover the mortgage payments. The house itself, run down as it was, in a poor part of town, had cost the Wests £6,500 in 1972 (about £90,000 today). They got a loan from the council, and

A PASSION FOR BONDAGE

Fred worked all hours to make ends meet. Shirley moved in around April 1977, renting a room on the first floor at the back, overlooking the garden. That October, just after she turned eighteen, she was recorded with the local Health Centre in Gloucester as being six weeks pregnant.

At the time, Fred was employed at Muir-Hill wagon works (later known as Winget Ltd), a factory that made railway carriages, tractors and other industrial vehicles. Fred operated a drill, doing his repetitive, dirty work with untiring energy. Shirley came to the factory to see Fred. His workmates knew that she was carrying his baby, at the same time that Rose was pregnant. 'It was quite a big joke,' Fred told the police. 'You know, having a wife and a girlfriend pregnant.' Fred seemed to transfer his affections to Shirley briefly. They had their photograph taken at a local photographic studio, posing in their best clothes, Shirley resting her head against his. It was a strange picture for a married man to have taken with his lodger.

The way Fred told the story, Rose didn't know at first that he had made Shirley pregnant. He said that he killed Shirley when she was threatening to tell Rose what was going on.

> **Fred West**: I turned round and just smacked her straight in the jaw, and she went straight on the floor. Then I went and got the piece of [electrical] flex and tied it round her neck ...
> **Howard Ogden**: Tell the officers.
> **Fred West**: I grabbed her on the throat and I held her. I turned her, something like that, over my knee, pushing her down ... and then [she] went limp [and] I put the flex round her to make sure she was dead. And that was it.

THE FRED WEST TAPES

He strangled Shirley, he said, because he had a fear of burying a woman alive. He wanted to be sure she was dead. He claimed he did the same with the other two victims. There were no more, Fred again insisted. He was making a clean breast of the three bodies in the garden because he knew that he was going to prison. He wanted to leave the house in good order for Rose and the children.

Shortly after 10:30 that morning, Hazel Savage and Darren Law took Fred back to 25 Cromwell Street to show them where he had buried Shirley and her 'mate'. The crime scene had been covered over with plastic sheeting, held up with scaffold poles, like a marquee. 'Right, Fred, what I want you to do is, can you show me first of all where you buried Shirley Robinson?' asked DC Law, to whom Fred was once again handcuffed.

'There, that slab there,' said Fred, taking a cigarette out of his mouth, and pointing to the patio slab under the back door, level with the cat flap.

'And now, can you tell us where you buried Shirley's friend?'

'Right by that,' said Fred, indicating a spot between the bathroom and the conifers.

'Whilst we're here, Fred, is there anything else you want to look at?' DC Savage asked him. Fred shook his head.

Fred West: That's it.
DC Hazel Savage: Are you sure?
Fred West: Yes. You can take it all apart. There ain't nothing else.

Meanwhile, Rose was being questioned again by Detective Sergeant Terry Onions, who asked her about Shirley Robinson and her 'mate'. Onions told Rose that Fred had admitted to killing the two women, in connection with which she was also

A PASSION FOR BONDAGE

arrested. Rose claimed not to remember Shirley, though the police had found Rose's 1977 pocket diary in the house in which she marked the dates when Shirley paid her the rent.

> **DS Terry Onions**: She was pregnant at the time, he [Fred] says ... does that ring any bells with you?
> **Rose West**: No. As I said, I don't remember that well.
> **DS Onions**: He also says that he was the father of that unborn child. Does that ring any bells with you at all now?
> **Rose West**: No.

Despite the evidence of her diary, which showed her to be the rent collector, Rose insisted that Fred dealt exclusively with the lodgers. She considered them to be a nuisance, causing damage to their property and attracting the police with their drug use. This introduced a sensitive subject. Gloucestershire Constabulary had been in contact with the Wests for years, and police officers had visited 25 Cromwell Street regularly on drug raids, as well as coming to the house on other inquiries. Yet they had failed to detect signs of murder. 'I got raided solid for years [by] the police,' Fred told his interviewing officers, naming two drugs squad officers who, he said, were in and out of his house frequently because of their young tenants and their drug use. 'I mean, it was unreal. Raided, raided, raided, raided.' Apart from gloating over police failure, Fred always spoke of drug use with opprobrium. So did Rose. Fred liked to say that he never imbibed more than 'an occasional shandy'. In this clumsy way the Wests tried to signal that they were better than their lodgers. 'I didn't want my children involved with that, so I cut my bit [of the house] off,' Rose told Terry Onions primly. 'I didn't have much to do with them.'

Onions remarked upon Rose's lack of emotion.

THE FRED WEST TAPES

DS Terry Onions: Are you shocked by this ... I [would] expect you to be shocked, if you've got no knowledge [of these crimes]. What about the pregnancy ... that he made this Shirley pregnant, and she was carrying his baby? What's your attitude to that?
Rose West: Something wrong with the bloke, isn't there?

As the police tried to question her further, Rose said less and less. Then she started to reply 'no comment'. Another detective attempted a different approach, going back to Rose's admission that Fred hit her, and controlled her.

DC Neville Smurthwaite: Does [Fred] frighten you, Rose?
Rose West: Sometimes, he does, yeah ...
DC Smurthwaite: Has he ever threatened to kill you at all?
Rose West: (silence)
DC Smurthwaite: What was that, a shrug of a shoulder?
Rose West: I don't know...
DC Smurthwaite: Has he ever choked you before?

Rose conceded that Fred had strangled her, for 'a couple of minutes, and then he's let go ... he's only done it when he's been angry ... more when he was younger ...' She didn't seem too bothered about it. 'Just when we argued, that's all.' She had the opportunity to portray herself as a victim, a woman who lived in fear of a violent and abusive husband.

DC Neville Smurthwaite: Have you ever seriously thought that he would do that to you?
Rose West: Do what?
DC Smurthwaite: Kill you, at some stage? Rose?
Rose West: Never thought about it.

A PASSION FOR BONDAGE

Although Rose may have been scared of Fred, she chose not to use that as a defence at this time. She did refer to it fleetingly later in court, claiming ultimately that Fred threatened to kill her. But Fred said the same of her.

Having reached an impasse, Det. Supt. Bennett decided that it was time to release Rose. Fred was delighted when he heard that his wife was being bailed. Rose went home to 25 Cromwell Street on Sunday, 27 February, spending the night at the house with May and Steve, but she couldn't stay at home with the garden being excavated and journalists starting to gather outside. What had begun as a domestic murder inquiry had made the front page of the Gloucester *Citizen* on Friday, and was beginning to gain national attention. On Monday, the police took Rose to a safe house in the city. May went with her, and Steve dropped in at times. Unknown to the family, the police had bugged the house, with the permission of the Chief Constable, hiding cameras and microphones.

Meanwhile, back at Gloucester Central Police Station, Fred was talking about Shirley Robinson. While initially insisting that Rose had never met Shirley, he contradicted himself by saying that the women not only knew but disliked each other. 'I think Rose knew she was a lesbian,' he said. The truth was that Rose was jealous of Shirley, and Fred fuelled her jealousy. Witnesses said that Fred taunted Rose about his affair. Fred told Rose that 'Shirley is going to be my next wife'. He now spoke to the police about the women being pregnant at the same time, under the same roof. It was a highly charged, complicated domestic situation. Shirley was having Fred's baby, but Rose was pregnant by another man – a black friend of theirs. 'We wanted a half-caste (*sic*) child and it was planned, so I mean I was quite excited about it.'

According to Fred, Shirley then started to make crude, racist remarks about his wife.

THE FRED WEST TAPES

Fred West: [She said] that bitch is having a black baby, and that got me really mad ... Shirley got a bit nasty about it and she said, 'Well, all right, Rose is going to know, I'm going to tell Rose I'm having your baby' [calling Rose] 'that bitch' or 'that cow' or 'that slag' or some[thing], which I'd warned her a lot of times about ... I had slapped her a few times before for it, for insulting Rose ... And, anyway, then she threatened to go and tell Rose. So I just lost all sense. I just went for her, and hit her flying on to the floor, and then I just strangled her.

As the Senior Investigating Officer read the transcripts of the interviews, he saw that Rose had said next to nothing of use prior to being released on bail, while Fred was leading the interviewing officers in circles, lying, contradicting himself, and getting everybody muddled. 'These interviews are crap!' John Bennett exploded, the pressure of the case starting to take its toll. 'He's taking over! We're getting nowhere.' DC Savage also lost her cool, complaining that she was sometimes at a disadvantage in the interview room with Fred because she wasn't kept fully informed of what detectives in the incident room were finding out about the Wests, as her CID colleagues chased down leads.

As tempers frayed at the police station, the search team at 25 Cromwell Street found a skull, buried below the bathroom window where Fred said he put 'Shirley's mate'. Later that day they found Shirley's remains behind the back door, where Fred told them to look. Despite inconsistencies in Fred's confessions, and the frustrations of dealing with such a slippery character, the police had now found three bodies roughly where Fred said they would be, and the bones provided vital forensic evidence of what had been going on.

When Professor Knight recovered the skull of Shirley's

A PASSION FOR BONDAGE

'mate', there was a brown leather belt looped under the chin, fastened with the buckle, which meant that the victim had been gagged. This pointed to a sex crime, not a row as Fred had said. Hazel Savage raised this with Fred. She reminded him first that she knew that the Wests were into bondage sex. Fred owned a bondage kit, including belts.

> **Fred West**: Yeah, that was only [used] with Rose …
> **DC Hazel Savage**: Is it possible that any of that bondage kit was used with this girl?
> **Fred West**: No, not actually used with her.
> **DC Savage**: Can you explain that a bit more?

He said that he collected belts and scraps of material to make bondage 'harnesses' for Rose. Their favourite fetish material was red PVC. 'It was summat new we tried, just me and Rose, this bondage thing.' He kept some rags and belts in his work van and conceded that he may have dropped rags in the grave with 'Shirley's mate'.

> **DC Hazel Savage**: But you would know if you specifically put a belt … around a certain part of a girl, wouldn't you?
> **Fred West** (after a pause): There might be a belt, or something tied round her.

Any straps found with the woman would have been used to truss her up before rigor mortis, he said, not to restrain her during sex. 'She wasn't stiff. She was loose.' He had to tie her arms and legs in order to lift her corpse without her limbs flopping about.

★ ★ ★

THE FRED WEST TAPES

Upstairs in his office, Det. Supt. Bennett had a visitor. Paul Britton was a forty-seven-year-old clinical psychologist from Leicestershire, where he worked out of a psychiatric unit. Britton advised the police on cases where officers wanted a psychological profile of an offender. His reputation had grown in recent years, so much so that he was said to be the inspiration for the criminal psychologist played by Robbie Coltrane in the TV drama *Cracker*. Britton had consulted with Birmingham police on a high-profile kidnapping, and the Metropolitan Police on the murder of Rachel Nickell on Wimbledon Common in London in 1992. In the Nickell investigation Britton assisted an unorthodox undercover operation whereby a female detective befriended a suspect, Colin Stagg, to see if he would confess to killing Nickell. As a result of this 'honeytrap', Stagg had just been committed for trial. Unfortunately, when the case came to the Old Bailey later in 1994 the judge threw it out, criticising the operation. It turned out that the killer was another man altogether, a fiasco which brought offender profiling into question. All that was in the future, however. 'He [Britton] was what I call the "in thing" for police at the time,' says Bennett. 'If you had a major investigation, and you didn't have a forensic psychologist, you hadn't done your job properly.'

Bennett told Britton that Fred had admitted to killing three women, whose bodies had been found dismembered and decapitated. Fred and Rose had been known to Gloucestershire police for years, and to some extent the couple had slipped through their fingers. Two years ago, the Wests were arrested for the sexual abuse of one of their daughters. Fred was charged with three counts of rape and one of buggery, committed with Rose, who was charged with 'causing or encouraging' unlawful intercourse with the child, and cruelty. In plain English, she allegedly helped Fred rape their daughter. The Wests walked

A PASSION FOR BONDAGE

when the child refused to give evidence at court. 'There are several embarrassing aspects to this inquiry,' said Bennett.

When they were free, Hazel Savage and Terry Onions joined Bennett and Britton in the police canteen, sharing their thoughts on Fred and Rose. DC Savage struck Britton as an unusual detective, a woman of junior rank who had become so immersed in the West investigation that she felt able to interrupt her SIO. 'At every opportunity, as we talked, Hazel would interrupt and comment not just on the facts but with opinions on how the different [West] children felt about what happened and to what extent they were frightened of their parents,' Britton later wrote in a book, *The Jigsaw Man*. Among Fred's eccentricities, Savage explained that the prisoner had an obsession with medical matters, and crazy ideas about breeding the perfect child by collecting semen from condoms Rose used with other men, then using this sperm to try to artificially inseminate their children.

When he had heard everything, Britton suggested that Fred may have abused and murdered his victims in cahoots with Rose. That much the police already supposed. He also said that there were human remains in the garden of 25 Cromwell Street, possibly because the house was full. 'You should take it apart, every square inch, the floors, the walls, the roof,' he advised the officers. 'There'll be more bodies. I'm sure of it.'

★ ★ ★

The most pressing task was to find out who 'Shirley's mate' was. When Fred said, 'I didn't know her' he seemed to mean it. He said that after he and Shirley had their photograph taken, Shirley had sent prints to her family and friends, including a girlfriend in Bristol, also writing to her to say that if she went quiet her friend should come to Gloucester to find her. One day when Fred was outside working on his van, a young woman approached him in

Cromwell Street asking about Shirley. Fred described her vaguely as a mousey woman in her twenties with a 'little round face' and blue eyes. In his first full account of her murder, on 26 February, he said that he sent this woman over to his father-in-law's café, the Green Lantern, in Southgate Street, while he got Rose out of the way. Then he drove to the café and brought her back. They had a row. He punched her cold, then he strangled her.

When Fred retold the story on 27 February, however, the details were slightly different. This time the woman was dead when he brought her back in the van, and Rose was at home. It was another moonlit night, as it was when he killed Shirley. He cut the engine and lights, so he glided the van soundlessly into a neighbour's garage. He then had to carry the corpse out of the vehicle and into the garden without alerting Rose.

> **DC Hazel Savage**: [But] why had she got a piece of belt tied around her skull, Fred?
> **Fred West**: Well, that probably had another piece through it, holding her head forward.

The image of Fred dragging a dead body into his garden while Rose was indoors, oblivious, was hard to believe. The house and garden were so small that if Fred had lit a cigarette in the back yard Rose might be expected to have heard the match strike. When Fred said that Shirley's mate was heavy, DC Savage remarked sarcastically: 'Most people are when they're dead.' Savage then reminded Fred of a conversation they'd had while she was finger-printing him. He admitted that he hoped initially to conceal the fact there was more than one body in the garden, and only confessed to the other two when he knew the police had stumbled upon more evidence and would inevitably find all three.

A PASSION FOR BONDAGE

DC Hazel Savage: So, you haven't been totally co-operative, have you? It's been like pulling teeth.
Fred West: Well, do you expect it any other way?

The detective laughed grimly. 'I mean, there ain't no more,' Fred assured her. But there was a lot Fred wasn't saying, and the police had further disturbing evidence to put to him. Professor Knight had examined Shirley Robinson's remains. She was eight and a half to nine months pregnant when she died, just about to give birth to Fred's baby. The police thought at first that the baby may even have been cut from her womb.

DC Hazel Savage: If you have removed the baby, now's the time to tell us about it.
Fred West: Hazel, what are you trying to say here ... did I move the baby? No! The baby was left inside the mother as it was ... I love children.

The pathologist ultimately decided that there was no evidence that the baby had been removed. Like Heather, Shirley had, however, been decapitated. 'For the length,' explained Fred. In digging the graves his concern was to avoid the footings of his house, making a small square hole, then cutting the victim down to fit the hole. It made for a grisly conversation. As Hazel Savage tried to get the truth out of Fred she noticed that the appropriate adult, Janet Leach, wasn't looking too well and asked if she wanted some fresh air.

'Yes, please,' gasped Leach. The interview then ended.

★ ★ ★

The fact that all three victims were found nude, Heather and Shirley's mate also with evidence that they were restrained, indicated that these may all have been sex crimes. The way into understanding what had happened, therefore, seemed to lie in the sexual activities of Fred and Rose. Fred had no problem talking about that. He told the detectives proudly that he and Rose 'weren't living a straight sex life'. They enjoyed all sorts of high jinks, including bondage, voyeurism and pornography, while he showed disapproval of other types of sexual behaviour, notably same-sex relations. From their first interviews, Fred and Rose had made it clear they weren't happy about the idea that Heather might be a lesbian, and Fred spoke of homosexual men with disdain. 'I felt right weird with him,' he told the police of a gay man he met when the Green Lantern later became a gay club. DC Savage asked if he had visited the premises after it became a gay club. 'No, I did not,' laughed Fred, as if this crossed the line for a murderer. 'What a question!'

The next morning, Thursday, 3 March, Fred appeared briefly again at Gloucester Magistrates' Court, where the police asked for him to be remanded into custody for further questioning. As he heard his daughter's name read out in charges, Fred lost his composure. 'West's face turned white then green as the blood drained from his features,' John Bennett later wrote in his account of the investigation, *The Cromwell Street Murders*. 'His knees buckled and he grabbed on to the rail in front of him.' When they got back to the station, Fred spoke about why he became upset at court. It was to do with everyone watching him, he said, as if he was a 'hero', and he didn't feel like one. 'That was my daughter,' he sniffed. 'It's just coming home to me now ... the thing that I held in my mind for all these years ... This is where everything in my mind is so smashed up. Because what I used to do for hours on end was try to put it right, in my own mind, that what I did was right.

A PASSION FOR BONDAGE

You know, put excuses in. That's the only word I can think of at this moment, why I done it, why I allowed it to happen.'

Hazel Savage said that she had never heard Fred talk like this.

'I mean, I didn't want to touch anybody. I mean, all I want is a quiet life with my family ...' he said.

This show of self-pity may have been a ruse to distract the police and give Fred time to think. They would continue talking in the morning.

Rather than remand Fred into custody at HMP Gloucester, the old gaol across the road from headquarters, it was more convenient for the police to keep Fred at the station where he could be brought quickly to the interview room or taken easily to Cromwell Street. It was also better for Fred not to be thrown into the rough house of prison. His daily life was much more comfortable at the station. By arrangement with HM Prison Service, he was held in segregation in a suite of cells at the station. Staff fed him from the police canteen (he enjoyed the police canteen chips); he could walk in the police yard and smoke as much as he liked; he was 'paid' £2.50 a week as a remand prisoner, from which he bought rolling tobacco and cigarette papers. His solicitor Howard Ogden brought in treats, including a tiramisu for dessert on one visit, and he took Fred's clothes to the laundrette. Fred was even allowed a TV and video recorder, Ogden bringing him rental movies including a murder mystery. Ogden tended to make jokes to diffuse the tension, and often impersonated Fred's 'Farmer Giles' way of speaking. Sometimes his humour verged on bad taste. One day he brought a book to the station as a supposedly funny gift for his client. 'I've got this, Fred,' he said, handing him *Butchery for Beginners*. Ogden had a business to run, so Fred was often left in the company of his young clerk, Scott Canavan, who spent hours with Fred playing cards. 'I'd only worked as a clerk for a month, you know, let alone [on] a murder case. It was almost like hearing somebody reading you a story,' he later said. 'It was hard to picture.' Scott and Fred became friendly, but what Fred told the clerk weighed on his mind for the rest of his life. A troubled man with a drink problem, Scott committed suicide in 2020. His widow said that he was haunted by what Fred told him in 1994, especially by the casual way in which he had talked about his crimes.

Fred spent a lot of time alone with Janet Leach, who also found the experience to be life affecting. Fred chatted freely with almost everybody he met in custody but he confided in Leach in particular, identifying her as a woman he might try to charm. She found herself drawn into a complex relationship with a man whom she considered to be mad, but who seemed to want to tell her things he could or would not tell others. Fred started to make significant claims and admissions to Leach, making her promise to keep what he told her confidential. 'After only two or three days of my involvement with Mr West, he began to tell me things about the murders, and implicated his wife, Rosemary West, as being involved in the murders,' she later said. 'He told me many things which he did not tell the police.' Most significantly, Fred told her that he and Rose had a pact. By the terms of their pact he would take all the blame for crimes that they had, in fact, committed together.

4
FRED'S EARLY LIFE

Thursday, 3 March 1994 • Day Eight
Gloucester Central Police Station

'Whatever you enjoy, do ... And make sure you don't get caught doing it.'
FRED WEST QUOTING HIS FATHER

The psychologist Paul Britton advised John Bennett that his officers should lead Fred back through his life to see what else might emerge. 'Let Mr West talk,' he said, suggesting that Fred should be made to feel at ease to encourage him to open up. At this stage, new interviewing officers were brought in to complement the strong-minded DC Hazel Savage. They included twenty-nine-year-old DC Barbara Harrison, who had the manner of a kindly social worker, and DC Jeff Morgan, a local man of around Fred's age with a similar softly-softly style, though both detectives were capable of asking penetrating questions. Morgan suggested to Fred that he should imagine that the police were writing his biography, and to start telling them his life story from the beginning. Fred enjoyed telling stories. 'Well, I was born in Much Marcle, Bickerton Cottage, and I lived with my parents ...' he began, seizing the invitation.

THE FRED WEST TAPES

> **DC Jeff Morgan**: Stop a sec ... How many brothers and sisters do you have?
> **Fred West**: I'm the eldest.

Frederick Walter Stephen West was born in the Herefordshire village of Much Marcle on 29 September 1941, to Walter and Daisy West, Much Marcle being half an hour by car from Gloucester, just over the county border, but a place lost in time with a sense of remoteness. Much Marcle was and remains a beautiful village surrounded by cider orchards, rolling arable fields and Herefordshire cattle, in a landscape that turns yellow with daffodils in the spring. There are wealthy people in the area, living in fine houses, but the Wests were poor, semi-literate farm workers who lived by the seasons and could appear almost as ignorant as the beasts they tended. There were eight children, two of whom died in infancy, leaving three sisters and three brothers: Fred, John, Daisy, Doug, Kitty and Gwen. 'And we were a very happy family ... Very close,' Fred told the police. 'We all protected each other.' He described a childhood with traditional values. He said that it was important to him to have been christened and confirmed in the village church, St. Bartholomew's. Hazel Savage sounded surprised by this, asking why it mattered to Fred.

> **Fred West**: Because I love my own village.
> **DC Hazel Savage**: You're a country lad?
> **Fred West**: Yeah.

Mother, or Mam as he sometimes called her, was a formidable woman. Short of stature, and overweight, Daisy West laid down the law.

FRED'S EARLY LIFE

DC Hazel Savage: So, who was the boss in your house?
Fred West: Mother. No doubt about that. Mother was the boss. Even with my father … Should I explain this bit now about my mother and father? What happened, apparently, when my mother lost her first child[3] my father took to drink and [he] let everything go on drink. And Mother stepped in and stopped it. So from that day onward, Mother was always boss.

Mother was 'a pillar of steel'. She wore a thick leather belt which she used to beat her children, a habit Rose West adopted, surely inspired by tales Fred told her of his childhood. Maybe this was also the genesis of Fred being sexually excited by straps and beatings. Fred would climb a tree to escape Mam's wrath. 'And she used to say, "You'll come down when you're hungry."' When he climbed down, she thrashed him. In contrast, Dad was easy-going. 'He was so placid it was unreal,' said Fred, who said that he worshipped his father. 'He didn't judge nobody.'

Much Marcle was a close community, where everyone knew one another, from the land owners to the village constable, John Rock. There was little privacy. The postman read their mail, spreading gossip as he did his round. The farrier who shod the horses also repaired their boots. 'And we used to go and sit by the horse, feed the horse shoeing there, and you'd sit there and he'd make your boots.' Fred grew up around livestock, and the breeding and slaughter of animals left an impression on him. Mam kept a pig, which was fed on household scraps like a pet and often given a name, such as Sally. Inevitably the day came when the pig had to be slaughtered and Fred took part in this

---

3 Daisy West's first born, Violet, died within days of birth in 1940. Fred was next.

bloody ritual, his first domestic killing. 'Just slit its throat and bleed him,' he said. 'I mean, the main thing is to get the blood out ... every spot of blood had to be got out.' They hung the carcass in the yard to drain. At fourteen, Fred learned to use a shotgun and he went hunting, 'rabbiting, and [shooting] crows and squirrels'. Rabbits were shot for food for the family table. Crows, squirrels and foxes were considered pests by farmers who paid the village children 'half a crown or summat for a tail for squirrels' as proof of their destruction. Fred thereby grew up with killing and butchery, and from childhood he was used to handling dead creatures. He was no doubt desensitised by these experiences. He treated his victims as if they were animals, telling Janet Leach that the women that were killed were slaughtered like pigs.

When he left the village school at fifteen, Fred was barely able to read and write. His parents took him into Gloucester at this time to buy his first suit, from Burton's at the Cross, in the centre of the old town. That first visit to Gloucester endeared the city to Fred for life, 'I've always loved Gloucester,' he told the police. Fred would spend time in Birmingham, Bristol and Glasgow in adult life but such cities were too big for him. Gloucester, with a population of under 100,000 when he was young, more like a large town, was Fred's size.

For now, however, Much Marcle was home. When Fred was still small, the family moved to Moorcourt Cottage, tied to the farm where Walter worked as a labourer. After he left school Fred joined his dad on the land and he learned to turn his hand to most farm jobs: hedge-laying, beet-pulling, lambing, hay-making. Moorcourt Cottage was on a bend in the road heading out of Much Marcle towards the village of Kempley, the Wests' cottage surrounded by coppices and fields, including Fingerpost and Letterbox fields up the road. This was where Fred worked

FRED'S EARLY LIFE

and played. Hazel Savage asked about early girlfriends. 'Yeah, they were all there,' Fred laughed. 'No problem there.'

As much as he loved his village, Fred found country life restrictive as he entered puberty, 'as the seasons changed, you just did the same thing like'. He was fifteen when he tried to break free, riding his bike to Hereford where he got a job on a building site. He stayed there for a month or two, sleeping rough, never washing his clothes or himself, despite doing hard manual work. When he biked home, he was filthy. 'When I stripped off, my body underneath was black ...' He was never a clean man.

Fred returned from Hereford with enough money saved to buy a small 125 cc motorbike. Fred and a pal of his, Brian Hill, often rode their motorbikes into nearby Ledbury where they hung about the town's half-timbered market building, youth club and milk bar, chatting up girls. The boys were arrested together in April 1961 for stealing cigarette cases and a gold watch strap from a couple of high street shops, impetuous crimes punished with fines. This was the start of Fred's criminal life. By 1994, his record was two pages long, and petty convictions followed thick and fast in his youth. He came before magistrates again a few months later, in October 1961, for stealing from a building site where he'd been working. The court report in the Gloucester *Citizen* revealed Fred to be a young man who didn't know the difference between right and wrong. 'In court, West said other men took things from the stores, so he thought he could do the same.' He pleaded guilty and was fined £20.

Fred omitted these convictions from the account of his life he gave to the police in 1994, while exaggerating or inventing stories to make himself seem more of an adventurer than he was. Apart from being a liar, Fred was a fantasist who saw the world through a magnifying lens. He claimed to have graduated from his 125 cc pop-pop to a 1,000 cc Triumph motorbike, 'a massive thing'. Massive was a favourite adjective for Fred who often described large men, of whom he was scared, and overweight girls, whom he viewed with contempt, as 'massive', as if they were truly gigantic. A friend had two daughters who were so 'massive', he said, that 'when they opened the door – shit! – they took the hinges and all off'. One night when he was riding his massive motorbike near home (his brother Doug says it was the little 125 machine, not a Triumph, which may only have existed in his imagination) Fred had an accident. A local girl named Pat Manns had rested her push bike by the road, and as he came roaring around the bend Fred collided with Pat's bike, which sent him headfirst into a wall. His crash helmet was split open and he was taken unconscious to hospital. 'I was splattered. I mean, me hands all damaged, me face all smashed, and I was paralysed from the waist down for twelve months.' His nose was broken, and when he got back on his feet he walked with a clumping limp. The police confirmed that this story was basically true, though embellished. 'I don't know if he was as seriously injured as some people have said,' comments John Bennett, though Fred's nose was scarred and crooked for life. More significant was a suggestion within the family that Fred suffered some form of brain damage when he came off his bike. Around this time he also hurt his head falling from a fire escape, which may also have had an effect. Doug West recalls that Fred was 'out near a week' after the bike accident and he said that his brother became moodier, and quick-tempered as a result. He was a changed man.

In the next chapter of his young life, Fred claimed to have run away to sea at eighteen after a row with his mother. 'I called her an old cunt,' he sniggered. 'I went to the docks and got a job on the ships.' Gloucester is a minor port with docks linked to the River Severn by the Gloucester and Sharpness Canal, leading in turn to the Bristol Channel and the oceans beyond, so this was not impossible, but Fred's seafaring stories sounded like make-believe. 'I went to Jamaica and the Far East … everywhere.' He said that he had been 'locked up in Australia once for drunk and disorderly.' There was no record of any of this. In fact, there is no evidence that Fred travelled abroad even once in his life. He boasted of having had sex with 'hundreds' of women during his supposed seafaring years. Even if he had never crewed anything larger than a rowing boat on the lake in Cheltenham, such comments were revealing. Hazel Savage remarked upon Fred's prodigious sexual appetite, which he took as a compliment. 'Well, I mean, it's nothing for me and Rose to have it twice a night,' he bragged. He said that he was even randier in his youth. 'I can remember times when I slept with three or four girls, and at least twice with each – a night.'

> **DC Hazel Savage**: Really? A night!
> **Fred West**: Yeah, one night … just gone from one to the other, and gone back over them.
> **DC Savage**: And 'gone back over them'?

Such absurd boastfulness suggested to a sceptical mind that Fred might not be as virile as he liked people to think. He was obviously a misogynist. Perhaps he was sexually inadequate. Perhaps he secretly liked men. Fred seemed to be obsessed with same-sex relationships, after all, constantly referencing lesbians, who both excited and disgusted him. He agreed that he had encountered homosexuals 'in the navy', but he said that he had rejected their advances. Naturally.

THE FRED WEST TAPES

DC Hazel Savage: You're a man's man?
Fred West: Woman's man (snigger) ... I don't get anywhere near 'em ... gays.
DC Savage: Gays ... But when you say 'gay', do you mean just men with men, or do you mean also women with women?
Fred West: Oh, I like that ... I like lesbians ... Two girls who go together ... I couldn't kiss a man ... that's wrong, [but] there's nothing dirty about two women being attracted to each other, is there?

He seemed to have forgotten having told the police how concerned he and Rose were that Heather might be lesbian. Now they were on the subject of sex – Fred's favourite subject – he talked of having enjoyed group sex, including sex with up to three women at a time. Once he had made love to them all, 'they start messing about [together]. Then I just sit and watch 'em'. And he said he enjoyed watching Rose 'making love with another bloke. I mean, it's a turn on.' Almost anything went with Rose, 'as long as it's not hurting'.

DC Hazel Savage: How do you mean ...?
Fred West: Well, like a girl taking a whip to me, or me taking a whip to a girl ...

That was a lie. The police found two whips and a flail at 25 Cromwell Street.

Fred West: I met Rose at sixteen[4] and trained Rose to what I wanted ...

---

4   Rose was fifteen when she met Fred.

FRED'S EARLY LIFE

DC Hazel Savage: Exactly … you've trained her down to letters and commands, and she's complied.

DC Jeff Morgan asked Fred if Rose was happy in such a marriage. Fred guffawed, asking the detective if he thought that Rose would have stayed with him all these years if she wasn't. 'She thinks just as much of me as I do of her.' Hazel Savage suggested that Fred had 'great sexual needs' and he had to have Rose under his control to fulfil those needs. 'Yeah, but she's also got great sexual needs …' They had sex all the time, he said, only missing a couple of days a month when Rose had her period. When he started to talk like this, Fred became extremely explicit, saying outlandish things. He described how he liked to have sex with Rose directly after she had been with other men. Fred sometimes collected 'the sperm in her' in condoms, as part of a plan to artificially inseminate their children. Sex with Rose went on 'for hours, non-stop'. They experimented 'to keep our sex life alive and change it'. As revoltingly fascinating as all this was, they had gone off on a tangent. This happened frequently during Fred's interviews.

Returning to the subject of his youth, he told the police that when he came home from sea his mother took her belt off and beat him with it at the garden gate, saying, 'Welcome home, son, now we're level.' As he told such stories about his mother, Fred sounded like the West children talking about Rose. Like Rose, his mother also had odd ideas about sex.

Fred West: Mother was very old-fashioned in her ways. I mean … girlfriends was strictly out until you were twenty-one. Not sixteen, like twenty-one you had a girlfriend and thought of sex … Whereas Dad was different altogether. You know, 'If it's on offer take it, son.' That was my father's idea.

THE FRED WEST TAPES

DC Barbara Harrison: Yeah.

Fred West: Whatever you enjoy, do. You know. And make sure you don't get caught doing it, you know? (laughs)

Village matriarchs kept their sons on a short leash, he said, wanting them to match with the right girl when they were more mature. Sex before marriage was therefore furtive and shameful. Fred said that he and his contemporaries went around in 'one massive village gang' and whatever sexual experiences they had 'was done hush-hush like … somewhere in the woods, or anywhere quiet in a field'. A complex picture was emerging, with Fred's attitudes to women and sex formed years ago in the country.

While Fred was giving the police glimpses into his formative past, he left a lot out of the story of his childhood, boyhood and youth, including significant matters that emerged from other sources, creating a far more sinister picture of his early life. Foremost among his dark childhood secrets was the sad story of his sister Kitty, six years his junior. One day in 1961 when Kitty West was thirteen she was talking to some girls outside the science laboratory at Ledbury Secondary School when her friends remarked that she had put on weight. 'I'm pregnant,' she announced. Surprised to hear this, her friends said that they didn't know that Kitty had a boyfriend. 'Oh, it's not a boyfriend, me brother did it.'

'Who?'

'Fred.'

Mention of Fred West's name created a titter of excitement among the schoolgirls. Fred was considered to be one of the handsomest lads around, says Jean Korbi (*née* Friedrich) who was one of the girls talking to Kitty that day, Fred being a bit older

FRED'S EARLY LIFE

than them and eyed as prime marriage material in a rural area where many girls aspired to marry young lest they be 'left on the shelf'. One day Jean and her mum were walking through the lanes when they saw Fred and his brother John ploughing a field. Fred called out to Jean, 'Hello Babby!' which was a local term of endearment. Her mother remarked on what fine lads they were. 'Yeah, I know,' said Jean, feeling herself blush. '"I like that one," which was Fred ... He had a lovely smile, a nice wide smile, it lifted up his face. He was just a lovely guy!' All the girls fancied him. 'I think I fancied Fred a little bit. A crush, just a schoolgirl crush.' Now Fred's little sister was telling her school mates that Fred – that nice boy – had made her pregnant. Jean thought the Wests a bit backward, what the Americans call hillbillies, introverted village folk, maybe even interbred. 'I mean she [Kitty] was a bit Dolly Dimple.' The whole family 'seemed a bit odd [but] I'd never heard of anything like incest, and then she proceeded to tell us how it was done, where it was done.' Kitty told them that she and Fred had sex in her bedroom at Moorcourt Cottage, they did it 'lots of times'. She felt nervous at first. 'But Fred said because I'm his sister I wouldn't get pregnant.' Now she was having his baby! Her friends suggested that she should have slapped Fred. 'She said, "I wouldn't do that ... I quite like it." Or, "I look forward to it." Something like that,' recalls Jean. 'She liked it, or looked forward to it ... she seemed quite cool about it, "It's normal, haven't you done it?" sort of thing.' Jean never forgot the conversation. 'I remember it to this day, even where we was when she said it, because we were all in shock.'

The story reached the local police, and in June 1961 a detective interviewed Kitty and Fred who admitted having had sex with his sister, as she was telling people. 'Yes, of course, it is right what she said.' They had done it four or five times since December. 'Well, doesn't everyone do it?' Fred asked the officer.

THE FRED WEST TAPES

By the time Fred was brought before a judge at Herefordshire Assizes in November, charged with incest, he had changed his tune. Fred, now aged twenty, pleaded not guilty in court and his mother spoke up in his defence saying that Freddy (her favourite child) 'took the blame for many things which were not his fault'. The family GP said in Fred's defence that the lad had suffered head injuries in a motorbike accident, and may be epileptic as a result. This is the only medical evidence, such as it is, that Fred had any form of brain damage. Hardly conclusive, it is nonetheless intriguing.

It all came down to Kitty West's evidence. 'In the box the girl refused to say who had associated with her,' wrote a court reporter at the time, covering the case for the local paper in Ledbury. 'She was given a piece of paper and a pencil and asked to write down the name of the person, but she refused to do so.' The judge then ruled that they could not continue with a hostile witness, and directed the jury to return a not guilty verdict. So Fred walked free. The repercussions were significant. Kitty was expelled from school and she had an abortion. She never got over what happened and died in 2006, haunted by her past. Also, Fred learned that he could commit a sexual offence and get away with it, even if the police became involved. This was the first time Freddy the Fox got lucky in such circumstances. It wouldn't be the last.

Fred didn't mention what he did to Kitty when he regaled the police with his life story in 1994, preferring to describe his childhood in Much Marcle as an old-fashioned country idyll, but the fact that he had raped his sister was on record. He hadn't been charged with rape, but that's what it amounted to.

There was another significant family matter Fred omitted, which also came to light. 'Fred was abused by his own father,' his daughter Anna Marie later wrote, while Janet Leach told the

FRED'S EARLY LIFE

police that Fred told her he was abused by both his parents, and Fred told his kids that his dad abused some of his sisters. 'He [Fred] said it was a father's right to break his daughters in,' his daughter May was quoted as saying in *Inside 25 Cromwell St.*, a book published in 1995 as part of a newspaper deal under her name. 'According to him, that is what his father had done.' The weight of evidence is that Fred grew up in an incestuous home. The fact that he had initially, casually admitted to the police to having had intercourse with his sister showed that he thought sexual relations between family members was perfectly normal. When he discovered that it wasn't acceptable, he tried to cover it up.

Despite having got his little sister pregnant, Fred remained a popular figure among his peer group in Herefordshire. '[Fred] was still liked,' says Jean Korbi. 'All the teenage girls, his age group, they were all like drooling ... a lot of girls were after him.' After a slow start Fred had girlfriends, though they tended to be younger than him. Around this time, Fred began to see a fourteen-year-old girl from the nearby village of Newent, a person who can't be named for legal reasons. Fred took her to dances. He talked of wanting to marry her, and gave her a ring. When she was fifteen, Fred was driving her home from his parents' cottage when he pulled over at a farm gate and attacked the girl. 'He pushed me on the bank and raped me,' she said. Afterwards, she said that Fred behaved oddly: 'he fell over on to his back [as if] unwell.' Then he said sorry. The girl felt numb. '[I] just didn't know what to say.' Not long after this Fred raped her for a second time, at a flat. She didn't report the matter to the police until she gave a statement to detectives on the murder investigation in 1994.

Then Catherine 'Rena' Costello entered the story. Rena was a young peroxide blonde Scot who came to stay in Ledbury in the early 1960s, causing a stir in the community. 'We were in awe of her, because we had never seen anyone quite like it,' says Jean Korbi. 'She had dyed blonde hair and she wore mini-skirts. She had this broad [Scots accent and] she didn't give a damn about anything.'

Born in Coatbridge, Lanarkshire, on 14 April 1944, to Edward and Mary Costello, Rena was the product of a broken home. Dad was a scrap metal dealer and her mother left home when Rena was young. Rena was in trouble with the police from the age of eleven, when she first appeared in juvenile court for theft. She was sent to an approved school at fourteen, and when she was sixteen she was warned for importuning. A month later she was sent to Borstal (a type of reform school) for theft and attempted burglary. Released from Borstal in May 1962, Rena briefly trained as a nurse, but was soon arrested for theft again. A girl she had met during her Borstal training was from Herefordshire, so Rena came south to visit her, lodging initially in the New Inn in Ledbury and getting a job in the milk bar on the high street.

'I went in [the] café and I met Rena,' said Fred, who was now working as a lorry driver for Ledbury Farmers, delivering feed. He worked predominantly as a driver in early adulthood, one of his filthiest jobs being sucking unwanted male chicks into a tanker for disposal. Fred took Rena for a ride in his lorry. In his police interviews, he turned this into a tall story about them being followed by a detective, Rena telling him that she was 'on the run' and pregnant. The last part was true. Rena 'told Fred that the baby was [going to be] half-caste, as the father was a coloured man,' according to a statement by Rena's girlfriend, Margaret Clarke, who told the police that Fred and Rena decided to abort the baby. 'All three of us went to a local wood [near Ledbury] called Dog Hill, and while I kept lookout Fred tried to abort the baby, but was unsuccessful.' As a result, Rena was examined by a doctor and the police were informed. Having failed to get rid of Rena's baby, Margaret Clarke says that Fred and Rena decided to marry, with Rena now telling people that the baby was Fred's.

'She was showing a bit, because she had a short black skirt on and it was so tight you could see, and a little jumper over the top,' recalls Jean Korbi, who asked Rena what her parents thought about the situation.

'They don't need to know, they wouldn't care anyway.'

'But you're on your own.'

'Fred's going to marry me,' Rena said, leaving Jean to assume that Fred was the father. 'It'll be lovely to have a little family at last.' Rena said that she and Fred were in love. 'I'm gonna be happy.' Local girls were jealous of her for having caught Fred.

When Fred spoke to the police about this in 1994, he denied that it was a love match. 'It was just a convenience thing,' he said, but Rena tattooed 'Fred + Rena' and a heart on his left arm, so maybe she had feelings for him.

They married hastily in Ledbury on 17 November 1962, when Fred was twenty-one and Rena was eighteen. His brother, John, who had been dating Rena's friend, was their witness. Afterwards, the little wedding party swigged from a bottle of sherry on the high street. 'Mam went mad,' Fred told the police. 'Calling Rena a lot of names.' Daisy West wouldn't have Rena in the house, so they decided to move to Scotland where Rena gave birth to a baby girl, Charmaine, at the Alexander Hospital in Coatbridge. The biological father was never identified, but Charmaine had dark skin. Fred suggested that the father was a Pakistani businessman, who was Rena's pimp. He nicknamed him Billy Boy. Police inquiries suggested a more prosaic explanation. Rena had worked on the buses in Glasgow, and Charmaine's father may have been an Asian-born bus driver.

THE FRED WEST TAPES

Typically, Fred painted a colourful picture of the time he spent living in Scotland. What he said didn't show him in a flattering light.

> **DC Darren Law**: Were you having a [sexual] relationship with Rena at that point, Fred …?
> **Fred West**: I weren't allowed to … I couldn't make love to her … I had to leave when told to leave …

He had married a prostitute, or a woman who dabbled in prostitution, and even if Charmaine's father wasn't a pimp Rena probably associated with such people, with Fred relegated to the role of driver. He was even told by 'Billy Boy' when he could and couldn't see Rena. 'He's the father [of Charmaine],' said Fred, characterising Billy Boy as one of those massive men who strode through his life like giants. 'He's the big boy. He's six-foot-something tall. I've never seen someone so tall in my life.' Rena and Billy Boy spoke in his language, 'I haven't got a clue [what],' said Fred, but he picked up a few phrases, 'words that was more protection to me than anything else, like "Get out of the way!" "Leave!"' The humiliation was glaring.

Rena was soon pregnant again, however, this time with Fred's child. Fred said that she never forgave him. Their daughter, Anna Marie, was born in Glasgow in 1964. All this happened during the period Fred also claimed to be travelling the world in the merchant navy, showing that to be a pack of lies, but it would be a mistake to assume that Fred lied all the time in his interviews. Some of his most colourful stories, though they were hard to believe at first, proved to be true.

Fred said that while Rena was prostituting herself in Glasgow he got a job driving a Mr Whippy ice cream van, touring the estates on the outskirts of the city, playing the tune of the

FRED'S EARLY LIFE

'Teddy Bears Picnic' to alert children that he was coming. He claimed to have had affairs with women he met on his round doing the job. One of the areas he visited was Castlemilk where cheap new homes had been built since the slum clearances. Fred said that he befriended a three-year-old boy in Castlemilk, a lad who regularly came to his van. He brought a ball for the boy to play with. One day when Fred was driving out of the cul-de-sac where the boy lived, he heard a dreadful sound. 'There was an almighty bang, and I stopped,' Fred told the police, sniffing back tears. 'I was on top of his head, and it was his head that made the bang.' He looked under his van. 'I see that the child was lying underneath the van, under the back axle ...' There was a commotion, people running to the scene, yelling, 'Stop!' It was too late.

Was this the first person he killed? The police struggled to confirm the story at the time. There was nothing about it on Fred's record. Much later, a Scottish family came forward saying that the story was true, identifying the victim as Harry Feeney, the three-year-old son of labourer Peter Feeney and his wife, Patsy. Young Harry had been playing in a close off Stravanan Street in Castlemilk with his cousin, Raymond, when the ice cream van appeared. 'I had seen people running up the street, a lot of yelling and screaming,' says Raymond's sister Isabel Kirby (*née* Corbett), who was twelve at the time, living yards away on the same estate. She now lives in Canada, and she recently told me the whole story for the first time. 'It was wee Harry lying in the street.' Harry's parents were alerted. Fred told the police that the distraught father confronted him. 'He was going to kill me ...' Isabel confirms this. 'Uncle Peter was gonna kill him.' In his police interview on Thursday, 3 March 1994, Fred remembered the incident well enough to give the detectives the date that it happened. 'I backed over a young boy and killed him,' he said. 'And that was 4th November [1965]. He must've been three or four.' He said this happened in Castlemilk, recalling a cul-de-sac near a street which he mispronounced slightly. Being semi-literate, Fred was not reliable on proper names, and usually he was hopeless on dates, but in this case he remembered every detail.

Fred was questioned at the time, but the Scottish police concluded that it was a tragic accident and he wasn't charged with any crime. The family do not agree, and they never forgot the name Fred West. To them, he was the ice cream man who killed wee Harry. When Fred made national news in March 1994 – the murder story was getting more attention now – Harry's father was still alive, and he recognised Fred from the coverage. 'The first thing my Uncle Peter said [was], "That's the fucking bastard that done it to young Harry,"' says Isabel. 'He said, "that fucking bastard murdered my boy."' The family don't believe that it was an accident, pointing out that Fred had space to drive his van out of the cul-de-sac without backing up. 'He done it for the thrill of it,' says Isabel. 'I think he was just plain evil.'

Fred told the police that he fled Glasgow after this incident – 'I run for it' – claiming that he was frightened for his life. Leaving Rena behind, he drove Charmaine and Anna Marie home to Much Marcle.

Where were Rena and Charmaine now? There was no sign of either one of them.

5
NINE MORE (APPROX.)

Friday, 4 March 1994 • Day Nine
Gloucester Central Police Station

> 'I don't think any of them were cut up. I wouldn't
> be 100 per cent on that, mind.'
> FRED WEST

The police were under growing pressure to identify the third body in the garden, the woman they were referring to as 'Shirley's mate'; and to account for members of Fred's family and other women and girls who had passed through 25 Cromwell Street over the years, including lodgers and their friends. The detectives had some names, which they put to Fred towards the end of the week. His replies were flippant and unhelpful. Asked about one ex-lodger, who had since suffered with serious health problems, he said callously: 'She's now a cabbage, isn't she?' He dismissed another woman as a 'big fat girl'.

The police had a third name.

DC Jeff Morgan: How about Lynda Gough?
Fred West: Don't ring a bell.

THE FRED WEST TAPES

Lynda Gough was the daughter of John and June Gough, Mr Gough being a senior fire brigade officer in Gloucester. Born 1 May 1953, Lynda was the eldest of three children. She had learning difficulties, attended a special school and left at sixteen to work as a seamstress for the Co-op in Barton Street. Just before she turned twenty, in April 1973, she unexpectedly left home. The police had found evidence of a link to 25 Cromwell Street. Asked if the unidentified victim in the garden could be Lynda Gough, Fred said, 'Wouldn't have thought so.'

On Friday, Hazel Savage told Fred that officers had been to see Lynda Gough's parents and her mother remembered a woman she thought was Rose West calling for her daughter shortly before she disappeared, inviting her out for a drink. After Lynda left home June Gough tried to find out where Lynda was staying and her investigations led her to 25 Cromwell Street, where she met both Fred and Rose. The Wests denied to her at first that Lynda had lodged with them, but then Mrs Gough glanced down at Rose's feet. 'I immediately noticed that [she] was wearing Lynda's slippers ...' Looking up, Mrs Gough also saw her daughter's laundry drying on the washing line.

Now Fred remembered. He told Savage that Lynda had come to them, asking to rent a room. The Wests 'interviewed' her to make sure that she was suitable, and 'dropped her home a few times'. Lynda hadn't stayed with them very long. She left with a boyfriend, bound for Weston-super-Mare in Somerset. That's what they told her mother. He struggled to explain why Rose might have been wearing Lynda's slippers.

DC Hazel Savage: We're going to conclude the interview in a minute. But I think it's only right to tell you that the police are actively involved in digging up the rest of your house. Are you aware of that?

NINE MORE (APPROX.)

Fred West: No …

DC Savage: The whole lot, the floor in the house, the conservatory[5] is being demolished, and the whole lot … They do intend to, certainly, dig up the whole of the basement. Do you want to ask any questions?

Fred West: You'll bring the house down, there's no footings underneath it.

When the police had left the room, Janet Leach told Fred that he should say if there were more victims. The strain was starting to get to her, and she told Fred that this had gone on long enough. Fred insisted that he had already told the police everything. Janet said, frankly, that she didn't believe him.

Fred stared into space, watched closely by Janet and the legal clerk, Scott Canavan. It was now clear that the police knew about Lynda Gough, and that they were going to search the house, whether Fred liked it or not. What was the best way for him to play the situation? Fred seemed nonplussed and lost in thought.

'Fred, is there any more bodies?' Scott Canavan asked him.

'There's a fucking load more.'

Scott alerted his boss, Howard Ogden, who hurried to the police station to consult with his client. When Fred was alone with his solicitor his manner changed from the deferential though crude man who spoke quite nicely to the police. 'He'd seek to be, he thought, reasonable in his interviews and courteous,' explains Ogden. 'He [was] very respectful of authoritarian figures, but then when he was with me [in private] he spoke at the speed of a machine gun, and every other word was an expletive.' After their confab, Ogden asked to

---

5   DC Savage must have meant the extension; there was no conservatory.

see Detective Superintendent John Bennett. He advised Bennett to sit down, then handed him a note. It was a new confession, which Ogden had written down:

> *I Frederick West authorise my solicitor Howard Ogden to advise Supt. Bennett that I wish to admit to a further (approx) 9 killings, expressly, Charmaine, Reena (sic), Linda (sic) Gough and others to be identified.*
> *F West*

Serial murder is sometimes said to mean three or more killings, with gaps between. Fred had already reached that threshold, but with this note, at a stroke of the pen, the Cromwell Street investigation was transformed into something huge. There was no doubt now that this was a serial murder case of the first magnitude. It was, indeed, mass murder. Not only had Fred killed his daughter, Heather; his pregnant girlfriend/lodger, Shirley Robinson; and a friend of hers (name unknown); he was also now admitting to killing his first wife, Rena; her daughter, Charmaine; the missing seamstress Lynda Gough; and six other females to be identified. Twelve in total, 'approx'. This was mind blowing. John Bennett faced a unique, career-defining job. Neither he nor any of his officers had any experience of investigating a serial murder case. The crime is so rare that the British police are not generally trained to deal with it. Now the superintendent found himself in the middle of such a huge and daunting inquiry, facing challenges that seemed almost overwhelming. 'It's a wave coming up the beach that bowls you over,' he said. 'The investigation was one of a kind.'

When interviews resumed forty minutes later, there was a lot to discuss. With the help of Leach and Canavan, Fred had

NINE MORE (APPROX.)

prepared a diagram of 25 Cromwell Street for the police, with the new graves marked. One was under the downstairs bathroom.

> **DC Hazel Savage**: Who's that ... under the floor in the bathroom?
> **Fred West**: Lynda.
> **DC Savage**: Lynda who?
> **Fred West**: Um, Gough, is it?

The previous day Fred had said that he had never heard Lynda's name. Less than twenty-four hours later he told the police where she was buried. Meanwhile, more of her story emerged.

Back in 1972–73, when the Wests started renting rooms out, most of their tenants were young men. One of these early lodgers was an eighteen-year-old youth named Ben Stanniland, who shared a bedsit on the top floor of the house with a friend of his, David Evans. Ben Stanniland met Lynda Gough in a café. They dated, sleeping together in his bedsit at Cromwell Street, where Lynda also slept with his friend, Evans, who slept with Rose West one night, as did Stanniland. It was that sort of place. The young men also smoked pot, which resulted in police raids, one of which earned Evans a conviction for possession of cannabis. As Stanniland later said, the boys were 'known to the police'. After her association with Stanniland and Evans waned, Lynda seems to have done some babysitting for the Wests. She may also have become involved with Rose sexually. One morning Ben Stanniland walked into Rose's room, when he was looking for the Hoover, and found Lynda and Rose together. It felt awkward, 'the reaction was shock ... it was the wrong time to actually knock on the door,' he said.

Fred did not offer an explanation for what happened to Lynda

Gough straight away, but he confirmed that he had killed her and said that she was buried under the bathroom floor.

> **DC Hazel Savage**: So that sorts [that] out. So when the police excavate this piece [of the house] it should be quite easy to recover Lynda Gough when they knock this down.
> **Fred West**: What, they're gonna actually knock the building down?

He squealed like a child who is told that his toy might be taken away. He didn't care a jot about his victims, but he cared about his house. Apparently motivated by the desire to limit damage to his property, Fred then told the police precisely where to look for the other bodies, stressing that there was no reason to search anywhere else. 'There's nothing on the other floors.' He explained who was buried in the cellar, as far as he could remember. 'That's the girl from Newent,' he said, pointing to where he had marked a grave under the stairs in the cellar. Newent is a village between Gloucester and Much Marcle.

> **DC Hazel Savage**: Do you know this girl's name?
> **Fred West**: No
> **DC Savage**: Alright.
> **Fred West**: I did know it at the time, but I forgot it now there's so many. I mean, I knew her well cos we'd had an affair.

He said that all these victims 'ended up this way because they threatened to tell Rose'. Another victim was a foreign hitch-hiker. He didn't know her name either, but he thought she might have been Dutch. So they began to refer to her in the

NINE MORE (APPROX.)

room as the Dutch Girl. He gave the Dutch Girl a lift, had sex with her, killed her and buried her in the cellar. His account of this series of murders was different to how he talked about Heather and Shirley Robinson. Those were domestic murders (Shirley being pregnant with his child was almost like a member of the family). These other women seemed to be strangers, or people Fred hardly knew. He spoke about them dismissively as if they were all the same, and what happened was their fault. He said that they all made the fatal mistake of not taking him seriously when he told them that it was a casual relationship, '[but] every one of them did exactly the same [saying] "I love you, I'm pregnant, I'm gonna tell Rose. I want you to come and live with me." And that was the problem.' This was a grotesque falsehood. Fred said that his next problem had been making sure that Rose didn't find out that he'd killed the women.

DC Hazel Savage: I expect she knows, really.
Fred West: Well, how does she know? ... she knew nothing whatsoever about this ... That's why she was sent out, and everything else.

Now that they were faced with twelve potential murder victims, the police had new questions for Fred; there were many details they needed to know, such as when these killings started. Making no mention of the little Scots boy, Harry Feeney (who didn't feature at all in the Cromwell Street inquiry), Fred said that the killings began when he did away with his first wife, Rena, after he left Scotland. They were fighting over Charmaine, who was living with Fred and Rose in Gloucester. Rena was drunk when he drove her and Charmaine out to the fields near Much Marcle, 'in the country where I know, and I strangled her and buried her'.

THE FRED WEST TAPES

DC Hazel Savage: And is Charmaine there, too?
Fred West: No ... I strangled Rena, dug the hole, cut her up, and buried her.

He went back to the car afterwards and saw Charmaine asleep on the back seat. 'I thought, shit, what am I gonna do now? ... She must have been six or seven, perhaps eight [years old] ... So, anyway, I strangled her while she was sleeping ...' The child wet herself when she died, just as he'd said Heather lost control of her bowels when he strangled her, horribly authentic details that no one would make up. He wrapped Charmaine in a blanket and drove home with the corpse. At the time, he and Rose were renting a ground floor flat at 25 Midland Road, across the park from Cromwell Street. Fred buried Charmaine in the coal cellar behind their old flat, telling Rose that Charmaine had gone off with Rena. Years later Fred did some building work on the Midland Road house, he was friends with the landlord, which gave him an opportunity to secure the grave.

★ ★ ★

There were so many admissions in Fred's '9 more' note, that the officers soon had to move on to the next crime. Fred was admitting to killing six victims whom he couldn't name, but the police suspected that they already knew who one of these women might be.

DC Darren Law: Lucy Partington ...?
Howard Ogden: Does that mean anything to you, Fred?
Fred West: Yeah, she's there ... Used to call her Juicy Lucy ... just a girl I was knocking off.

NINE MORE (APPROX.)

In contrast to most of his victims, Lucy Partington's background was one of comfort and privilege, though she came from a broken home. Lucy's parents Margaret and Roger Partington were professional people. Margaret worked as an architect, Roger was an executive with ICI. He left home when Lucy was twelve. The family were related to the novelist Sir Kingsley Amis. His writer son, Martin Amis, was one of Lucy's cousins, a couple of years her senior. Born 4 March 1952, Lucy was a twenty-one-year-old student at Exeter University in 1973, studying medieval English, when she came home to her mother's house in Gretton, a village outside Cheltenham, for Christmas. Lucy was friendly with a disabled girl named Helen Render, who lived near Pittville Park in Cheltenham, and Lucy visited Helen almost daily during the holidays, including 27 December, when she wrote an application letter to the Courtauld Institute of Art in London, where she hoped to study for an MA. Lucy left Helen's house that evening at 10:15, carrying her letter which she intended to post on her way to Evesham Road, where she would catch her bus home. 'It was quite a lonely bus stop,' says Lucy's sister, Marian. 'And that particular night it was very dark because there were miners' strikes at the time, so the [street] lighting was off.' The weather was also bad. It was sleeting.

Evesham Road led to Bishop's Cleeve, where Rose's parents lived. The police surmised that Fred and Rose may have been visiting Rose's mother the day after Boxing Day. If so, they may have been driving home, in their grey Ford Popular ('Vote Conservative' stickers on the back) when they saw Lucy waiting at the bus stop. Steve West was a baby at this time and it is unlikely that he would have been left at home. The offer of a lift from a young family with a babe in arms may have seemed safe to Lucy. 'She was renowned for being sensible,' says sister Marian. By coincidence, Lucy had recently visited

THE FRED WEST TAPES

St. Bartholomew's Church in Much Marcle. Fred's mother Daisy was buried in the churchyard, having died five years previously, and Fred sometimes visited his widowed father in the village. It is conceivable that he had bumped into Lucy. She would have been far more likely to accept a lift from someone she had met, however briefly.

Marian stayed out with friends that night. When she got home the next day she found her mother in a distraught state. 'My mum rushed out of the house and said "Lucy didn't come home last night!" in terrible panic. Mum had gone in to wake her up ... to discover that she wasn't there.' Sensing at once that something terrible had happened, one of Marian's brothers started swearing, saying that he would kill the man responsible. 'He immediately went to that place,' she says, meaning her brother made the assumption straight away that a man had killed their sister. The family contacted the police and there was an extensive, well-publicised search for Lucy, with missing posters and television appeals extending into the new year. Several of the older officers in the Cromwell Street inquiry, including John Bennett, took part in the 1973–74 search for Lucy Partington.

A cold case was reopened. DC Savage asked Fred what he meant when he spoke about 'Juicy Lucy'.

> **Fred West**: It's just that she was juicy, what I call juicy ... wet juicy, like.
> **DC Hazel Savage**: You're talking about sex now?
> **Fred West**: Yeah, yeah.

The officers had to suppress personal feelings of disgust and outrage. The Partington family was informed that Fred was confessing to having killed Lucy. Her mother had kept her bedroom unchanged all these years in the dim hope that she

NINE MORE (APPROX.)

would turn up one day. Mum didn't want to admit that Lucy was dead. Now all hope was extinguished. 'They said that Frederick West had been talking to them,' says Marian. 'There were five more young women in the basement, and one of them was called Lucy.'

The story Fred proceeded to tell about Lucy was, however, a pornographic fantasy. He said that he met her when he was visiting Pittville Park with his family, feeding the ducks on the lake. 'Rose was there somewhere,' he said, then quickly tried to cover up a slip of the tongue that might implicate his wife, 'but I think Rose was down on the swings with someone.' With Rose out of sight, he chatted Lucy up. They met regularly for months, making love in the park. Fred seemed to be borrowing memories to fabricate this tale. Pittville Park was where he and Rose met, in secret when she was underage. In a 1969 love letter, Rose wrote to him:

> *Dear Fred,*
> *I'm glad you came to see me after all ... I love you Fred, but if anything goes wrong again it'll be the end of both of us for good ... we mustn't be seen together ... Anyway, if I don't see you before Sunday then meet me outside the boating hut in Piteville (sic)[6] Park at approx 2:30 to 3:00 PM Sunday afternoon. Kep saying those pray's and remember I'll always love you,*
> *Lot's of Love, Rose xxxxxx*

Fred said that his 'affair' with Lucy was doubly secret, because she had a boyfriend. In fact, Lucy had never had a serious boyfriend, in addition to which she was a recent convert to

---
6 Retaining her misspellings.

Roman Catholicism. 'Her sexual status was innocent,' notes Marian. Fred told the police that after they had been seeing each other for a while Lucy 'come the loving racket', saying that she wanted to give up her boyfriend to be with Fred. When Lucy got 'nasty' about this, Fred 'grabbed her by the throat' and strangled her. He brought her body home to bury.

> **DC Hazel Savage**: Is there anybody else involved with you?
> **Fred West**: Nobody at all.

This interview ended just before 9:00 PM. Having agreed to show the police where he had buried these other women – including Lucy and the ones he was referring to by nicknames (the Dutch Girl, the Girl from Newent) – Fred was then taken back to 25 Cromwell Street. This time they took him inside his house.

Since the 1970s, Fred had altered his home considerably. The front door now opened on to a new hall leading to a tool room, which in turn gave access to an enlarged kitchen-cum-living area. A small downstairs bathroom was incorporated into this shack-like extension (the roof leaked when it rained), having been built over a car inspection pit which was behind the house when the Wests moved in. The pit had served as a ready-made grave for Lynda Gough. There was a floor panel in the living area, covered with carpet, that revealed an old set of steps, which was the original outside entrance to the cellar, now inside the extension. A sideboard had been placed over the trap door, as if to hide it. It had been used by the children in the past, though. There had also originally been a front area entrance to the cellar, but that had been filled in. Primary access to the cellar was now via a flight of steps in the middle of the house.

NINE MORE (APPROX.)

Descending these steps with Fred, the police entered a cramped, dank tomb that had also served as a dormitory for his children. The younger ones were locked in the cellar at night, using a bucket for a toilet, which they slopped out in the morning like prisoners. They had put stickers on the walls and drawn cartoons in the manner of prisoners who put graffiti on cell walls. The police called the cellar area with stickers 'the nursery alcove'. Two other walls were papered with images of Marilyn Monroe from her films, with the film titles printed as part of the wallpaper: *Niagara*, *The Seven Year Itch* and *Bus Stop*. Monroe was one of the world's great sex symbols when Fred was young, and bus stops were significant in the murders. Fred also stored tools and building materials down in the cellar, and he seemed to be in the process of converting the space again. He proudly pointed out some of his DIY work to the officers. Head clearance in the cellar was low, at five foot nine inches, because he had poured in so much concrete. The police noticed four holes drilled through the ceiling joists in the rear part of the cellar, as though to hang something. Or someone. The holes were positioned so that a body might be suspended – spreadeagled – by hands and feet. The edges of the holes were worn, as if by ropes rubbing the timber.

The police gave Fred a can of red spray paint and invited him to mark the concrete floor where he had buried his victims, covering the graves over with the concrete. 'That line there ... She's there, or somewhere just on the edge of there,' Fred muttered as he sprayed. 'That's the second girl.' He marked five graves in total: Lucy in the nursery alcove; another grave under the stairs; two in the front part of the cellar (nearest the street), and one in the back. 'He would say, "Yes, I think I put [Lucy] here" and the other girls' names. He went round [and] we marked everything on the floor,' said an officer who was at the scene. Fred sprayed 'bodey' in one place. That was how he spelt the word. 'He was an odd sort of character,' added the officer, understating the case. As creepy as the cellar was, it had been even more insalubrious when the women were murdered. In the 1970s it was 'a cold, wet, damp cave', as Rose had told the police before she was bailed. The floor was originally paved with bricks, and when the drains flooded the cellar filled with water. It stank. It still did. Janet Leach had accompanied Fred and the officers on this visit and when she went home that night she couldn't get the smell of damp and decay out of her nostrils.

The search team started to excavate the cellar the following morning, Saturday, 5 March, using Ground Penetrating Radar to identify voids, then drilling down through the concrete. Fred had constructed a false fireplace in the front part of the cellar. He had spray-marked a grave in what might be thought of as the hearth. 'That's the girl in the fireplace,' he said. They started digging here. By noon the police had broken through the concrete, and a blue plastic membrane Fred had laid down to keep the water out, opening a stinking waterlogged hole, filled with adipocere and bones. This was all that was left of the Dutch Girl. She had been decapitated, and her legs had been removed. Fred told police that he cut the head off over the hole, to drain the blood, as his family had bled the pig. There was a knotted scarf with the skull, rolled and tied to make a loop.

On the opposite side of the cellar was a real fireplace. The fireplace and the surrounding walls were decorated with the Marilyn Monroe wallpaper. Fred had put a gate across the fireplace. The juxtaposition of funereal ironwork with voluptuous images of Marilyn Monroe, the words *Bus Stop* still visible, was extremely creepy, creating a grave and a sex shrine. When the police dug down in front of the fire a skull was uncovered.

NINE MORE (APPROX.)

* * *

Everybody involved in the investigation was astonished by what Fred West was saying, and what was being found at 25 Cromwell Street. As grim as the work was, there was a sense of excitement within the murder squad, officers remarking to their colleagues that they felt fortunate to be working on such a unique and fascinating case. People privy to the facts naturally wanted to talk about it, and one person with inside knowledge decided to share that information with my newspaper.

'Howard, can you take this call?' asked my news editor that Saturday morning. I was at work at the multi-storey *Mirror* building on Holborn Circus in London, where I was a general news reporter for the *Sunday Mirror*, sister paper to the *Daily Mirror*, when newspapers like ours sold in the millions. Saturday was production day and the news room was full of people putting tomorrow's paper together. 'It's someone ringing from Gloucester about that murder case.' I had been a journalist for ten years by 1994, having started in the business almost straight from school, working mostly for tabloid newspapers. Much of my time was spent investigating leads about TV celebrities, errant politicians and the younger members of the Royal Family. I travelled all over the UK and abroad doing that. Sometimes the stories stood up. Often they didn't, and you got nothing in the paper. Crime was part of the editorial mix of the *Mirror* and there was more emphasis on hard news stories on Saturday, writing for a Sunday paper, but most of what I did during the week didn't seem important and I was feeling jaded with my job as I approached thirty, thinking I should be doing something different. I was so fed up, in fact, that I almost hadn't come to work that Saturday. As I picked up the phone, I didn't know that I was taking a call that would reinvigorate me and change the course of my career.

THE FRED WEST TAPES

I struggled to think what the murder case in Gloucester was all about. In police terms this was Day Ten of the Cromwell Street investigation, but the news story had developed gradually, starting as a missing person case which attracted mostly local interest. The national press started to pay attention after the police confirmed the discovery of human remains on 27 February (Day Four), but it was still a domestic murder inquiry. The story had become bigger on 1 March (Day Six), when the police announced that they had recovered three victims from the garden. The nationals started to call the case the Garden of Evil. It was not yet a sensation, however. That was about to change.

The caller – our 'source', whose identity I've never revealed – told me that they had inside information. The previous afternoon, Fred West had confessed to nine more murders, and everything he said I was now told. There were six bodies under cement in 25 Cromwell Street, one under the bathroom, the rest in the cellar, including one under a fireplace, while Fred's first wife and her daughter were buried elsewhere. The source said that the victims included lodgers and women who had gone missing years ago, including a known missing person, Lucy Partington. 'A number of the victims may have been dismembered.' I scribbled all this down, thanked the caller, then spoke to my news editor who summoned Chris House, our crime reporter.

Chris was an older journalist, gruff, ruddy-faced and world-weary, speaking with what might be described as a Cockney accent. He telephoned Gloucestershire police who confirmed that what I had been told was true, though the press office didn't seem to be very pleased that we had found out. Then Chris and I sat down at a large, beige-coloured word processor to write the story together. 'What shall we call it?' Chris asked me, as my fingers hovered over the keyboard. 'Garden of Evil is no

NINE MORE (APPROX.)

good anymore. Most of the bodies are inside the house. Any ideas, 'Oward?'

'I don't know.'

'Let's call it 'ouse of 'orrors.'

So we wrote a story beginning, 'Murder squad detectives are searching for nine more bodies in the House of Horrors investigation …' The story was published under a joint by-line, my name printed first because I took the call. It was some time before I realised that several previous addresses in criminal history, including the abodes of 'Doctor' Crippen and John Christie, both of whom buried their victims at home, had also been described as a house of horrors. The name was far from original, but it stuck.

As Chris and I wrote our story, Fred was talking again to Jeff Morgan and Barbara Harrison in the interview room in Gloucester. He had drawn a diagram of his previous address, 25 Midland Road, marking where he had buried Charmaine with a C. He said he buried her shortly after he got out of prison in 1971. Dates turned out to be important in Charmaine's murder. Fred's record showed that he was arrested in November 1970 for stealing from a Cheltenham tyre fitters, having been arrested the previous month for driving on a stolen tax disc without an MOT, vehicle licence or insurance. On 3 December, he was remanded into custody, shortly after which he was sentenced to ten months in prison (including a six-month suspended sentence for yet another conviction), and held initially in HMP Gloucester. On 27 January 1971, he was moved to HMP Leyhill, an open prison in Gloucestershire, the relevance being that he couldn't have murdered Charmaine while he was locked up. His release date was 24 June. He claimed that the crime was committed just after that date, in the summer of 1971, half a lifetime ago when the world was watching the last Apollo moon landings.

THE FRED WEST TAPES

Fred West: What happened was, Rena came round [to] see Rose when I [was] in prison and Rose said, 'Look, you'll have to wait until Fred's home.' It was only a couple of weeks.

He claimed to have killed Rena first, after a row, then he killed Charmaine, but he said that he didn't cut Charmaine up. 'I couldn't touch a small child, and hurt her.' While he repeatedly said that Rose knew nothing about the killings, contested custody of Rena's eldest daughter seemed to create the problem that resulted in double domestic murder. Fred agreed to take the police to where he had buried Rena. It was in Letterbox Field, up the road from his parents' cottage. 'The reason I know all these fields now is because I worked them when I was young,' Fred told them. DC Harrison fetched an Ordnance Survey map, which they pored over together in the interview room like a treasure map. 'That's the road ... that's the woods ...There, just there,' said Fred, pointing to the spot. He drew a circle.

'It would be nice to do it now,' said DC Morgan, checking his watch. The time was just after 1:00 PM.

Within the hour they were at the scene, on a bend in the lane to Kempley. Letterbox and Fingerpost were adjacent arable fields belonging to two farms. Fingerpost Field on the left, named for the mile post on the corner, was part of Bridge Farm; Letterbox Field on the right, named after a post box at the entrance, over which grew an oak tree, was part of Stonehouse Farm. It was a pretty place, even on a damp March afternoon. The police brought Fred to the scene in a truck marked 'Underwater Search Unit' to fool the press. He had an anorak draped over him, the hood up to shield his face, and once again he was handcuffed to a large policeman to make sure that he didn't escape. He pointed

NINE MORE (APPROX.)

to the hedgerow not far from the gate, saying gnomically that he had a 'feeling' Rena was thereabouts, no more than a feeling. 'The area that the prisoner was indicating is under the nearest tree,' said the officer filming on videotape. Fred was behaving strangely again.

Back at the station he spoke of having had a supernatural experience in the field. Rena's spirit had come before him in a white evening dress, he said, under which he could see her bra. She gave him a kiss. 'Rena come fucking straight into me, man.' He tried to hold her with him, but she disappeared back to the spirit world.

What was more, he sensed a second ghost in the field.

That evening Fred was interviewed again. As the police strove to identify his victims, he began to refer to two 'Worcester girls', saying that he met these victims in the Worcester area, about thirty miles from Gloucester, in the 1970s. They were among the five women buried in the cellar. Fred's account of the Worcester crimes was confusing. He said that he picked the women up separately as hitch-hikers back when he was a lorry driver, but he also suggested that they knew each other. He claimed never to have known their names, when they died, or which was which among the graves in the cellar. All he could say was that they were young, aged seventeen to nineteen, one had a bandaged hand from a firework burn, and they both wore heavy make-up. He suggested that they were prostitutes, of which there was no evidence. In fact, throughout his interviews, Fred revealed an obsession with prostitutes. He had married a prostitute in Rena, and encouraged Rose to prostitute herself, even getting Rose to use the same working name Rena had used, which was Mandy. But he also spoke of prostitutes with contempt and anger. He said that he was outraged when one of the Worcester women asked him for money after sex.

THE FRED WEST TAPES

Fred West: I said to her, 'I don't carry money …' 'Oh no,' she said, you'll pay me or I'll report you.' I said, 'Report me for what?' She said, 'You raped me.'
DC Barbara Harrison: Yeah.
Fred West: I said, 'You can piss off and all.' So, I mean, I stopped the lorry and we had a right set-to, and the next minute I smacked her up against the window and she just dropped … anyway, I strangled her, or held my hands around her neck … and that was it. She just slid down to the bottom of the lorry.

As the interview continued, he embellished his confession while adding to the confusion about which Worcester victim he was referring to. He thought that he had 'made love' to one of them twice. He never admitted to raping any of his victims, which was what really happened.

His story about the other Worcester victim was much the same as the first.

Fred West: I picked her up just outside Worcester … I was just generally talking to her as I was going along, and the next minute [she's] got me fly undone, and messing about, so I did the same. I just pulled in and, um, er, I made … we made love … then she said, 'That'll be £10' or something, and I said, 'Well, I don't carry money [and] anyway I wouldn't pay a prostitute … If you had said that in the first place,' I said, 'I'd have told you to get lost.' And then she started shouting and she said … 'You're the sort of person who goes with slags' or something …
DC Barbara Harrison: Hmm.
Fred West: And I just lost the (*sic*) head with her. Because as soon as she said that I thought of Rose, and Rose is no

NINE MORE (APPROX.)

slag as far as I was concerned. So I went for her, and the same thing happened with her.

He drove the body home. DC Harrison asked Fred if he cut this victim up. He became bashful, as he did occasionally when speaking to female police officers.

Fred West: I ain't sure.
DC Barbara Harrison: Do you remember what you did?
Fred West: I ain't sure ... I don't think any of them were cut up ... I wouldn't be 100 per cent on that, mind.

Fred often used this quaint local phrase – 'I'm not 100 per cent on that, mind' – when he wanted to hide or blur the truth, the unnecessary addition of 'mind' being characteristic of Gloucestershire and Herefordshire dialect. Such equivocation was frustrating for the police, considering that Fred had previously admitted to cutting up four victims. Professor Knight said that every victim he'd examined so far had been decapitated and dismembered. Fred gave a clue as to why he may have been changing his story in this perverse way. He had let slip that Rose was home when he brought at least one of the Worcester girls back to the house, which created a problem if he meant to keep his wife out of it. 'I can't see how I could have cut her up with Rose asleep above.'

He said that he met the Dutch Girl when she was travelling. He had punched her out in his lorry, and brought her home alive before strangling her in the cellar. The police would find her naked, 'but I don't think she's cut up'.

DC Barbara Harrison: OK, what did you do with the clothes? Last question.

THE FRED WEST TAPES

Fred West: Er, black plastic bag, and chucked out front for the dustman.

It was now late on Saturday evening, time for the police to leave Fred to his thoughts. By the casual way in which he spoke about his crimes, it seemed unlikely that he would lose sleep over what he had said. On the contrary, he appeared to have enjoyed talking about the murders.

A lot had happened during this Saturday. The police had recovered two more bodies, and they had taken Fred to the country where he identified Rena's grave. Meanwhile, I had received inside information about the investigation, something that was beginning to bother the Senior Investigating Officer. 'Questions were coming in from reporters, principally Howard Sounes of the Mirror Group, who said the following day's *Sunday Mirror* would report that the investigation had found [more] bodies and that the police were going to search at places other than Cromwell Street,' John Bennett later wrote. He wondered how much information had leaked out to me. He found out in the morning when our story ran on the front of the *Sunday Mirror*, turning to two pages inside. We also published a detailed diagram of 25 Cromwell Street, as Bennett noted, 'pointing out exactly where each of them was buried. It also coined the headline, "The House of Horrors", the first time the Wests' home had been described like that, and a name by which it became universally recognised from then on.' Bennett wanted to know who had leaked this information to me. He accused Howard Ogden and Scott Canavan. Annoyed, Ogden advised the superintendent to look to his own team first. Bennett reminded his officers that they must not talk to the press. He trusted them when they assured him that they hadn't breathed a word, but he had their bank accounts and phone records checked to see if they were selling stories, and he had me followed, and my records checked. 'I make no apologies,' Bennett told me years later, when he revealed this to me. 'We were trying to establish how this information was getting out.' He never did find out.

The case was now classed as a 'major incident'. The lecture room on the fourth floor of divisional police headquarters was converted into the Major Incident Room (MIR), with extra phone lines and computer terminals loaded with the latest Home Office software. An expanding investigation team numbered over thirty officers, and it would soon double. Bennett worked out of an adjoining office. Meanwhile, journalists were flocking to Gloucester to cover the breaking story, teams of reporters and photographers, TV crews from the UK and around the world, all booking into hotels and taking up positions outside 25 Cromwell Street. There were so many journalists and onlookers that the local authority erected crowd barriers to keep everyone in order. I arrived in Gloucester for the first time in my life, bought a map of the city to orientate myself (this was before smartphones), and started to look for an exclusive line for the following weekend's paper. Within hours I was talking to family members and various people who had known the Wests. The stories they told about Fred and Rose were extraordinary. I felt like I was uncovering the secrets of a sex and murder cult, which is a good way of imagining life at 25 Cromwell Street.

As the press pack gathered in Gloucester, the search team worked out of sight down in the cellar, digging now in 'the nursery alcove' where the West children had slept. This is where they found Lucy Partington's remains. Her missing poster described Lucy as she was when she was last seen alive on 27 December 1973:

THE FRED WEST TAPES

21 years. 5'4" Long dark curly hair, gold rimmed specs, dressed in rust coloured raincoat, pink jeans, red mittens, carrying faded brown canvas satchel.

There was no sign of these clothes in her grave, nor her spectacles, or satchel, which had her name inside, and in which she was carrying a poetry book and a Christmas gift from her sister. There was no sign of the letter she had written to the Courtauld Institute of Art, where it was never received. Fred had thrown Lucy's belongings away, like rubbish, and buried her naked.

There was disturbing evidence that Lucy had been restrained, dismembered and decapitated. Her bones were, once more, in a jumble. There were two braided cords in the grave, tied with a reef knot. There was also adhesive tape, which had seemingly been wrapped around her head, with strands of Lucy's hair and her hairgrips still stuck to the tape. The Partington family was told all this before the press. 'There were many details that shocked me profoundly,' says her sister Marian. 'One of them was the detail about Lucy being gagged, and realising that she couldn't use her voice ... She had just become flesh and bones for the gratification of others.'

Uniquely, there was also a knife in Lucy's grave. It was an old bread knife, worn where it had been sharpened. Asked about this, Fred admitted that he had dropped a knife of that sort. It seemed likely that he cut himself while dismembering Lucy – though Professor Knight said that Fred would have needed heavier tools, too – because just after midnight on 3 January 1974, Fred presented himself at Accident and Emergency at Gloucester Royal Hospital with a laceration to his right hand. This might explain dropping the knife in Lucy's grave. It also suggested the terrifying scenario of Lucy being kept alive for up

NINE MORE (APPROX.)

to six days, from her disappearance on 27 December to Fred's emergency hospital visit. Paul Britton told the police that it was likely the Wests learned to prolong their pleasure with the victims, taking their time in the cellar.

Marian came home to countless messages on her telephone answer-machine from journalists wanting to interview the Partington family, and she was upset and angry by what she saw as media intrusion. She called the journalists 'Pain Vultures'. 'That's what it felt like. You know, what do they want to hear from us? What's it going to add?' Marian asked me years later when I got to know her. 'What is in the public interest?' Margaret Partington once told Marian that it might be better for them not to know what had happened to Lucy. Marian started to understand what her mother meant. 'At that point, I remember feeling this terrible thought that we're in for the long haul.'

Later on Sunday, the police recovered the remains of the victim known as the Girl from Newent, though her proper name remained a mystery. She was buried opposite Lucy in the cellar, under the stairs. Decapitated and dismembered, there was a depression in her skull as if she had been hit with a hammer. This victim had been trussed up with a clothes line, ten feet of plastic-covered rope, some of which was still wrapped around what had been her arms. There were also loops that might have gone around her wrists and ankles. Unusually, there were a few items of clothing in the grave: socks, a bra and tights, which had been tied and wound around her skull. Also, a pair of knickers. They could have belonged to the victim. They could have been Rose's.

That afternoon the police drove Fred around Worcester to see if he could pinpoint where he encountered the Worcester victims. Fred tended to describe places by landmark rather than proper names. 'She was by that motor place,' he told the police, describing where he met one girl. He didn't know the name of the garage. 'Something Motors,' he said. 'You know where I said the roundabout was, there's traffic lights now.' While he insisted that he meant to be helpful, he got the police more muddled.

Fred said that he first met the Worcester girls when they were thumbing a lift together. He dropped them off where they wanted to go. He then picked them up separately. This was when they had sex, he said, in a lay-by.

> **Fred West**: I can't remember which girl said what but one of them said, 'Alright then, when I get out I'll scream rape, I'll just say you raped me.' And I just slammed her one … I just turned and hit her with my fist in the face, like that.
> **DC Jeff Morgan**: What, with your right fist?
> **Fred West**: Yeah … her head went out the window … that girl probably [will] have bruising across the back of her neck where it went over the window … I got a vague idea she broke her neck [but] I strangled her after …
> **DC Morgan**: To make sure?
> **Fred West**: Yeah.

This was the body he brought home when Rose was upstairs (asleep, he now said). He thought she was the girl with the firework burn. He pushed her down into the cellar through the old back steps, then dug the grave. 'I dug it out ever so quiet,' he said, so silently that Rose didn't wake up. This was too incredible for DC Morgan not to challenge.

> **DC Jeff Morgan**: So … hmm … Alright, I won't argue with you, Fred, but that sounds a bit hard to believe. Because Rose is upstairs, and you're digging a bloody great big hole to put a body in!

NINE MORE (APPROX.)

Fred West: Yeah. Rose is not above me. Rose is in another [bedroom] away from me.

Meanwhile, the police had found a possible name for the Girl from Newent.

DC Jeff Morgan: Juanita Mott?
Fred West: Yeah, that's her …
DC Morgan: How did you meet her?
Fred West: At Cromwell Street … she had friends there …

He said that he and Juanita had an affair. She told him she was pregnant and threatened to tell Rose, so he strangled her after having sex in the cellar. Her clothes 'would have been shoved in a bag and shoved out for the dustman.' Behind this foul and misleading confession – the same old story – was a real person with a family who loved her. Like Lucy Partington, Juanita Mott's family had been searching for her for years. The women met the same tragic fate, but their backgrounds were at opposite ends of the social spectrum.

Born 1 March 1957, Juanita Mott was the daughter of an American serviceman, Ernest Mott, stationed in England, and Mary, his Gloucester girlfriend. Juanita was the middle daughter of three girls with an older sister, Georgina (born 1955), and a younger sister, Belinda (born 1959). Juanita was four when Ernest went back to the United States. Her mother then married and had a fourth daughter, Juanita's half-sister, Mary-Ann (born 1968). They lived in the Coney Hill area of Gloucester. Mum suffered with depression and underwent ECT at the local psychiatric hospital. When she was unhappy, she seemed to live on coffee and cigarettes. 'My mother was ill around about this time, resulting in both myself and Juanita spending periods in the care of the local authority,' Belinda told the police on 7 March, when they took a statement from her.

As soon as she saw the search of 25 Cromwell Street on the TV news, Belinda had rung the police and told them: 'I think my sister might be one of them.'

'What makes you think that?'

'Because I've tried every source there is to try and find her, and nothing has come up.'

A detective came to the house and asked Belinda for a photograph of Juanita. The only photos Belinda had were made in a photo booth years ago, four little black and white pictures of Juanita posing for the camera, printed in a strip. As these simple photos showed, Juanita was a pretty girl with high cheekbones, hazel eyes and olive skin. She liked jewellery. Boys were attracted to her, but her sisters thought that she chose the wrong ones to date. Juanita was naughty, but loveable. She clashed with her stepfather and was sometimes kicked out of the house. One night Belinda heard stones being thrown against her bedroom window. She looked out and saw Juanita, who said that their mum wouldn't let her in. So Belinda let her climb in through her window. 'And I said, "Well, you know the window will always be open to you."'

After leaving school at fifteen, Juanita lived an unsettled life. In 1974, when she was lodging at 4 Cromwell Street, she was convicted of stealing a pension book and remanded into custody. That summer she lodged briefly at 25 Cromwell Street. The following spring, when she was eighteen, Juanita was staying with a friend of her mother, Jenny Fraser-Holland, in Newent. Jenny was getting married on Saturday, 12 April 1975. Juanita agreed to babysit Jenny's younger children on the wedding day. Friday night, before the wedding, Juanita went into Gloucester.

NINE MORE (APPROX.)

She may have hitched into the city, as she often did. 'She left the house in the clothes she was wearing, and I do not believe she took any extra items with her,' Jenny told the police in 1994. 'By the following day she had not returned, [which] was totally out of character ...' and they never saw her again.

As her sisters got older, they made efforts to find Juanita. Belinda went on local radio to appeal for news of her sister, and she spoke to the *Daily Star* and *Take a Break* magazine. She visited the register of births, deaths and marriages in London, to look for public records that might reveal what had happened to her missing sister, but she couldn't find any record of Juanita marrying, having children, or dying. In 1977, a friend of Belinda's, Gill Britt, lodged at 25 Cromwell Street. Belinda went to the house to visit her. Rose was sitting on the front step, a pram nearby, children running around.

'Who are you here for?' Rose barked at Belinda.

'Gill.'

Fred popped his head around the door, took a look at the visitor and said that she could come in. So Belinda entered the house of horrors to see her friend, 'and we'd have a laugh and a joke, not knowing at that time that my sister was under the stairs – buried.'

6

EVIDENCE OF TORTURE

Monday, 7 March 1994 • Day Twelve
25 Cromwell Street

> 'I don't believe in suffering.'
> FRED WEST

On Monday, the remains of Lynda Gough were recovered from under the bathroom at 25 Cromwell Street. Professor Bernard Knight was unable to say whether Lynda had been decapitated, because her bones were in such a poor state, though he was certain that her legs had been disarticulated. The thigh bones showed signs of fine cut marks, caused by a knife. A ring of adhesive tape was with the skull, seemingly having been wrapped around Lynda's head; and once again there was a gag. There were no clothes. Fred told the police that he flushed Lynda's underwear down the loo, which was the final act of disrespect.

For John and June Gough this was news that they had long dreaded. It was a Thursday in April 1973 when Lynda left home. Her mother found out that Lynda had gone when she returned from work at lunchtime. 'Lynda had left a note to say that she had found herself a flat,' June explained to detectives, showing the officers the note which she had held on to all these years.

Dear Mum + Dad,
Please don't worry about me, I have got a flat, and I will come and see you sometime.
Love Lin xxxxxxxxx

Although her daughter was old enough to make her own way in the world, June was concerned about her. 'I wanted to know where she was living. I wanted to know if she was happy, if she was alright.' When her inquiries led her to 25 Cromwell Street, she tried to speak to Rose West as one mother to another. 'I really talked about Lynda. We were feeling very hurt that she had gone, she hadn't contacted us, almost abandoned [us] but I got no feedback.' The Wests told Mrs Gough that Lynda had gone to Weston-super-Mare, so she and her husband went there. 'We went to the Job Centre and made inquiries as to [whether] she had been there trying to find work. We knew she didn't have much money, you see.' The Goughs consulted a neighbour who was a police officer, but they did not report Lynda as a missing person so there was no official police search. Meanwhile, they had two other children to raise, and family life went on. 'Perhaps I've been blessed with being tough,' June told me when we spoke about this years later. 'In order to survive you've got to get on with things.' Looking back, she saw that Lynda was immature, which made her vulnerable. 'Girls of [that age] want to be loved, and they want adventure.'

When June was told the tragic news, that Lynda had died at 25 Cromwell Street in 1973, killed by the man she met, and probably his wife, whom she also faced on the doorstep,

EVIDENCE OF TORTURE

June realised that she too may have been in peril. 'I was lucky to get away from that house.'

While the search team recovered Lynda's remains, detectives took Fred back to the fields near his childhood home on a ghost hunt. After his first visit to identify Rena's grave, Fred had spoken of sensing the spirits of two dead people out in the country. He was now saying that there might be a second body in Fingerpost Field, the adjacent field to where he said they would find Rena. It was just before 7:00 PM and dark when officers escorted Fred back to the scene. A rutted field rose ahead of them, then fell towards the woods in the distance. It was spooky. Janet Leach, who was part of the entourage, didn't like the dark, and Fred was behaving like a freak, saying that he felt the ghostly presence of an old girlfriend flying around in the night. She was wearing a long white dress, he said. He wasn't sure where exactly her remains were buried, or how she had died, but he felt her presence at a drinking hole for cattle down near the trees, a place where he and his father had once laid concrete for cattle to stand on. Turning to Leach, Fred said that his handcuffs felt loose. He might slip them off and run into the woods. 'Nobody'd ever find me.'

When they got back to Gloucester, the detectives tried to get Fred to talk rationally about what had just happened.

> **DC Jeff Morgan**: Right, [I] would like you to tell me the truth, in your own words, why you took us across that field [this evening], and why you indicated where ... who ...
> **Fred West**: Anne.
> **DC Morgan**: Anne?
> **Fred West**: Anne McFall ... I felt Anne's presence up there ... I know she's there by feeling, only...

THE FRED WEST TAPES

DC Barbara Harrison: How did she die?
Fred West: I don't know.

The full details didn't emerge at once but Anne McFall – who Fred sometimes called Anna, and was also known as Annie[7] – was a friend of Rena's from Scotland. Born out of marriage in Glasgow on 8 April 1949, to an alcoholic cleaner and her mechanic boyfriend, Anne McFall had a rough early life, including a period living in care. She came to Gloucestershire to stay with Fred and Rena after Fred fled Scotland in 1965. Fred told the police that he and Anne became lovers, and he soon made her pregnant. 'She's pregnant, and she's chuffed, and I'm happy,' he told the police. But in 1967 Anne went 'missing'.

Fred West: I was looking frantically for her...
DC Barbara Harrison: [The] day Anne went missing, what happened?
Fred West: Well, when I went back to the caravan to see her, there was a note that said she'd gone to Scotland.

He claimed that he drove to Scotland to find Anne, and when he couldn't locate her there he reported her as missing to the police. (Anne was not reported as missing.) He asked his parents if they had seen her. 'And that was when my father said that Rena was seen up at the Fingerpost ...' He suggested that Rena had killed Anne.

DC Jeff Morgan: And you are now saying that you didn't kill Anne?
Fred West: No, I did not kill Anne.

---

7   Anne's name is spelt without an e in some sources, but she is Anne on her birth certificate.

EVIDENCE OF TORTURE

Morgan decided to end the interview here, asking everyone in the room first if there was anything they wanted to add. 'All I hope is that efforts are made to find Anne,' said Fred, playing the victim.

★ ★ ★

The next day, Hazel Savage joined Jeff Morgan in the interview room. With many parallel lines of inquiry, the detectives were going back and forth over the identified and unidentified victims trying to figure the whole case out. There were many loose ends. They had not recovered all the remains yet. They didn't know the identities of some of the victims. They needed to establish the true circumstances of the deaths and, crucially, the extent of Rose's involvement.

A recurring feature of the case was the repeated evidence of restraint being used on the victims. The only Cromwell Street victim not found with evidence that she had been tied up was Shirley Robinson, who was in a consensual sexual relationship with Fred and, as the detectives were discovering, Rose as well. Witnesses told them that the three shared a bedroom at Cromwell Street at one stage. Shirley became 'part of the West family' said an ex-lodger. They didn't need to tie her up. The presence of ropes, cords and other binds with the other victims, however, indicated sex crimes. The women had evidently been raped while tied up, suggesting a link to Fred's and Rose's mutual passion for bondage sex.

Fred claimed not to know which victims had been bound and gagged.

DC Hazel Savage: Well, why don't you know? You put them there, didn't you? You don't know whether you put them there?

THE FRED WEST TAPES

Fred West: No.
DC Savage: Buried these people.
Fred West: Yeah, buried the people – yeah, yeah – but I mean ... it was done quick and a long time ago ... I didn't sort of take notes ...
DC Savage: Right, so you don't know how [body] number four[8] got this cloth around her head, is that what you're telling us? So that means, then, that somebody else might be involved, if you didn't put it there?
Fred West: Hazel ... there is nobody else involved. I did it all on my own ... Let's get that straight now.

Although the police were becoming used to recovering ropes and gags with the dead women, the state of one victim was surprising and especially disturbing. When the police excavated the grave under the Marilyn Monroe fireplace in the cellar, the skull that emerged was cocooned in parcel tape, wrapped round and round the head like the bandages of an ancient mummy, the plastic tape preserved while the flesh had rotted. This had been one of the Worcester girls. The cocoon, or head mask, was a hideous sight, terrible enough to make a seasoned detective wince. Fred admitted that he had wound the tape around her head. 'That was to keep it (*sic*) quiet, I think, in case her (*sic*) made any noise.' He suggested that he masked her to keep her silent while Rose got ready upstairs to go out for the evening. Could he have forgotten what else he had done to this woman?

DC Hazel Savage: What's all this tubing around her, then ... Remember?
Fred West: Tubing?

---

8 The Dutch Girl was the fourth body recovered at 25 Cromwell Street. There was a rolled and knotted cloth with her skull, which would have been used as a gag.

EVIDENCE OF TORTURE

DC Savage: Yeah … It would seem to have been up her nostrils. Now, this is something new. I would hope you'd remember that, Fred.

A U-shaped piece of plastic tube was sticking out of the tape mask, where it had seemingly been forced into the victim's nose. There was also a second tube in the grave. It seemed that Fred had kept his victim alive with a breathing tube, her face completely wrapped so she could not speak, or scream. In that state she died. This was evidence of a crime so terrifyingly dreadful it was almost beyond comprehension.

'Whatever's done on these girls, I done,' Fred admitted carelessly, 'but for what reason I can't think.'

As everyone in the room contemplated this new horror, Fred suggested that the tubing may have been from a home brew kit. It was typical of Fred to throw in extraneous and misleading details like this. Hazel Savage retorted that Fred had used tubes of that kind to syphon petrol, not brew beer, which made the clerk Scott Canavan laugh, easing the awful tension briefly. Fred was just the sort of dishonest individual to steal petrol by syphoning fuel from cars, as he used other people's tax discs on his vehicles. Apart from being a rapist and a serial killer, he was a common thief. Half the stuff in his house was nicked, even the kids' bikes (he had convictions for theft of a pedal bike and handling a stolen bicycle). At the same time, he was capable of extreme, dehumanising cruelty.

Despite brief moments of dark humour, DC Savage never lost sight of what she needed to know. 'Who was first?' she asked suddenly.

Fred West: Pardon?
DC Hazel Savage: Who was first?

THE FRED WEST TAPES

Fred West: Rena, and Charmaine.

That wasn't true either. If Anne McFall died in 1967, she came before either one. Then there was the series of murders at 25 Cromwell Street. '[That] all started with Lynda Gough,' said Fred the next day. That may have been true, but the story Fred proceeded to tell was far from accurate, though he indirectly revealed some clues as to what may have happened. 'Lynda was way kinky. She went into anything, she was way out. And this is where it all started with her: the bondage business,' he said, 'it was their own fantasies that I set up for them [and] Lynda was the first one.' He claimed that Lynda owned books on the supernatural and wanted to bathe in 'virgin's blood'. Fred seemed to be channelling the tropes of low budget horror films when he spoke like this, movies like *Sex and the Vampire* which was showing at the ABC in Gloucester in 1973, just before Lynda disappeared. Some of his confessions seemed to be coloured by that kind of gory entertainment. What is seen by most people as harmless fantasy Fred acted out in real life. He said that he tied Lynda up in the cellar, which he also referred to as his 'dungeon', lashing her to the joists, where the police had noticed holes.

DC Hazel Savage: What's that beam got a slot in it for?
Fred West: Well, for hands and that to tie up to. [Lynda] wanted to be tied upside down.

He said that this bondage session took place while Rose was out visiting her mother. At the time the cellar was a glory hole stuffed with all manner of items including fairground chimes, which made the murder scene sound even more grotesque. 'She was tied up across the beams,' he repeated, possibly telling the

EVIDENCE OF TORTURE

truth about that. But the story he wrapped around this admission revealed the workings of his mind, not Lynda's. 'We started this fantasy thing ... she stripped off and oiled herself [and] said, "I'm ready" ... And then she wanted her bust tied up ... she was all roped up, [as] she wanted, and [she] kept laughing her head off ...' That would have been Fred laughing, or Rose. Fred said that Lynda was 'enjoying every minute of it', wanting him to pour 'love potions' over her. Suddenly, they were interrupted by the front door bell. Somebody shouted 'Fred!' He went upstairs to see who it was. 'When I got back down there, the flipping rope that was holding her legs ... had snapped [and] she was hanging there, she was strangled, hanging by the neck ...'

> **DC Hazel Savage**: So, what you're saying now is she was strangled accidentally, and not that you killed her?
> **Fred West**: No, I never killed any of them outright.

Hazel Savage had been listening to Fred patiently, but she'd heard enough. She reminded Fred that he had previously admitted to killing Lynda Gough. Now he was inventing a ridiculous and insulting lie.

> **DC Hazel Savage**: You don't have to be afraid. We are not going to ask you about your kinky habits ...
> **Fred West**: I had no kinky habits at that time ... I was trying to explain ...
> **DC Savage**: I don't believe any of that crap you've just given us about this woman hanging herself. It doesn't matter. I'm not here to judge you. Doesn't matter at all. But I'm telling you this, because I feel very strongly about what you're saying now.

THE FRED WEST TAPES

Scott Canavan leapt to his client's defence, reminding Savage that she had asked Fred for an explanation but she had dismissed his answer as bullshit. 'Yeah,' she replied, 'I thought it was bullshit.' Having been told that the police had found evidence of gags and binds with the victims – a ring mask of brown parcel tape was found alongside Lynda Gough's head – Savage thought that Fred was inventing a story to explain this away and, in passing, he was suggesting that he hadn't actually murdered anyone.

> **Fred West**: Yes, that's exactly what I'm saying ... I never killed anyone deliberately.
> **DC Hazel Savage**: Well, that's not what you've told us until now. You've said, 'I strangled them' ... You're now saying [it] was an accident. She hung (*sic*) herself ... I think we better conclude this interview, because this is stupid, isn't it?

That evening the remains of the second Worcester victim were excavated from the cellar. The police now had a name for one of the two Worcester girls. They put the name to Fred on Tuesday.

> **DC Hazel Savage**: [There was] a missing girl called Carol Cooper, from Worcester, and she had firework burns on her hands ...
> **Fred West**: Quite possible.
> **DC Savage**: [From] an injury she received on the tenth of November [1973], which of course is five days after firework day. Do you remember you told us about a bandage?
> **Fred West**: Yeah. It was her left hand, wasn't it?
> **DC Savage**: I can't tell you that at the moment. How old do you think she was?

EVIDENCE OF TORTURE

Fred West: Seventeen, eighteen.
DC Savage: Well, this Carol Cooper is fifteen.

One of the saddest aspects of the West case was how young many of the murder victims were. Carol Ann Cooper was one of the youngest of the twelve, still a girl at the tender age of fifteen. Born 10 April 1958, Carol was the only child of Mary and Colin Cooper, an RAF serviceman. She was four when her parents separated. Her father moved to Scotland, leaving Carol with her mother. 'In 1966, after I had moved to Scotland, I was informed that my wife, Carol's mum, had died. We had never divorced,' Colin told the police in 1994. He returned to England with his new partner, and Carol came to live with them in Worcester. 'Between my separation from her mother and the time I was reunited with Carol in 1967, I had had no contact with her at all. Unfortunately, my second marriage disintegrated. I had tried to set up a home for Carol, but unfortunately too much time had passed.' Carol, aged ten, was put into the care of the Pines Children's Home in Worcester. Her dad only saw her a couple of times after that, but he said that she 'seemed to have settled in'.

On the contrary, Carol, sometimes known as Caz, was so unhappy at her care home that she often ran away. On Friday, 9 November 1973, she was given leave to visit her doctor, and spend the night at her grandmother's house in Warndon, outside Worcester. Carol kept her GP appointment and then went to the cinema with a group of teenagers, including a boy named Andrew Jones, with whom she had been 'knocking about' for a few days, as Andrew told the police. After a film, fish and chips and a drink in a pub, Andrew walked Carol to her bus stop at Trinity Passage. They'd had a tiff during their date. 'Carol put her arms round me and wanted to kiss me, but I wouldn't. I was still feeling a big niggly, and she went and stood across the other side of the passageway, and I think she was crying. I went over to her and we made it up.' They arranged to meet the following evening at six. At 9:15, Carol got on her bus, and waved goodbye to Andrew.

When she didn't arrive at her grandmother's house, Carol was reported as a missing person. There were appeals for information, as there were for Lucy Partington. When Carol's remains were recovered from the rear cellar at 25 Cromwell Street in 1994, she was decapitated, with her legs removed, a now familiar pattern. There were the same distinctive knife marks on the bones. An elasticated cloth was wrapped around the lower part of her skull, where it would have gagged her. There was another piece of looped fabric under one of her arms, and two braided cords, evidence that Carol had been tied up after she had been snatched from the street. Or maybe Fred had been on her bus and managed to talk her into going home with him, just as he had chatted up Rose on a bus. These are things that aren't known, and probably never will be known. In retrospect it seems surprising that Carol Ann Cooper's disappearance in November 1973 was not linked more directly at the time to Lucy Partington vanishing from a bus stop in a neighbouring county the following month. Serial killers were at work in the area, though no one realised it at the time, killers so insatiable that they struck twice within seven weeks.

★ ★ ★

It was becoming clear that these killings stretched back decades, way back to Fred's first marriage to Rena and the tumultuous seventeen months they spent together in Scotland. The detectives asked Fred more about this period of his life, trying to elicit what really happened to Rena and Charmaine, who Fred

EVIDENCE OF TORTURE

had admitted to killing in his '9 more' note; also Rena's friend, Anne McFall, who he now suggested might be buried near to his first wife.

The police established that Fred lived in Scotland from July 1963 to December 1965. His account of the period was his usual mixture of fact and fabulation, few of his stories more preposterous than his claim to have had sex with the Scottish pop singer Lulu, whose youthful good looks would have appealed to Fred ('a gang bang job,' he sniggered as he told this lie). He claimed to have had many extra-marital relationships in Scotland, and described several lovers, including a married woman who had a candle-lit steak dinner ready for him when he swung by in his Mr Whippy van. He said that he kept the van's engine running while they had sex, so the ice cream didn't melt. When he spoke like this, he was simply ridiculous. He made it clear to all these women that he wouldn't stand by them if they got pregnant. 'No way I want to settle down like that. Well, you can't marry them all, can you?' Much of this sounded like bullshit, but some of it proved to be true.

Fred had an affair with a Scotswoman named Margaret McAvoy, whom he made pregnant. Fred's description of Margaret was intensely misogynistic. 'They always used to call her my spaniel because she was always behind me, you know. She was no oil painting, or nothing. She was just sort of a lap dog for me. When I would tell her to do something – go here, go there, do this, come here, go there – she just went.' Margaret gave birth to a son, Steven, in July 1966, after Fred had gone back to England. Steven later came to live at 25 Cromwell Street briefly, going to school with the other West children who remembered a Scots lad who looked like Dad. There were allegations that Rose mistreated the boy, grinding her stiletto heel into his face when she flew into a rage. When Steven's mother wanted him back, however, Rose tried to hang on to him, a situation akin to Rena and Rose both wanting custody of Charmaine. In this case, the Wests backed down when Margaret got the authorities involved. 'And then Margaret came down and got him ...' said Fred. The police were trying to locate Margaret and Steven. Asked how Steven had been returned to his mother, if she had picked him up in a car for example, Fred cracked a joke. 'Margaret couldn't drive,' he said, 'only me up the wall.'

> **DC Barbara Harrison**: She's alright, is she? You haven't killed Margaret?
> **Fred West**: No, no, no, no.
> **DC Harrison**: And/or Steven?
> **Fred West**: Not Steven, no ... There is certainly nobody else, to my knowledge, that you will find dead. Nobody else has to be found ... apart from Anne. I want her found, and I want her back ... she means more than anything.

Having told a corny joke moments ago, Fred now turned sentimental.

> **DC Barbara Harrison**: Would you mind telling me why Anne is so special to you? Just to help us understand.
> **Fred West**: Anne ... I don't want to talk about it too much ... She's a saint as far as I'm concerned.

He sniffed back a tear. It was hard to tell whether Fred was revealing genuine feelings here, or play-acting. On one level he seemed to have convinced himself that he was a bereft lover and a bereaved father, a victim of all that had happened. That delusion may have helped him to live with himself. Like most people who do wicked things, Fred did not appear to see himself

EVIDENCE OF TORTURE

as a wicked person, for the most part, but somebody who was swept up in events. Nonsense, of course. Also, there was always a hint that the man was unbalanced to some degree. His volatile mood was one symptom of his instability. He said many strange things. He continued to speak of feeling the 'presence' of women he had killed, for instance, which was barmy if he meant it, talking about the spirits that rose up to greet him. Ghosts don't count in police work. The officers were concerned with evidence that would stand up in court and Fred's supernatural feelings and visions did not help them. As they asked him about one set of remains in the cellar, he said: 'I'm getting the feeling that [is] Lucy.' DC Savage reminded Fred that they had previously agreed that Lucy Partington was in another grave, but Fred was communing with the spirit world. 'Perhaps we will conclude the interview while the feelings ... get put together,' Savage remarked wearily. 'It's four minutes to five ... and we'll turn the tape off.'

Fred was still vague and unhelpful when they resumed talking the next day. 'The thing is, all these [victims] are so mixed up in my mind, I haven't got a clue which is which,' he said. Hazel Savage tried to get him to focus on the facts, reminding him of distinctive restraining items found in the graves, including the grave of young Carol Ann Cooper.

> **Fred West**: I mean, they all had ... what we refer to as kinky sex ... not bondage, it was just kinky sex ...
> **DC Hazel Savage**: Was the kinky sex responsible for this girl's death [Carol Ann]?
> **Fred West**: Well, it all led up to it.

Savage waded deeper into the unfathomable horror of what had been done to these women. 'Things are involved here that we don't understand fully, OK?' she said. 'We just hope that you might be able to explain what has gone on here, because I don't understand it …' She was going to the heart of the case, what Joseph Conrad called the heart of darkness, a place where human beings commit acts of unpardonable cruelty and wickedness. Many people would use the word evil.

> **DC Hazel Savage**: I don't understand why people have got masks on, or tubes coming from them, and the mask being such to prevent the person … seeing, or shouting, or screaming, in my view, and the tube coming from them to allow them to breathe … I'm asking if you can help me understand why these people are tied up in this way, and why these things have happened to them. With regard to Body Number Nine,[9] why her bones are cut up, her wrists are tied together, and an elastic headband is around her head?
> **Fred West**: But I mean, each one was their own fantasy, where they wanted bondage sex, or kinky sex … it wasn't done for any particular reason. That's why you probably finds it hard. It was their thing they wanted to do … What they all wanted was the actual [bondage] harness that you can buy, but I mean have you ever seen the price of that stuff? … This stuff's hundreds of pounds …

Before Fred could expand on the extortionate cost of commercially-made bondage gear, Savage directed him back to the forensic evidence. Professor Knight had now had an opportunity to study the human remains in detail, and he had discovered further disquieting facts about the state of the dead women.

---

9   Carol Ann Cooper was the ninth body recovered.

EVIDENCE OF TORTURE

DC Hazel Savage: So why is Body Number Nine's toe bones and finger bones missing ...?
Fred West: I never ... I never cut no toes or fingers off.
DC Hazel Savage: Did I suggest you had?
Fred West: Well, I mean ... If they were cut up, it was just their heads and legs. Nothing else took off.
DC Savage: You sure about that?

Not only were the women cut up, their skeletons, when reassembled by the professor, were incomplete. Every one had bones missing, many small finger and toe bones, but also larger bones that could not possibly have rotted away, or been accidentally overlooked by the searchers. These bones represented body parts that had been removed when they were clothed in flesh, that is to say cut off when they were actual fingers, actual toes. There was no sign of these body parts at 25 Cromwell Street, which had been searched outside and in, from the cellar up to the attic. 'I mean this was straight kinky sex that went on,' Fred blustered, 'nothing ... I don't know, what do you call it ... something like that?'

'Masochistic?' suggested Scott Canavan.

Hazel Savage had the apposite word. 'Torture?' she said.

'No, no. I couldn't hurt anybody like that,' said Fred. 'I don't believe in suffering anyway. I mean, I couldn't torture anybody.'

7
SEARCHING EVERYWHERE

Friday, 18 March 1994 • Day Twenty-three
A police house, Dursley

'I shall always protest my fucking innocence, no matter
if I do spend the rest of my life in fucking nick.'
ROSE WEST

All this time Rose had remained free on bail living in a police house in Gloucester, accompanied by her daughter, May, with visits from her son, Steve. Almost immediately the siblings had a fight. 'The pressure was starting to get to me and Stephen,' May wrote in *Inside 25 Cromwell St.*, a book co-authored with her brother and two *News of the World* reporters, who bought their story. 'He hit me after my cat walked over the puzzle he was doing on the table.' The next thing May knew, she was on the floor. Rose rang the police, telling them that 'she would rather be locked up if her son was going to act like his father'. The fact that Steve was now talking to the *News of the World* (also to me for the *Sunday Mirror*) was a problem for Detective Superintendent John Bennett, who feared that his safe house may not be a complete secret from the press. So, Rose was moved to another house in the town of Dursley. Within a week, a press photographer had found the address and snapped Rose and May out shopping, a picture which made the front page of the *Today* newspaper. The police immediately moved Rose again, to Hales Close, Cheltenham. I was given the new address, not by Steve but one of my other sources, and a photographer and I parked a camper van outside, peering at the house through the curtains of the van windows.

Unlike us, the police heard every word being said inside the house because they had it bugged. Between games of Scrabble, often speaking with her mouth full, the TV blaring in the background, Rose insisted to May that the murder investigation had come as a total surprise to her. 'When they arrested me, I was devastated,' she said in extracts from the surveillance tapes that have entered the public domain. 'May, look, I told you, as you know well, [I] thought Dad was a very sick man, and it's come out he is a very sick man, and the worst liar I ever could have dreamed of! But nobody could have known [the truth].' She described a marriage in which she was 'brainwashed' into doing what Fred wanted, including prostituting herself. 'I was in love with your father. Whenever I made love with your father, that was it for me ... but I had to go out with this bloke I didn't like, and climb into his bed, and make love all night.' If she chose to have sex with a man she did like, Fred became jealous, which she considered unreasonable of him. However, she said that she would never have left Fred. Rather, her fear was that Fred might throw her out on the street. 'I mean, look, if I got near the bastard now, I'd put me fucking hands round his throat, and somebody would have to fucking pry them off me,' she said. 'This is something you don't fucking forgive.'

What was lacking in Rose's conversation was also absent from her police interviews: she expressed virtually no compassion for the daughter she had lost, and didn't mention the other victims. Like Fred, Rose was principally interested in herself.

SEARCHING EVERYWHERE

'They'll never get a confession out of me for something I haven't done!' she shrieked, being a woman whose every other sentence seemed to demand an exclamation mark. 'If they think I've got fuck-all to do with this, then the best thing they can do is put me in the cells, and fucking throw the key away! Because I shall always protest my fucking innocence, no matter if I do spend the rest of my life in fucking nick!'

As the police listened to Rose's conversation, distraught families were contacting the Major Incident Room fearful that their missing loved one might be among the victims buried at 25 Cromwell Street, the so-called House of Horrors having captured the country's attention. The murder squad had swollen to eighty-four officers, and police forces nationwide were assisting in the search for the names of the women Fred had killed, but could not identify, and looking into the possibility that there might be more victims somewhere. The police were working with organisations including the National Missing Persons Helpline, sifting through the 10,000 missing females on the charity's books.

Detectives beseeched Fred to tell them if he was withholding information. 'There are people, parents, ringing up crying,' DC Jeff Morgan told Fred on Monday, 14 March. 'It's not only people with daughters either, is it? It's people with sons as well that are gone missing ...'

'I'm not into that!' snorted Fred. 'Well, as far as I know, at this moment, I mean in all seriousness, there is no more. You've got them all. That's the lot.'

He said that the Cromwell Street murders began when he felt that Rose was threatened by the women he was having 'affairs' with. 'I mean, that's really [the] whole problem right there,' he said, 'that fear got so great to me that somebody was going to touch Rose that I would've done anything. You know, there was no limits to protect her.' This was dangerously close to an admission. 'Whatever we did, we did together ...' He and Rose were so close, he said, that they read each other's minds. He referred back to the start of their relationship. On their second date, when Rose got tipsy, she became 'loving [and] cuddling', so they had sex against a gate in Tewkesbury. The connection they made then was profound and enduring. 'We stood at that gate and summat happened to us both,' he said, 'we crashed into each other, and locked so solid in each other's minds, it was unreal.'

As much as he was infatuated with Rose, Fred claimed to have had an equally strong bond with Anne McFall, whose memory Rose had supplanted until recent events brought her back to his mind. 'Anne was the very first girl in my life that really was for me,' he said. 'We never quarrelled. We never had a mis-word together. [We] worshipped each other.' They got together in the short space of time between Rena leaving him, and Fred meeting Rose. Fred recalled playing his acoustic guitar and serenading Anne, as she combed her long hair. Their special love song, he said, was 'Kiss an Angel Good Mornin'', made popular by Charley Pride. Like so much of what Fred said, that couldn't be right. The record wasn't released until after Anne's disappearance, but the lyric must have chimed with Fred – being about making love like the Devil with an angelic-looking girl.

Morgan tried to drag Fred back to the job of identifying his victims, but Fred was stuck on Anne. It was Rena who had done for Anne, he suggested, that tough Glaswegian lass who carried a blade and associated with a biker gang, the Skulls, who she set on Fred. Rena had been too much for him. 'I'm an absolute coward, if you want to know.' While there was no doubt that he was a vicious psychopath, Fred was also revealing himself to be

SEARCHING EVERYWHERE

an inadequate coward who could not cope with the pressures of life. 'I had too many people to watch at once, that's what went wrong,' he said, pathetically.

Anne's body was in the fields, he was sure. At least her skull was there.

DC Barbara Harrison: How did she die?
Fred West: I have a horrible feeling she was stabbed through the heart.

As yet the police only knew half the story, but social services reports had been recovered, from December 1966, showing Fred's relationship with Anne McFall to be under strain just before she died. She had told a social worker that Fred wanted to make her pregnant by artificial insemination. Unsurprisingly, she planned to leave him. Asked about this in 1994, Fred insisted that he and Anne never argued.

It was impossible to rely on Fred's word alone, so the police were talking to as many witnesses as they could find to check his stories, including Fred's siblings and his children. Fred gave the impression that he didn't mind the police making such inquiries. This was bluster. He had made strenuous efforts to prevent his kids talking to the authorities. 'Whatever May says will be the dead truth,' he told the detectives, referring to his second child. 'May will not tell lies for nobody.' The police were also talking to Fred's boss, Derek Thomson, and his workmates, who said that when Fred was on a job he boasted about properties he owned, foreign trips he took with rich friends, and sex, talking so much crap to his workmates that they hardly listened to him. One co-worker described Fred like this: 'Fred West was an out-and-out pervert who was always inviting men to have sex with his wife.' Fred took exception.

THE FRED WEST TAPES

Fred West: Where did he get the 'pervert' bit from? What's 'pervert' about making love?
DC Hazel Savage: I can only tell you that this bloke said: you are an 'out-and-out pervert'.

Starting on Wednesday, 16 March, a police artist named DC Bob Wilcox, joined the interview room. He encouraged Fred to describe 'Shirley's mate', who they still had not identified, in the hope that Wilcox's drawing might spark a response from the public. Fred was happy to co-operate. As he drew, DC Wilcox referred to a police dictionary of facial features, known as the Penry Facial Identification technique. 'That's her eyes,' said Fred, picking a pair of eyes (image B558) from the reference book. Fred had previously been shown crime scene photos from his garden, which featured human remains with long dark hair, and he was trying to get Wilcox to draw that woman. Twenty minutes into the session, DC Savage realised that they had blundered.

DC Hazel Savage: Unfortunately, those photos relate to Heather.
Fred West: Heather! That's Heather's hair ... I'm building up a photograph of Heather.

When they started over, Fred's description of Shirley's mate shaded into a sexual fantasy. He said that she had been young with 'a schoolgirl look'. Most of his victims were teenagers, while Rose dressed like a schoolgirl, wearing long white socks and pinafore dresses into middle age. ('[Rose] made me feel unnerved at times, because she stared a lot and she dressed like a child,' one witness told the police.) 'She wasn't big-busted or nothing ... She was a young girl which is going to grow up to be a big girl,' Fred said of Shirley's mate. 'She had very soft skin.

SEARCHING EVERYWHERE

Baby's skin ... She wore very tight jeans ... about two sizes too small for her.' Her hair was lacquered. She fixed her hair in his van. 'I said, "For God's sake don't spray that stuff in my eyes. I'm driving!"' The artist moved on to the unidentified Worcester victim. 'She wasn't that good-looking,' said Fred, 'she had quite a few spots.' He started to get mixed up with Anne McFall, who he also described as having 'a very young look to her'.

It didn't require Sigmund Freud to wonder whether Fred's feverish sex talk was the outlet of a man who, in reality, might be sexually dysfunctional. In 1992–93, when he was charged with raping one of his daughters, Fred was obliged to live away from home at bail hostels in Birmingham, where he and Rose were interviewed by a clinical psychologist. The detectives had obtained the psychologist's report, which contained an intriguing reference to Fred's virility, or lack of it.

> **DC Hazel Savage**: You've told him [the psychologist] that you've got this injury to your genital areas, and because of that injury you have problems getting an erection.
> **Fred West**: I don't know what that is about.

Fred told the Birmingham psychologist that he and Rose had a good sex life until about 1980, when he suffered a groin injury at work, having been 'struck between the legs by an iron bar'. Since then he had struggled to get an erection. That's why the Wests used pornography and sex toys. When Fred failed to impregnate Rose again, because of his impotence, they arranged for Rose to sleep with a friend of Jamaican background. This man was apparently the father of three of the younger West children.

DC Savage was curious to know if Fred really did suffer from impotency. 'I think I was taking [the psychologist] for a ride, weren't I?' Fred laughed. 'He was a prat anyway.' Savage read through the rest of the report, which included Fred denying any 'deviant sexual interests' and having been monogamous in his marriage.

> **DC Hazel Savage**: I mean, that doesn't sound true ... I don't know if you remember when you were at Gloucester prison [in 1992], and I came to see you, [and] you then said to me certain things which included the fact you were going to say you couldn't get an erection, so how could you do these things that were alleged, and that you were charged with? So, you were telling me that as well ... Do you remember that?
> **Fred West**: Well, no, but I mean I must have done if you say so ... I've never been injured, not sexually anyway.

In a candid moment, he admitted that he sometimes lied in interviews when he wasn't sure what to say.

> **DC Hazel Savage**: To fill in the gap?
> **Fred West**: To get away from it.
> **DC Savage**: And you're good at that, aren't you ... You're ever so good at going off and saying something else that is totally irrelevant.
> **Fred West**: Yeah ... there's a reason for that ...

It gave him time to think, he explained.

'It's really great you can actually say this, Fred,' replied Savage, 'because you haven't said this before.'

Within moments, however, Fred was lying to the police again. He was by nature as crooked as a corkscrew.

★ ★ ★

SEARCHING EVERYWHERE

The next day, Paul Britton returned to see Detective Superintendent Bennett. The psychologist found the Senior Investigating Officer buried in paperwork in his office, the Major Incident Room humming with activity. Bennett brought Britton up to date on their progress. All but three of the victims had been identified, but there were aspects to the case which the police still found puzzling, including missing bones and knife marks on thigh bones. Britton thought that he might have the answer. 'When you carve meat, you often leave marks on the bone,' he told Bennett, as he later wrote. 'I suspected that cannibalism might be part of the ritual. It would explain the missing bones.' As wild as this may sound, serial killers do sometimes consume their victims, or bits of them. The American mass murderer Jeffrey Dahmer said that he cooked and ate human flesh because he wanted his victims to be part of him. Fred was fascinated by bodies. He had played at artificial insemination, and abortions, while he routinely butchered his victims. Perhaps Britton's theory had merit.

While Bennett pondered this horrible idea, his deputy took Britton over to 25 Cromwell Street. The psychologist walked through the house, looking for clues that would help him understand the Wests. He found a photograph album, with little evidence of the warmth normally captured in family snapshots, and noticed odd items in display cabinets, some of which looked as if they could have belonged to the women who were murdered.

Britton was coming to conclusions about Fred and Rose. In his childhood in Much Marcle, Fred had probably not had the 'moral guidance and structures' that most people receive as children, and had developed into a crude, selfish man. 'For him, women were sexual objects to be exploited in whichever way he chose.' There was something lacking in Rose's childhood, too, so when they met she accepted Fred as he was. Moreover, she found that she enjoyed the same activities. 'The key to all that follows is that Rose responds with delight and sexual excitement,' Britton wrote in *The Jigsaw Man*. 'She discovers that her own sadistic potential can be unleashed and revelled in by Fred. For her, this form of sexual expression makes up for all of the emptiness in her early life.' The unification of two such strange people led to a joint campaign of abduction, rape and murder, maybe even cannibalism.

It is important to remember that married serial killers who commit murder as part of their relationship are rare. There are only a handful of cases in modern history in the world, such as Ray and Faye Copeland who killed five homeless men in the United States in the 1980s, but those were not sex crimes. A better comparison closer to home was Ian Brady and Myra Hindley, who killed five young people in the Manchester area in the 1960s as part of their depraved sex life, though Brady and Hindley were not married. The cases have many similarities. Like Myra Hindley, there was evidence that Rose was infatuated with Fred who, like Brady, was the older partner in the relationship, and probably the initiator. Hindley claimed in later life to have gone along with what Brady wanted, because she was terrified that he would kill her if she crossed him. Rose never played that card with conviction. Nevertheless, she may have gone along with Fred partly as a form of self-preservation, at least at first. One of the mysteries of the West case is why Fred didn't kill Rose, as he killed other women he made pregnant. Joining Fred in murder may have been Rose's way of staying on his right side. But as Britton noted there was also evidence that she enjoyed the same violence and abuse.

Something else the psychologist said unsettled John Bennett. Britton suspected that there could be even more bodies

SEARCHING EVERYWHERE

somewhere, and he suggested that the police should search everywhere Fred had lived or worked. Bennett almost threw up his hands in dismay. 'Now, what a simple thing to say, and what a ridiculous conversation to have,' he sighs. 'It is completely and utterly ridiculous.' Fred had lived at several addresses, and worked at innumerable locations. Recently, Carson Contractors had been sending Fred all over the country for work, while he had the run of a home for autistic people near Stroud, and Prinknash Abbey, a monastery outside Gloucester, both places where the company had contracts.

In addition, members of the public were calling the incident room saying that Fred may have done some work on their house. Fred confirmed that he had worked in many private houses, including work in the cellars.

> **Fred West**: And patios.
> **DC Hazel Savage**: I know. And there's people saying, 'In 1968, he did our roof ...'
> **Fred West**: Yeah. I've done loads of roofs. Hundreds of them ... I mean it's just endless ...

The police compiled a list of ninety-six places Fred had access to where he could conceivably have buried something, or someone.

> **DC Jeff Morgan**: So, we've got a lot of searching to do, have we, Fred?
> **Fred West**: I shall have done my life sentence and [be] back out, or buried or something by the time you got round to them [all].

However, Bennett would not countenance digging anywhere else without additional information. 'I never would have gone anywhere, unless there was some evidence. That he had been there, didn't mean anything.'

Meanwhile, there was a breakthrough with the victim known as 'Shirley's mate'. Detectives had come across a name while researching former care home residents. Having checked it out, they were fairly sure that she was the unidentified woman. Still hopeful that Fred would volunteer the name, the police gave him some clues. The victim's family were in Wales, and she had lived latterly at Jordan's Brook House in Upton Lane, Gloucester, a home for disturbed girls. 'I been there,' said Fred. She was a runaway who wrote to her parents in 1979, saying she had moved in with a local family. DC Morgan read from a letter her mother had received. It didn't sound like Shirley's mate as described by Fred: an older woman who came from Bristol to find Shirley Robinson, then threatened to go to the police. When Fred still failed to provide a name, Morgan told him that the woman in question was Alison Chambers, sometimes known as Ali. Now that she was identified, Fred showed neither surprise nor compassion. In fact, he continued to speak of her in disparaging terms, referring to her 'stringy hair' and 'manly' walk. 'She wasn't very feminine at all.' He suggested that he may have picked her up when he was driving and taken her for a 'shandy' to clear the road dust from their throats. 'I mean there was so many girls I was picking up on the way through all the time.'

Alison's story was one of the most poignant of the victims. She was born in Germany in September 1962, to Robert and Joan Chambers, both parents serving in the British Army. Several of the victims were the daughters of service personnel, whose parents had lived unsettled, peripatetic lives ending in family break-up. Alison was the middle child of three sisters. After her parents split, in 1972, her mother remarried and Alison clashed with her stepfather. '[Alison] rebelled. She would be out to one o'clock in the morning, and then our parents would phone the police ... that sort of thing,' her younger sister Dezra says in *Fred & Rose West: A British Horror Story*. 'All of a sudden, [it became] too much and you get told she's been put into care.' Alison was about fourteen when she was made a resident of a home in Wales. 'She's crying, she's upset, she wants to come home.' In January 1979, Alison was transferred to Jordan's Brook House, which specialised in working with exceptionally troubled teenage girls. Alison's mother didn't know why her daughter was moved there, and she hadn't seen her since a pub lunch in January. 'Alison was very clinging to me. It was as if she wanted constant affection, and wanted to belong to something secure,' said Enfys Davies, a member of staff at Jordan's Brook, who noticed a van was often parked at their gates around this time. Some of the care home girls would go to this van. 'I don't know who was in the van, or remember what the attraction was.' It was Fred, surely.

Alison started to talk about an older man who was her boyfriend. 'Alison was a really lonely person,' a woman who was in the home told me. 'Alison had a vivid imagination ... she was talking about this older man who loved her and was buying her this and buying her that.' Then she got a trainee position in a solicitor's officer in Gloucester. If she had not already met Fred, Alison began to visit 25 Cromwell Street at this time. Lodgers remember seeing her there. Alison absconded from Jordan's Brook House on 5 August 1979, taking her belongings. It seems that she went to stay at 25 Cromwell Street, where she thought she had found a loving second family. The Wests told her that they owned a farm where she could live. They showed her pictures of this idyllic property, possibly estate agent literature. Ali was easy to deceive. The following month her mother received a letter postmarked Northamptonshire. 'I am at present living with a very homely family and I look after their five children and do some of the housework. That I would like you to understand is something I do purely voluntarily. They know that I was in care and are more than willing to help set me up on my feet.' The stilted English of the letter reads as if it was written under direction. It may have been posted by the Wests after Alison's death to fool her family into thinking that they had no need to look for her, and mailed from a different part of the country to cover their tracks.

Although they were buried close together in the garden at 25 Cromwell Street, the police could find no personal link between Alison Chambers and Shirley Robinson, who may never have met. It seemed that Fred had concocted the 'Shirley's mate' story to disguise how he and Rose ensnared Alison Chambers, fooling that sad young woman from the local care home into thinking of them as friends, before raping and killing her. Another young woman from a Gloucester care home who was abused by the Wests around this time told the police that Rose befriended her by saying that she was a 'shoulder to cry on'. That was the game they played. There was, however, a broader connection to Shirley Robinson and other victims in that several of these girls had been in care. Anne McFall was in care. Rena West had been in care, and Borstal. Shirley Robinson, Juanita Mott, Carol Ann Cooper and Alison Chambers were all care home girls. Fred and Rose understood this world, for it had been part of their story, too. When Rose became pregnant by Fred in 1969, her parents placed her into the care of the local authority, which caused Fred to drive around the county asking if anyone knew which home Rose was in. 'Because most of the girls that I met had been in homes, you know.'

SEARCHING EVERYWHERE

In their search for the identity of the last two women in the cellar, the police were reviewing reports of young women registered missing from Gloucestershire, neighbouring counties and beyond, going back years, and some of these girls had been in care. One name that emerged was Shirley Hubbard. Born out of marriage in June 1959, to Owen John Owen and Glenys Lloyd, from Wales, Shirley was taken into care as a toddler. When she was about six, she was placed with a foster family named Hubbard in Droitwich, between Worcester and Birmingham, all within a fairly short drive of Gloucester. She took their surname. Shirley didn't see her birth mother again until 1974, by which time she was a teenager. She was a pretty, slightly-built girl whose front teeth were out of alignment, giving her a distinctive smile. 'Shirley was aware of her sexuality and had a number of boyfriends,' said her foster mother, Linda Hubbard. Shirley wore cheap costume jewellery and she upset Mrs Hubbard when she had her own name tattooed on to her forearm. When she was fifteen, Shirley ran away – twice. The second time she was found camping in a field with a man. Around this time Shirley was taken on by Debenhams in Worcester. She met a teenager named Daniel Davies at the fair in November 1974. They dated for three weeks during which time Shirley visited Daniel's home. He sensed that she had problems, but said that she was 'a bubbly girl who enjoyed life to the full'. On Thursday, 14 November 1974, he and Shirley had a date in Worcester. They ate chips and watched TV at his home. He walked her to her bus stop around 9:00 PM, making arrangements to see her the following evening. When Shirley didn't show, Daniel rang Shirley's foster mother who reported her as missing.

As the police researched this case, they suspected that Shirley Hubbard might be the girl in the mask under the Marilyn Monroe fireplace, one of the so-called Worcester girls, the other having now been identified as Carol Ann Cooper. Fred had implied that these two victims knew each other, and it seemed that their paths may have crossed. Apart from both being in care, with links to Worcester, Shirley Hubbard and Carol Ann Cooper dated members of the Davies family. Carol dated Alan Davies, after meeting him at the fair in Worcester in 1972; and Shirley dated Alan's brother Daniel, who met her at the same fair two years later. Both girls visited the Davies home, though Daniel didn't think that they had met.

Proving the identity of the girl in the mask was down to forensic dentist, Dr David Whittaker. 'There was an identification problem. My name came up. John Bennett was on the phone to me, chasing me around. He said, "We need you ..."' Whittaker had worked on hundreds of police cases, identifying dead victims from an examination of their skulls and teeth. 'It was what I would call an upside down murder, and a mass murder ... Fred was talking and giving names, but in a legal sense they still had to be identified and some of them no one had any idea who they were, including Fred.' The whole case was highly unusual in Whittaker's experience. 'It's a very rare event, is mass murder. There were only eight in the whole of the United Kingdom in the *whole* of the twentieth century, it's as rare as that.' Whittaker was brought into the heart of the investigation, setting up a special laboratory at Cardiff University, where both he and Professor Knight were based. While Knight studied the remains of the bodies, Whittaker was given the skulls of the dead, which in most cases came out of the ground in fragments with missing teeth. His team confirmed the sex of the victims from the extant teeth, rebuilt the skulls, then looked to the police to provide dental records and photographs to continue the identification process. Only three sets of dental records were available in the West case. In the absence of files, Dr Whittaker

SEARCHING EVERYWHERE

needed photographs of the missing women, smiling for the camera, which he could superimpose on to images of the rebuilt skulls to see if they matched. 'I said to John Bennett at the start, "What I need are photographs and good ones."' Faced with up to 10,000 missing females, Whittaker suggested that they focus on young women and girls aged twelve to twenty-five. 'There were hundreds still.' So began a painstaking process of collecting photographs of missing women and comparing them to the reconstructed skulls. Shirley Hubbard was one of the most challenging cases.

The identity of the so-called Dutch Girl remained a mystery. Fred assumed she was Dutch, because she had a European accent and she carried foreign money. He thought they had met twice, firstly in Worcester, or maybe Evesham, when she was hitchhiking. 'She was going to Monmouth, to see some particular site, or scenery, or summat,' he said. 'Because she had a map of [places] she wanted to see.' He gave her a ride. They stopped and 'made love', arranging to meet again on her return journey. 'She said, "I'll come back next week." Because we were planning on going somewhere else and do this fancy thing she had [in mind].' He still insisted that all these women shared his perverse sexual interests, the sort of sex depicted in hardcore pornography. 'She had these magazines,' he said, suggesting implausibly that this woman was travelling around the UK with a backpack full of hardcore porn, which then came into his possession. 'It's a pity the magazines have been destroyed. There's been more evidence in this case destroyed by the police,' he teased the detectives. Fred was referring to the previous child abuse investigation in 1992–93 where the police had seized a quantity of pornography from 25 Cromwell Street, books and videos, some of the videos recorded by Fred and Rose. When that case collapsed, the police destroyed almost all this obscene material. In doing so they may have lost vital evidence. 'Don't tell the press,' Fred told Morgan and Harrison.

When he next picked up the Dutch Girl, he said that she was so excited 'to get this flippin' bondage thing going' that she stripped off in his vehicle. 'I look around and she's absolutely starkers, except for her earrings … it was unreal.' It was that indeed.

'The Dutch Girl,' mused DC Morgan. 'Europe's a big place … That's the problem we've got.'

While they went back over the details Fred sat grinning at the officers, puffing on a roll-up cigarette. Although he had told them stories that would shame the Marquis de Sade, Fred seemed to think that the detectives would see him as the decent bloke he believed himself to be: a local Good Samaritan. 'I mean, anybody around Gloucester anywhere knows if they were in trouble, during the night, they only had to ring me and I'd be out of bed and going [to] help them out, you know, with any plumbing, anything at all.' If your toilet flooded, your ceiling collapsed, or the lighting fused, Fred would answer an emergency call 24/7. The fact that he wasn't qualified to do 'anything at all' didn't stop him mucking about with plumbing and electrics. 'I mean, I've got a good reputation for my work and everything I do. I haven't gone out to destroy and injure and maim people, or anything … I wanted a good life … I was getting my own life in one hell of a mess helping others …'

★ ★ ★

Staring at his charts in the Major Incident Room late into the evening, John Bennett had a brainwave. It seemed that Lynda Gough had been the first murder victim buried at 25 Cromwell Street. Fred buried her in the most convenient place available, which was the old car inspection pit behind his house. When he killed again he moved indoors to conceal the evidence.

SEARCHING EVERYWHERE

There were five victims in the cellar, distributed along its sides. If Carol Ann Cooper, the care home girl from Worcester who disappeared in 1973, was the first victim buried in the cellar, in the back, and Lucy Partington was next, to Carol's right, buried in the nursery alcove in January 1974, perhaps Fred had worked his way around the cellar clockwise as he killed, filling the available spaces with bodies: the one in front of the false fireplace, then the Marilyn Monroe fireplace, finally burying Juanita Mott under the stairs in 1975. With the cellar full, he went back into the garden to bury Shirley Robinson, Alison Chambers and finally his daughter Heather. Bennett could hardly write his theory down fast enough. If he was right, he now presumed that the Dutch Girl must have disappeared between 1973 and 1975. This narrowed the search.

There were still three more victims to recover outside 25 Cromwell Street. On Sunday, Darren Law and Hazel Savage took Fred on another outing, accompanied by Howard Ogden and Janet Leach. They visited Fred's former allotment in Gloucester. Fred spoke of burning the clothes of a victim here. The police asked Fred what else he might have done at the allotment. Fred became distracted by memories of the old boy who kept the neighbouring allotment and grew 'the most beautifulest chryanths (*sic*)'. He said that he couldn't remember whose clothes he burnt. As he rented the allotment in 1975, the most likely victim was Juanita Mott. He didn't have the allotment long. The council cancelled Fred's tenancy because he didn't keep his plot in good order. The police searched the strip of land but didn't find anything buried there. It emerged that Fred also had the use of an allotment in Glasgow in the 1960s. However, that plot had since become part of the M8. There was no hope of digging up a motorway.

That afternoon, the police also took Fred to 25 Midland

Road, asking him to show them where he buried Charmaine. They walked through the flat into the kitchen, part of the new extension that had been added since Fred and Rose lived at the address.

DC Hazel Savage: Fred, do you realise why we are here?
Fred West: Yeah ... to tell you where Charmaine is.

He marked a wall to indicate that Charmaine was buried in the old coal cellar beneath the mark. Fred had previously admitted to strangling Charmaine in the car after he killed Rena in 1971, but he now insisted that the police would not find Charmaine at Midland Road because of subsequent building work. He said that Charmaine's bones would have been removed and dumped 'on a tip somewhere'. The police could knock the house down, but they would not find anything, although he wanted Charmaine found.

DC Hazel Savage: Why do you say that?
Fred West: Because I want her buried with Heather ... at Much Marcle.

When Savage remarked factually that Heather wasn't at Much Marcle, Fred sighed deeply as if the detective just didn't understand. He then explained tearfully that he wanted Heather and Charmaine buried together at St. Bartholomew's Church in the village, near his parents' grave, his father having died two years earlier in 1992. He became especially emotional as he spoke about this, as if his deepest feelings were stirred up. Savage pointed out that they had to find Charmaine before any funeral could be planned, and Fred was now saying that Charmaine wasn't where he had put her.

SEARCHING EVERYWHERE

* * *

The search for Charmaine wasn't the only mystery that the police faced. As the team researched Fred's background they saw that he had links to Bristol Road in Gloucester, an arterial road running parallel with the canal. Fred was employed for years at two factories on Bristol Road: Permali, where he worked with asbestos; and Muir-Hill wagon works (later Winget Ltd) where he was a machinist. He worked at these jobs with manic energy, though he also stole shamelessly from his employers. In fact, he left such a bad impression at Permali that his personnel file was marked with this note: 'If anyone thinks of re-employing this man, do not'. The police had a suspicion that Fred had committed yet another murder on Bristol Road.

> **DC Hazel Savage**: Back in 1968, Fred, [a] fifteen-year-old girl went missing from the Bristol Road.
> **Fred West**: Yeah.
> **DC Savage**: Do you know about that?
> **Fred West**: Nope. Nothing to do with me.

Mary Bastholm was a waitress at the Pop-in café in Southgate Street, which was an extension of the Bristol Road. Mary's mother didn't want her working at the café, which attracted a rough crowd, but Mary asserted herself. 'It was a place where she used to hang out with her friends, and her boyfriend,' said her sister-in-law, Denise Bastholm. Mary was seeing a lad named Tim, from Hardwicke, and they had a date on the evening of Saturday, 6 January 1968. 'It wasn't a night to be going out. The snow was coming down. It was cold.' Mary insisted on keeping her date and walked to her bus stop on Bristol Road. Tim was going to meet her at the other end. Due to the bad weather, buses were taken off the road that night and the buses that ran were delayed. The next thing the Bastholms knew Tim was at their door asking what had happened to Mary. 'And that was when panic set in,' says Denise. A police search revealed evidence that Mary may have been snatched from the bus stop. She was carrying a Monopoly set, pieces of which were found scattered in the snow.

For years Mary's mother had been reluctant to leave the house in case Mary came home. Now journalists were contacting the family, asking if Mary could be a victim, and the family thought that it was very likely. 'The circumstances are so similar to a couple of the [other] girls,' says Denise. 'Cos Lucy [Partington] went missing from a bus stop, and I believe one of the other girls went missing from a bus stop.' Fred also met Rose on a bus, or at a bus stop. It was a pattern, like the care homes.

Asked about Mary, Fred remembered the search for the waitress. There were posters about it all over Gloucester in 1968. He and Rena had been stopped at a road block by police and asked if they had seen Mary. As he told this story, Fred started to refer to Rose being in the car with him that night, not Rena. He sometimes got the names of his wives muddled, but was it possible that Fred knew Rose in 1968, over a year before he said that they met? Rose would only have been fourteen. Decades later, Rose's solicitor came to believe that Fred and Rose may have known each other as early as 1968, and that Rose may even have helped Fred bundle Mary into his car. 'There was clearly a struggle because Monopoly pieces were left in the snow. It would have been seconds. Unless someone else was there, he couldn't have got round to the other side to drive, without Mary Bastholm getting out,' says Leo Goatley, speaking to me since 2004, which is when he

SEARCHING EVERYWHERE

stopped representing Rose. 'So just on a practical level, there would have to have been somebody else [involved].'

> **DC Hazel Savage**: What do you know about that missing girl, Fred?
> **Fred West**: Nothing ... Every girl who went missing, it ain't me who gone and collected them up, mind!
> **DC Savage**: I know that Fred!
> **Fred West**: Oh good (laughing) ...
> **DC Savage**: But there's a few that have gone missing that have ended up in your cellar, too.
> **Fred West**: Yeah, but I've told you them all ... Hazel, I'm telling you, I know nothing about that girl on Bristol Road ... What I want [is] anybody's that's been harmed by me to go to their resting place properly now. That's my ambition at this moment, to get them all back with their parents, have burials. Plus my own daughters.

Speaking of which, Savage had news for Fred. They had, as he knew, been speaking to his children, which had revealed important information. 'May has made allegations against you,' she said.

Fred seemed very surprised. 'I don't believe it,' he said.

8
OUR FAMILY OF LOVE

Monday, 21 March 1994 • Day Twenty-six
Gloucester Central Police Station

'We don't want any bullshit. We only want the truth.'
DC HAZEL SAVAGE

Fred had told the police that his daughter May would never lie. With that in mind, Hazel Savage now turned the tables on him. May didn't have as high an opinion of her father as he had of her, characterising him as a 'dirty, thieving, filthy-minded man' and she had made a statement that showed him to be all that and more. As May and her older sister Heather had grown up, she said that their father groped and molested them both, to the extent that the sisters went to bed with their clothes on to protect themselves from their dad's filthy hands. They stood guard for each other outside the bathroom, making sure to come out of the shower wrapped in a towel. Fred then drilled holes in their bedroom doors, so that he could spy on his daughters when they were naked.

DC Hazel Savage: What about that then, Fred?
Fred West: No comment.

THE FRED WEST TAPES

DC Hazel Savage: You're not denying that this happened?
Fred West: I've no comment on it.

Fred made it plain to Heather and May from when they were young that he intended to have sex with them – 'break them in' he said – when they were sixteen, if not before. He said that his father had done this, and he intended to repeat history by taking his daughters' virginity. He said this to them in a bantering way, as if he might be joking, but the girls knew that their dad meant it.

Heather turned sixteen first, and Fred pestered her relentlessly as her birthday approached. When Heather resisted him, he accused her of being a lesbian.

DC Hazel Savage: You've talked about Heather and lesbians, haven't you?
Fred West: (silence)

After Heather 'disappeared', Fred switched his attentions to May who lived in daily fear of being raped by her father, never sure whether Heather had managed to resist Dad or not before her disappearance. Until the murder inquiry, May said that she thought Heather had run away. After her disappearance, Fred became more aggressive, touching May in front of her mother, who did not seem to care. Incest was the family tradition, it is the vice at the heart of the West case, and to Fred and Rose it was normal. Finally, May lost her temper and told her father to stop touching her, slamming a door in his face. His smirk was replaced by 'a dark threatening glare'.

'Don't you dare speak to me like that,' he said, 'you little bitch!'

May was interviewed by the police in 1992, when Fred was

accused of raping one of her sisters. At that time she said that her father hadn't touched her. She didn't want the family broken up. Faced with overwhelming evidence that her dad had murdered Heather, probably after raping her, May had now decided to tell the police everything. Hazel Savage reminded Fred that May had signed her statement as being absolutely true.

> **DC Hazel Savage**: Each statement here is signed on the bottom, do you see there? Each page ... That's very difficult, isn't it, Fred?
> **Fred West**: There's no comment.

This was the first time during the interviews that Fred had been so quiet, the first time that he had replied 'no comment' to police questions. Not for long, though. When Savage finished reading, Fred said that his daughter's allegations were all 'rubbish'.

Family was important to Fred and Rose, though their family values were twisted and intertwined with sex, regardless of the conventions of normal parental behaviour. Rose had been obsessed with children since she was a child. Her parents considered Rose to be slow-witted and essentially childish, while Rose's mother believed that the fact Fred already had children was what drew Rose to him initially. 'She had this attraction for playing with young children always,' Daisy Letts told me. When she saw Rose with Fred's children 'it was like a child looking after a child'. Babies were living dolls to Rose. But when the dolls grew up, she became short tempered, flustered and abusive towards them.

When Rena came to reclaim her daughter Charmaine in 1971, Rose didn't want to give her up. Fred and Rose considered moving home to shake Rena off, but they couldn't afford to move. 'We were bloody flat broke, and that was it, we had no money to do nothing,' said Fred. Then he went to prison, leaving Rose in poverty at 25 Midland Road, a teenager with three children to care for: eight-year-old Charmaine, who knew that Rose wasn't her real mother and resented it; an unhappy Anna Marie, who was seven; and baby Heather. Although Rose had wanted Fred's children, she was unable to cope with them. The flat became squalid. She was irritated when Charmaine wet the bed.

Meanwhile, Fred wrote to Rose from prison about 'our family of love', and made her the model gypsy caravan that had been on display at home ever since. The caravan opened up as a jewellery box, inscribed with the words *Our Family of Love*. Fred's semi-literate prison letters were cobbled together with the help of fellow inmates and gaolers and, as he explained to the police, he copied phrases like 'our family of love' from books to pad out his letters to Rose. In one letter he wrote that his love for Rose was like a diamond 'never to be lost or hurt'. 'I called [Rose] "my diamond" and that, and she was precious to me,' Fred explained. 'I mean, if anybody tried anything with her, then they'd have had to answer to me, simple as that.' Such crudely expressed sentimentality impressed Rose, when she could make out Fred's handwriting, and she saved his letters in a box in the attic, together with the letters she sent him. The police had now found them all. They were very useful evidence.

In 1971, Rose wrote to Fred about problems she was having with Charmaine:

Darling about Char, I think she likes to be handled rough, but darling why do I have to be the one to do it. I would keep her for her own sake, if it wasn't for the rest of the children. You can see Char coming out in Anna [Marie] now and I hate it ... Oh! Love! About our son. I'll see the doctor about the pill,

OUR FAMILY OF LOVE

and then we'll be safe to decide about it when you come home. Well love, keep happy, Longing for the 18th ...
Your ever worshipping wife Rose.

Here was evidence that Rose was mistreating Charmaine while Fred was in prison, treating her 'rough'. The fact that Rose signed off as Fred's 'wife' was also interesting. Fred and Rose weren't married at the time, he was still married to Rena, but Rose evidently saw herself as Fred's wife. She also made it clear in the letter that she wanted another baby with him, a son this time. Fred wrote back to Rose as 'your ever worshipping husband'. When Rose wrote to Fred, she drew their names in a love heart pierced by an arrow.

The couple were besotted with one another. Scratching at his arm with a needle and ink, Fred attempted to change Rena's heart tattoo from 'Fred + Rena' to read 'Fred + Rose'.

DC Hazel Savage: You'd go to the end of the Earth for [Rose], wouldn't you?
Fred West: Yeah. And over the top.
DC Savage: And over the top?
Fred West: Yeah ... I worship that girl ... we got married because we love each other, and that's the thing that's gone all through our life together.

Their love had grown. 'I mean ... it can't get any stronger, I don't think it can. It's gone too far as it is,' he told the detectives, revealing perhaps more than he intended. 'Half the things have gone wrong was [me being] too much protective to Rose ...' In another interview he said that, when angry, Rose was as fierce as a tiger. In truth they could both go berserk: attacking their kids, strangers, even each other. One witness said that they saw Rose at 25 Cromwell Street with broken glasses and a black eye after being smacked in the face by Fred. The kids remembered Rose running after Fred with a carving knife in hand in 1974, after he teased her beyond her patience. When Fred slammed a door in Rose's face, she plunged the knife into the door with such force that her hand came down over the blade and she almost severed two of her fingers. Fred took Rose to hospital where she underwent surgery, having told the staff that she had injured herself 'cutting wood'. Broadly speaking, however, Fred saw himself as Rose's protector. As he said to the police 'anybody threatened to say anything to her or anything, that's when the trouble started'. When Rena posed a threat to Rose, regarding custody of Charmaine, the result was murder.

Most of the Cromwell Street murders were sex crimes, however, and some of the victims had been lodgers, or visitors to the house when the Wests rented rooms out. Fred claimed that he and Rose didn't socialise with their tenants, implying that the young people who lived upstairs shunned them. 'We never had no actual visitors from them lot,' Fred told the interviewing officers. 'They come to see somebody in the house, upstairs ... nothing to do with us ... Rose don't mix with nobody.' On the contrary, the police were gathering evidence that the Wests had a lot to do with their lodgers, including having sex with some of them. Rose bedded male and female lodgers. Fred hotly denied that Rose became sexually involved with any of the women in the house. 'Rose was not a lesbian,' he insisted. 'I've tried several times to get her into it, but without success.'

DC Hazel Savage: So, you're into that, are you?
Fred West: Yeah, I like watching them ...

OUR FAMILY OF LOVE

After the Wests stopped taking in lodgers, around 1981 – partly because Fred didn't want to comply with strict new rules that had come into place governing landlords – he turned the first floor of the house into a self-contained prostitute's flat for Rose, with the Black Magic Bar. 'She had her own bathroom, kitchen and everything up there,' he said proudly.

Such intense conversations in the interview room were alleviated with lighter moments, even humour. Fred made occasional jokes, while DC Savage made sarcastic remarks at his expense, and interviews often veered off on absurd tangents. A prime example was when Fred was asked, at this stage in the interviews, about information received from a member of the public that he had done building work at a convent school where he supposedly became 'involved' with a nun.

> **DC Barbara Harrison**: So what happened with this nun?
> **Fred West**: Story of my life (laughing).
> **DC Harrison**: So go on … where is she now?
> **Fred West**: There was about four of them, actually.
> **DC Hazel Savage**: There would be, wouldn't there!
> **Fred West**: And, um, one used [to] cover for the other. There was a saying that one nun would get none.

Fred was killing himself laughing. Unimpressed, Savage suggested that this was mere fantasy. 'I don't live in fantasy worlds. I live in this world,' retorted Fred, insisting that he'd had sex with several nuns. 'I went out with one in Manchester … I went with one in Glasgow.' He met his first nun when she was collecting for charity outside a pub; not inside the pub because of course nuns don't drink. 'Good thinking, Fred,' said Savage.

Some of his falsehoods were so demonstrably untrue that they helped the police. Fred claimed that he dated Lucy Partington for months in Cheltenham. She knew him as Stephen (one of his middle names) because 'I didn't want anybody to know that I was carrying on with anybody.' Other pseudonyms he used included Fox, Chief and Wilf. One day Lucy came to him in a bad mood. '[She] said, "I've been bloody looking for you!" And I said, "What for?" She said, "I'm pregnant and I want £1,000 off you," or something, or £800 or something, or whatnot, "for an abortion." And that's where the row [began]. Because I don't reckon she was pregnant. I think she was having me on. So then we had a violent row and that's how it … all happened.' The police told Fred that his story could not possibly be true, because Lucy was away at Exeter University when Fred said that he was dating her in Cheltenham. Also, as a chaste Roman Catholic, Lucy was one of the least likely people to have asked for money for an abortion. Fred's lie helped build a case against him.

When the police defeated Fred in a lie, as they did here, he quickly tried to divert the conversation in a new direction. There were other women he saw in Cheltenham, he said, when his imaginary affair with Lucy Partington had been debunked, one girlfriend being 'a little fat bird with straggly hair'. Maybe he was getting his Cheltenham girlfriends mixed up. 'There's so many flipping girls I've met through the time, that's the problem.' This other Cheltenham woman was 'a poor class girl,' said Fred, whose imaginary world was populated with a cast of peculiar characters. He seemingly invented them as he jabbered away to the cops. The neurologist Oliver Sacks had a verbose psychiatric patient who exhibited similar behaviour, a case Sacks described in his book, *The Man Who Mistook His Wife for a Hat*. 'Unable to maintain a genuine narrative or continuity, unable to maintain a genuine inner world, he is driven to the proliferation of pseudo narratives, in a pseudo-continuity, pseudo-worlds peopled by pseudo-people, phantoms.' Dr Sacks's patient was suffering with brain damage. While Fred had sustained head injuries in his youth, and brain damage was suggested as a possibility at the time by the family GP, people who dealt with Fred in custody in 1994 were generally of the view that he was not mad. John Bennett and Howard Ogden both saw Fred as a manipulator who lied as it suited him. Yet Fred did and said things that were so peculiar that they pointed to a man who was, to some degree, out of his wits. Rape and murder aside, does a rational man play at abortion, as Fred did, and try to artificially inseminate children? Throughout his time in custody he showed repeated signs of mental instability, talking about visions and ghosts, and he escaped with more and more frequency into fantasy. Some of this behaviour may have been deliberate to confuse the police, some was no doubt to titillate himself, but there was also a sense that Fred was lost in his own pseudo-world.

DC Harrison asked Fred what he called this second Cheltenham girl. 'Screamer!' he exclaimed. 'For the reason you're thinking,' he laughed, 'that was the turn-on with her. I mean, you have to be careful where you touched her because she screamed ... she wanted [the] whole of Cheltenham to know she was making love ... I never met a girl that noisy in my life before.' He said that she worked in Woolworths. 'I didn't want anybody to see me with her.'

DC Jeff Morgan: Why not?
Fred West: Because I was scraping the bottom of the barrel, like, you know. I mean, she was rough.

There was a café near to where this woman worked, and Fred said he used to play fruit machines in the café. As he told the story, the café became a 'casino' where he won large sums of money. DC Morgan reminded Fred that the café was merely a greasy spoon with a fruit machine, but Fred was away with the fairies. 'We will close the interview there, the time is 12:54,' sighed Morgan, before lunch on Saturday, 26 March. There was little to be got from Fred when he was in this mood.

When they resumed talking that afternoon, Morgan and Savage tried to get a tighter grip on the discussion, quizzing Fred about gaps in the timeline of murder. The twelve known victims disappeared between 1967 and 1987, but the murders weren't evenly distributed over the twenty years. Anne McFall vanished in 1967; Charmaine and Rena were seemingly killed in 1971; Carol Ann Cooper, Lynda Gough and Lucy Partington disappeared in 1973; the police believed the other Worcester victim and the so-called Dutch Girl were killed in 1974–75; Juanita Mott also disappeared in 1975; Shirley Robinson was killed three years later, in 1978; Alison Chambers the year after that. Then there was an eight-year gap until 1987, when Heather disappeared. The Wests had been fiendishly busy at times, especially in 1973–75, when six murders occurred, but there were no known victims in 1976, 1977, or the six-year period 1980–86.

> **DC Jeff Morgan**: What we were saying, Fred, was that we find it very, very hard to believe someone is killed [almost every year], and there's a six-year gap ... We just find that totally hard to believe ... I'll be quite frank with you, and look you straight in the eye. I am not happy that you haven't killed anybody in those [gaps]. I just find it unbelievable.
> **Fred West**: Well, it's right ... I haven't killed anybody in the gaps. You got all the girls, or anybody that I've had anything to do with ...

Morgan was not satisfied. A psychological profile of Fred had been created. 'And the experts tell us that you haven't stopped killing in those years,' he said.

> **Fred West**: Well, they're wrong ...
> **DC Jeff Morgan**: Do you know what the main reason [is], I think, you could be not telling us about others?
> **Fred West**: Go on then.
> **DC Morgan**: Because I think that you'd be frightened it would implicate Rose.
> **Fred West**: Rubbish ... Rose knew nothing of what I was doing at all. Ever.
> **DC Hazel Savage**: Was she ever in the house when you were killing somebody?
> **Fred West**: No.
> **DC Savage**: Or cutting them up?
> **Fred West**: No.
> **DC Savage**: Never once?
> **Fred West**: No. Only once. Yes. Once, sorry. I think the Worcester Girl, when I brought her in the back way, and [Rose] was in the front room ...
> **DC Savage**: Because I just think of the horrific noise ... of killing somebody... and of dismembering them ...

The police believed that the bodies were probably dismembered in the bathroom at 25 Cromwell Street, where Fred had privacy and running water, which he would need to clear up afterwards. The pathologist Bernard Knight had advised the officers that dismembering a human body was not a quick or easy task for a layman, though Fred would probably have got faster at it with practice. There would be an appalling mess. Hazel Savage struggled to believe that Rose could have been unaware of what was happening as Fred turned her downstairs bathroom into an abattoir. After death, without the heart pumping, blood would ooze rather than spurt from the victims, assuming the victims were cut up post-mortem. There would still be a lot of blood, though, blood in the bath, blood on the taps and tiles, blood smeared along the skirting boards, on the door frames and on the floor as Fred dragged bodies about. His hands and clothes would have been covered with blood and he would have left sticky marks on every surface that he touched. Such marks had disappeared over time, with years of cleaning and redecorating, but how could Rose not have been aware of this when it happened? She must have known.

'Rubbish!' said Fred. He suggested that a body could be dismembered very easily, in a few minutes. Savage said that the professor estimated it would take half an hour, not counting the clean-up and burial.

Fred West: He probably hasn't done it then.
DC Hazel Savage: Well, he probably hasn't murdered, no.

One of Fred's annoying characteristics was that he always thought that he knew best, even when he spoke nonsense.

★ ★ ★

The officers now changed the subject, while maintaining the pressure. Jeff Morgan and Barbara Harrison had been to the Forest of Dean to interview an important new witness named Caroline Owens. She had given the detectives a statement that seemed to shed light on the joint activities of Fred and Rose. Indeed, her evidence would prove to be crucial to the whole investigation.

OUR FAMILY OF LOVE

The story went back to 1972 when Caroline Raine (Raine being her maiden name) was a trendy sixteen-year-old girl who melded the fashion styles of glam rock and skinheads, cutting her hair short, wearing flared jeans, puffer jackets and platform shoes. Caroline wasn't happy living at home with her mum and stepdad in Cinderford, an isolated town in the Forest of Dean. She was dating an apprentice engineer from Tewkesbury named Tony Coates, also sixteen. Tony only had a push bike and public transport was bad, so Caroline hitch-hiked the twenty-four miles to Tewkesbury to see her boyfriend. After their dates, it was her habit to walk to the Gupshill Manor pub in Tewkesbury to thumb a ride home. One night in September 1972, the driver of an old Ford Popular stopped. When Caroline saw a young woman in the passenger seat of the coupé she felt reassured that it was safe to accept a ride. Caroline was small and pretty, young-looking for her age. Men were attracted to her, not always in a good way. When she was thirteen, she was assaulted in a public toilet, so she was wary. 'The girl rolled down the window and asked me where I was going ...' This was Rose, soon to celebrate her nineteenth birthday. Fred was driving. Caroline got into the car.

On the drive to Cinderford, Caroline revealed that she was out of work and keen to leave home. 'After I had finished explaining this to the pair of them, they both looked each other in the eye and [said], "We need a nanny to look after our three daughters."' The job paid three pounds a week, plus room and board. Caroline was cautious enough to ask the Wests to meet her mother first. They brought Anna Marie, Heather and baby May to Cinderford to see her mother. The meeting went well. Caroline thought that the kids were 'cute', and Fred and Rose seemed nice. 'I had always wanted to be a nanny.' She wasn't the first or last young woman the Wests caught with the lure of nannying.

THE FRED WEST TAPES

Caroline moved into 25 Cromwell Street, sharing a bedroom with Anna Marie. There was a free and easy attitude among the tenants. Caroline had a one-night stand with Ben Stanniland (the same lodger who later brought Lynda Gough to 25 Cromwell Street). Directly after sex with Ben, she had sex with one of his friends. Tony also stayed over with her, and she received an overnight visit from a sailor, who left her money in the morning. The Wests paid close attention to Caroline's liaisons. Rose began to make sexual advances to her, walking into the bathroom when she was naked, 'playing with my hair, [saying] I had nice eyes'. Fred engaged Caroline in smutty conversation, some of it disturbing. He told Caroline that Anna Marie, who was eight, had lost her virginity. 'I thought, that is a bit of a strange thing to say, and I asked him, "What do you mean, how did that happen?"' She'd an accident on her bike, said Fred, sitting on the frame when the saddle was off. Caroline looked at little Anna Marie, saw her blush and guessed that something sexual had taken place with her father. Fred reminded Caroline that he knew that she had slept with two or three boys at the house, but Tony didn't need to know this. 'It will be our little secret.' Shortly afterwards, Fred and Rose put a proposition to Caroline. They asked her to join their 'sex circle'. This circle comprised Fred and Rose and their Jamaican friends. When Caroline demurred, Fred muttered something about 'fucking lesbians'. Caroline quit the job and moved back home.

She continued to see Tony. At around 10:30 PM on Saturday, 6 December, having just turned seventeen, Caroline was once again thumbing a lift home outside the Gupshill Manor pub when the Wests cruised by in their Ford. 'Rose got out of the car and said, with a disarming smile, "Hello Caroline, how are you? I'm sorry that you left. We have missed you. Haven't we, Fred?"' Caroline's instinct was not to accept a lift again, but the Wests were very charming. 'Rose got out and pulled the seat forward for me to get in the back and then she said, "Fred, I will sit in the back with Caroline so we can have a chat," and she got into the back with me.' When they neared Gloucester the conversation turned sexual. 'Fred asked me if I had sex with Tony that night ... Rose had her arm around the back of me, and she started touching my breasts over my clothes ... Fred said, "What are her tits like?"' He was grinning and laughing, 'not a nice laugh'. Rose put her hand between Caroline's legs. 'I started panicking, and I was struggling with her.' The Wests were discussing Caroline's body, 'smutty talk'. Fred pulled over near a roundabout. 'Fred turned around and started punching me around the head ... He was calling me names ... "bitch" and that.'

When she came to, Caroline was still in the car. Her hands were tied behind her back with her scarf, 'and they were putting tape around my head – all the way round ... Over my mouth, all around the back of my hair ... a gag.' It was brown parcel tape, of the type found in the graves at 25 Cromwell Street. Fred stole the tape from work. They were wrapping her head so Caroline could only breathe through her nose. Rose pushed her down on the floor, then sat on her 'to keep me down', while Fred turned the car around and drove into Gloucester, 'talking and laughing' with Rose.

When they got to Cromwell Street, they led Caroline inside the house and up to the front bedsit – later to become the Black Magic Bar, at this time a doss hole with a mattress on the floor. 'They told me to keep quiet, and said if I was good [Fred] would take the tape off.' Fred cut the tape. He apologised when he nicked Caroline with the blade. '[Fred] was being very gentle,' Caroline later wrote. 'I couldn't grasp what was going on –

one minute they were attacking me, the next they were being nice to me and saying sorry.' Rose then kissed her. When Caroline told her to fuck off, Fred ordered Rose to 'get the cotton wool'. Rose did so quickly. 'They [then] tied my hands back up again, and they gagged me ... with cotton wool.' They also blindfolded Caroline and lay her down on the mattress.

'Keep fucking quiet, you stupid fucking bitch.'

Caroline felt fingers inside her. '[Fred] said if he could flatten the vagina lips the clitoris would be showing more and I would get more pleasure,' she recalled. 'Fred got a belt, a leather belt, and Rose held my feet apart while Fred beat me between the legs.' He hit her with the buckle in a frenzy. Then Rose became calm again. Several witnesses spoke of Rose's weird mood swings. Fred was also volatile. The next minute he was threatening. 'You shout, and we'll fucking kill ya, bitch!' It was like a nightmare. Rose then performed cunnilingus on Caroline. 'You're enjoying that, aren't you ... you dirty cow?' Fred asked Rose, while masturbating.

'Yeah, and you can join in now if you want.'

Fred penetrated Rose from behind. When they were finished, Fred said he had work tomorrow and so he needed to sleep. Caroline could stay in the room with them if she behaved. If not, he would put her down in the cellar.

Around 7:00 AM a visitor came to the house and Fred went to talk to them. 'Help me!' Caroline cried, but Rose smothered her face with a pillow. Fred was furious when he came back into the room. '[He] told me that he would keep me in the cellar and let his black friends use me, and when they were finished with me they would bury me under the paving stones of Gloucester. He said there were already hundreds of girls there, and the police wouldn't find them.' When Rose left the room briefly in the early morning to feed May, Fred raped Caroline.

OUR FAMILY OF LOVE

Afterwards Caroline was crying. Fred started crying, too, 'apologised for hurting me [and] said I was there for Rose's pleasure.' He told Caroline that she couldn't tell Rose. Caroline decided that her best hope of survival was to say that she would come back and live with them. Fred immediately told Rose, who was so delighted she gave Caroline a hug. The Wests then allowed Caroline to have a bath to get the tape glue out of her hair, after which Caroline got dressed. The children and lodgers woke up. Ben said Hi. Fred and Rose said they had to go to the laundrette, and Caroline offered to go with them. While Fred parked the car, Caroline walked out of the laundrette and hitched a ride home to Cinderford.

When she arrived home, Caroline's mother noticed that her face was puffy and bruised and so she called the police. Caroline was examined by a doctor and photographed by a police photographer, showing the officers the abrasions on her back where Fred cut her, and the bruising on her face. The police didn't seem wholly sympathetic. So much had happened that Caroline forgot to mention initially that Fred had also raped her. When she gave a second statement the next day, adding the rape, the police seemed frankly dubious. When DC Kevan Price went to 25 Cromwell Street to speak to Rose, though, he found a roll of masking tape and a button from Caroline's jacket in the Wests' car. Asked if she had attacked Caroline, Rose told the detective: 'Don't be fucking daft, what do you think I am?'

This was the story detectives Morgan and Harrison had now taken from Caroline Owens, twenty-two years after the attack, as evidence for the murder inquiry. There were striking similarities between Caroline's ordeal in 1972 and what appeared to have happened to the victims buried at 25 Cromwell Street: young women of a similar age, often with the same elfin look, who were bound and gagged. Caroline's experience seemed to be the template, the women who came after her being killed, perhaps, because the Wests didn't want to risk another woman going to the police as she had done. Or partly for that reason. 'I believe you've been bringing them back to the basement and torturing them there,' Jeff Morgan told Fred.

'Rubbish,' Fred replied. He put the tape on Caroline's face to 'calm her down' after Rose put her hand up her skirt. 'But that was all.'

'Fred, that was 1972. We're now 1994,' said Hazel Savage. 'Have you been taping up people ever since, twenty-two years on?'

Fred West: I know what you are trying to imply, but you're wrong ... I never went out looking for girls [to] injure [and] I was always on my own when I went out ...
DC Jeff Morgan: You weren't! ... You went out with your missus, to Tewkesbury, and you picked up Caroline Owens outside the Gupshill Manor. The two of you were in the car ... she stood on the side of the road hitch-hiking ... you and Rose pull up a second time, and that's when [you] abducted her, pulled into a gateway at Highnam,[10] and you whacked her. She was taped up and taken back. And when she came round, Rose was touching her up, as you have more or less said.
Fred West: Rose only touched her once ...
DC Morgan: Get to Highnam on the way to Cinderford. Pull into a gateway, you turn round and whack her one. She's semi-unconscious.
Fred West: Rubbish!
DC Morgan: And, then she's tied up and taped and taken back ...

---

10   A village on the A40 outside Gloucester.

OUR FAMILY OF LOVE

> **DC Hazel Savage**: Rose sat on her, that's the truth.
> **Fred West** (excited): No, she did not. Rose never touched her.
> **DC Savage**: That's what the lady says in her statement.
> **Fred West**: Well, she's lying ...
> **DC Morgan**: The truth is, Fred, that you will write Rose out of anything you can in respect of this ... there's all these people buried in your basement, in the garden, and your wife didn't know anything about it. It's just too ridiculous.

Fred accused the police of pursuing a 'vendetta' against Rose. He insisted that what happened with Caroline was his only attempt to get Rose involved in this part of his life, and when she didn't go for it he left her out of his subsequent activities. 'I kept her pregnant. I kept her with other men.' The police suggested that, on the contrary, the Wests remained locked together in all things.

> **Fred West**: Yeah, well, there's [a] lot of difference between evil locking together and love. I mean we're not evilly-locked together at all. I mean, Rose might look a bit hard-faced and that, but Rose is as soft as a kitten.

He said that the 'killing instinct' got into him before he met Rose. If Rose had been up for it, he would have taken Caroline home and 'put her in bondage'. She may have died. 'I would have let it go too far again, [but] Rose backed out completely on me.'

Furthermore, he denied raping Caroline.

> **DC Jeff Morgan**: Are you saying she agreed to [sex]?
> **Fred West**: Well, she didn't do a lot about it, put it that

way. I mean, she could have screamed then, and the whole house would have heard her.
DC Morgan: Women don't always scream when they're being raped, they're terrified very often.
Fred West: Rubbish.

Back in 1972, Caroline didn't want to give evidence in a rape prosecution, where she would be cross-examined in court. So when the police informed her that the Wests were prepared to plead guilty to lesser offences she settled for that, though she came to regret it. The lesser charges were assault occasioning actual bodily-harm (ABH) and indecent assault. 'I don't know why I did it, it just happened,' admitted Rose when the case was heard at Gloucester Magistrates' Court in January 1973. The Wests' lawyer suggested that Caroline had offered 'passive co-operation'. The chairman of the bench said that he didn't think it would do any good to send the Wests to prison. He fined them £50 each instead. Twelve years after he walked free from court after getting his sister pregnant, Fred got away with another serious sex crime. In years to come people involved in the 1973 case admitted that it was mishandled, that the Wests should have been prosecuted for rape at crown court, in which case they may well have been gaoled. One of the lawyers involved admits that he was astonished that the matter was dealt with by a magistrate, and wondered if a secret deal was done with Fred, rumoured to have been a low-level police informant at the time. But there was justice of a sort. When Tony Coates spotted Fred in the Albion pub in Tewkesbury, he chased him outside and thumped him.

Fred and Rose West were unknown in 1973, and the court report of their assault on Caroline Owens only made a small article in the local paper: 'City pair stripped and assaulted girl'.

OUR FAMILY OF LOVE

Twenty-one years later the Wests were notorious. Their case was filling the national newspapers and the tabloids were offering big money for exclusive insights into the Wests. Caroline had a dramatic story to sell, if she chose, and I was one of the reporters trying to 'buy her up', as we used to say. 'This girl at Cinderford now, she's in it for a packet,' Fred said in the interview room. He either knew or was shrewd enough to guess that Caroline was receiving offers from journalists like me. 'That's evil to say that,' said DC Savage, as if profiting from the case would be wrong.

> **DC Jeff Morgan**: Not everybody's in this to make money.
> **DC Hazel Savage**: That's like saying you're in it to make money …
> **Fred West**: What good's money to me when I'm away [in prison]?

Ultimately, Caroline signed a deal with the *Sun* for £20,000. Many people involved in the case were making money, or thinking about it. Steve and May West signed with the *News of the World*; Anna Marie received a down payment of £3,000 from the *Daily Star*, part of a deal that would include a book. More media deals would emerge, some of which caused embarrassment for the police. Fred was sharp enough to use this to his advantage. Told that another woman had made an allegation of rape against him, he accused her of cashing in.

> **DC Hazel Savage**: You find things like that very difficult to cope with, don't you … allegations of rape?
> **Fred West**: Yeah, cos I never raped nobody.
> **DC Hazel Savage**: And yet you killed people.
> **Fred West**: Yeah, see, you've even got the killing wrong.

THE FRED WEST TAPES

You're trying to make out that I just went out and blatantly killed someone ...
DC Savage: They went through Hell, actually.
Fred West: No, nobody went through Hell. Enjoyment turned to disaster.

* * *

Looking at more recent events the police were concerned about what Fred might have got up to in Birmingham in 1992–93, when he was living there in bail hostels. He described empty days without work in Birmingham, living on benefits, during which he mooched about the city, loitering around New Street Station in particular, where he would scavenge the pavements for dropped coins. 'You could pick up ten pounds on a good day.' One day he found a watch. He mentioned that he kept some of his street finds in a display cabinet at 25 Cromwell Street.

DC Hazel Savage: So let me get this clear. Are you saying that all the stuff you found in Birmingham [is] in your house, in a glass cabinet?
Fred West: Yeah.
DC Savage: Why?
Fred West: It was keepsakes.

A thought crossed the detective's mind. 'Is this souvenirs from people that you have offended against?'

'No! No, no, no, no, no, no. Rubbish,' said Fred. 'It's stuff I picked up on the street.'

The story became more suspicious when Fred said that he found women's rings in Birmingham, rings that 'got run over by cars'. These might be at home, too. 'So suddenly we now got a street full of rings as well?' asked Savage. This might explain

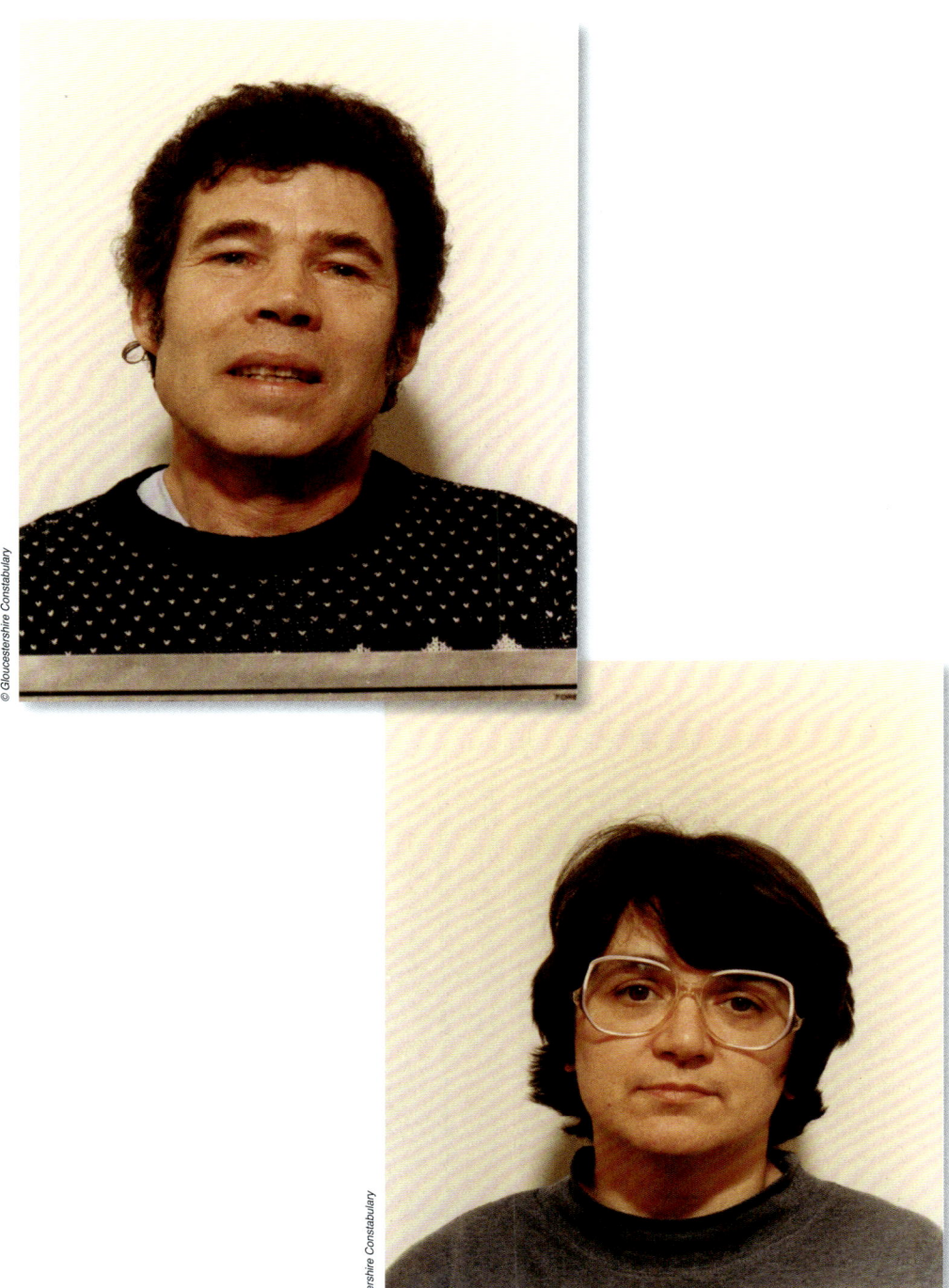

The police custody photographs of Fred and Rose West – taken soon after they were arrested in February 1994 – are among the most famous images in criminal history. Fred made admissions from the start, insisting that Rose knew nothing. She was belligerent, evasive and then said 'no comment … I'm innocent'.

Young Fred is seen here with his parents and siblings on a trip to Barry Island, Wales, in the 1950s (which apparently inspired the writers of the sitcom *Gavin & Stacey* to give their Barry Island family the surname West). Kitty West, the sister Fred later sexually abused and made pregnant, stands front centre. His sinister brother, John, stands right. Read about Fred's childhood in Chapter 4.

Rose West was a strange child who rocked herself manically back and forth.

Young Fred grasps Rose as if frightened to lose her, in this unique picture of the couple at the start of their relationship.

Mary Bastholm disappeared from a Gloucester bus stop in 1968, and has never been found – dead or alive. She was almost certainly one of the first victims.

Fred and Rose lived in the ground floor flat here at 25 Midland Road, Gloucester, 1970-72, with Charmaine and Heather. After her murder in 1971, Charmaine's mutilated body was buried in the coal cellar. She was eight.

As the House of Horrors started to make international news, crowds gathered outside 25 Cromwell Street in Gloucester. Inside, the police were finding human remains – in the garden, cellar and under the downstairs bathroom.

The twelve known murder victims are seen here in order of demise. Reading left to right, the top row shows Anne McFall, murdered 1967; Fred's step-daughter Charmaine, murdered 1971; her mother and Fred's first wife Rena West (*née* Costello) also murdered 1971; and Lynda Gough, the first Cromwell Street victim, murdered 1973.

Second row left to right: Carol Ann Cooper (murdered 1973) was one of the 'Worcester girls'; university student Lucy Partington disappeared 27 December 1973, and may have been murdered as late as 3 January 1974; Swiss student Thérèse Siegenthaler, was murdered in 1974; and the second Worcester girl, Shirley Hubbard, murdered 1974.

Bottom row left to right: Juanita Mott was murdered in 1975; lodger Shirley Robinson was murdered three years later in 1978; Alison Chambers was murdered 1979; and finally Heather West was murdered in 1987.

While the Wests abused women and children and committed mass murder, they continued to live as a loving married couple, apparently happy and devoted to each other. Here they are in their Black Magic Bar in the 1980s, Fred wearing his good suit.

Det. Supt. John Bennett led the police investigation with determination and integrity.

DC Hazel Savage deserves credit for bringing the Wests to justice.

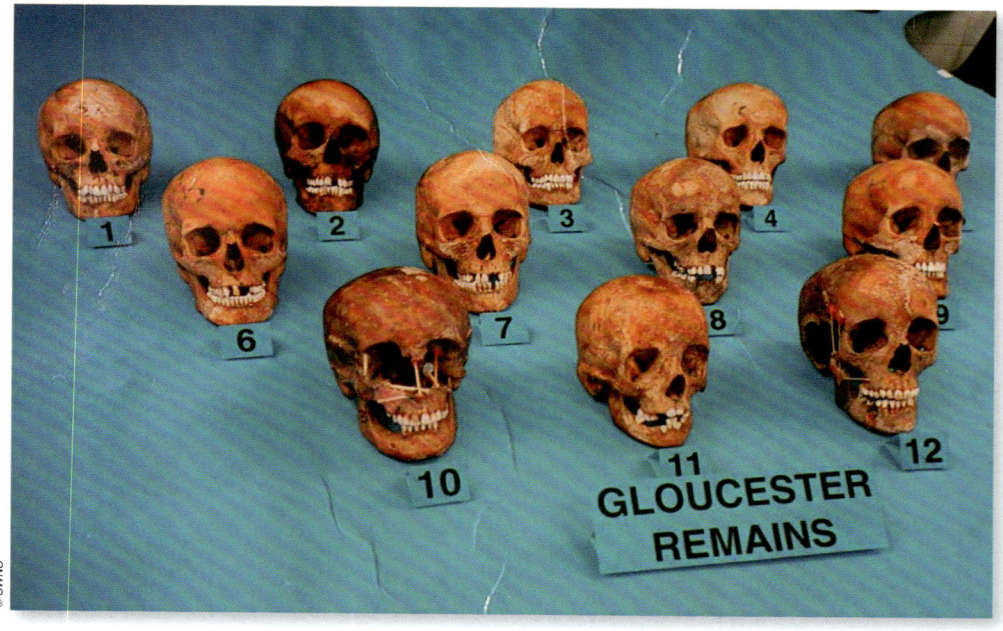

This unique picture of the skulls of all twelve murder victims – assembled and photographed only once – illustrates the scale of the crimes committed by the Wests, and the tragedy of twelve young women and girls whose lives were ended so brutally.

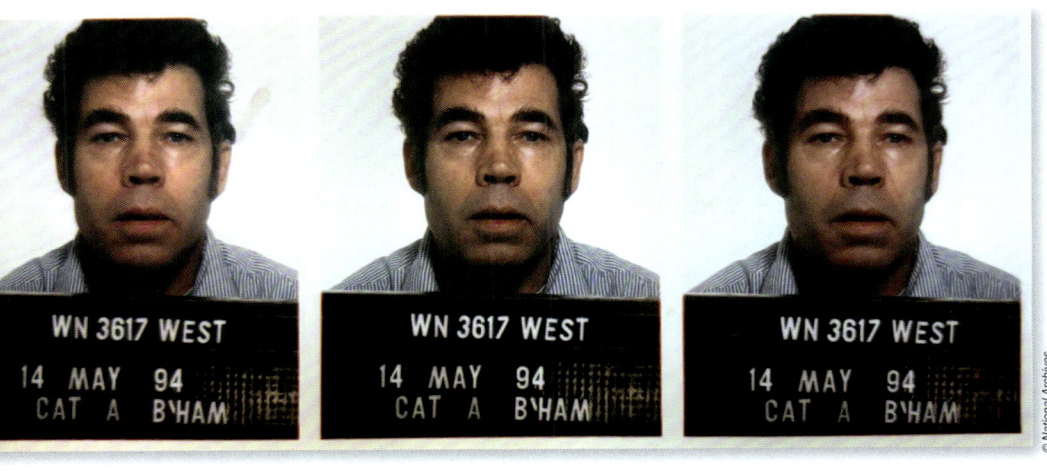

In Chapter 12, I describe how Fred was transferred from Gloucester Central Police Station to HM Prison Winson Green, Birmingham, on 13 May 1994. The next day he had his photo taken.

Meanwhile, I was investigating the case for my first book, *Fred & Rose*. On the coffee table behind me is a pair of plaster dogs which were ornaments in Fred West's childhood home. I bought them from a junk shop to help me think and write about his early life.

One of the most dramatic moments in the case was when Fred and Rose were reunited at Gloucester Magistrates' Court on 30 June 1994. She blanked him.

Caroline Owens, the victim that lived to tell her story at Rose West's trial in 1995.

Janet Leach, the appropriate adult, who told the court she hadn't sold her story to the press – but she had.

OUR FAMILY OF LOVE

why victims like Lynda Gough, Carol Ann Cooper and Shirley Hubbard, all of whom were known to wear a lot of jewellery, were found ringless. Fred could have broken their rings off during the attacks, then kept them in his cabinet, the violence he used explaining why they were mangled. Meanwhile, Rose picked over the dead girls' clothes, stole and washed what she wanted, and chucked the rest. Like many serial killers, Fred seemed to enjoy playing with the police. Keeping evidence in plain sight at home would amuse him. If this was the case, however, none of the families were able to identify any of the items as belonging to the dead women.

Fred seemed to be teasing the cops in the interview room. He said that he often chatted to the police in Birmingham, too. 'I knew so many of them, just to speak to, like, on that road [where I was living].'

This prompted a telling admission from Hazel Savage.

> **DC Hazel Savage**: Yeah, but you knew so many Gloucester policemen. But it took twenty-five years for you to be arrested for murder.
> **Fred West**: I didn't know that many Gloucester police [just] you and ...
> **DC Savage**: Kevan Price ...
> **Fred West**: Well, that was because they raided my place ...
> **DC Savage**: Well, Vince Castle, Bob Price, you know loads of 'em, far more than your average citizen ... But you were still burying people in your cellar.

Despite being in and out of his house for years, the police had not seen what was really going on, and now they feared that Fred may have committed other crimes – in Birmingham and elsewhere. 'Day after day, you walk the streets. You had every opportunity in the world to befriend or take somebody off the street and do whatever you wanted to with them,' said Savage, referring to Birmingham. Fred insisted that she had nothing to worry about. He stopped killing after Heather in 1987, 'after that, I never had anything to do with any girls ... Getting mixed up [with girls] and having affairs with other women, that was what caused the problem.' Savage pointed out that he wasn't having an affair as such with his daughter. 'No! Heather was an entirely different thing. But, I mean, that was what gave me one almighty shock ... after that I never had nothing to do with any other women at all.'

Again, the police had evidence to the contrary. For the past twelve years, Fred had worked for Derek Thomson at Carson Contractors, a family firm near Stroud. Derek was a nice man and a loyal boss, even giving Fred his job back after he was found not guilty of raping his daughter. In recent years Fred had driven one of Derek's vans, taking it home at night and parking it outside his house. Derek had given a statement saying that he was driving behind Fred recently, on the road between Stroud and Gloucester, when Fred stopped to give a female hitch-hiker a lift in his van. 'Ah, yes,' said Fred, 'you're right.' She was a New Age type. He dropped her by a wood with a water tank. Savage was surprised that Fred knew about this secluded place.

Fred West: Yeah ... we've been there quite often.
DC Hazel Savage: Who's 'we'?
Fred West: Me, Rose, the kids.

Suddenly, a new line of inquiry opened up. Criminologists say that serial killers keep offending until they are caught, or they die. If so, it was unlikely that Fred stopped killing in 1987.

OUR FAMILY OF LOVE

Had he been offending into the nineties? Returning to the interview room, DC Darren Law told Fred that his latest revelation about picking up the New Age traveller was another 'cause for concern'. They tried to get Fred to identify the woman. As he told the story Fred elaborated, now saying that she had an Alsatian dog with her. Derek Thomson hadn't mentioned seeing a dog. The next day Fred had told one of his workmates that he'd had sex with the traveller he gave a lift to. 'I didn't actually say [I] give her one,' corrected Fred, when reminded of this conversation. 'I said, I *could've* give her one.' Alarmingly, he suggested to the police that this woman was into rough sex, 'her fantasy was sex and violence'. It was Fred who was excited by violence. He appeared placid in the interview room, but when he assaulted women he was another man. Caroline Owens had given the officers a vivid insight into his other side. She was not the only woman to say that Fred also seemed to crumple after sex, crying and begging her not to tell Rose.

As the police went back and forth over Fred's life, they discovered another alarming story. In the 1960s, Fred worked on the lorries with a teenager named Robin Holt. Robin was a tall, good-looking boy who was friendly with Fred and Anne McFall, when she lived with Fred. In the summer of 1967, when he was fifteen, Robin was found dead, his body hanging in a cow shed, along with pornographic magazines with nooses drawn around the necks of the models.

> **DC Hazel Savage**: What did you know about it?
> **Fred West**: Not a thing. All I knew – somebody told me – that he committed suicide. And that was nothing to do with me ...
> **DC Savage**: Are you connected in any way with that young boy, Robin?

THE FRED WEST TAPES

Fred West: No.
DC Savage: Dying?
Fred West: No, none whatsoever.

The police weren't sure. First there was the lad in Glasgow. Now here was another boy known to Fred dying in violent circumstances, this one linked to Anne McFall, the first woman associated with Fred to have gone missing.

Meanwhile, a witness had shared some startling new information about Anne. The police told Fred that they had been to see his former sister-in-law, Catherine Jones, John West's first wife. Catherine remembered Anne. Fred brought her to meet the family in the summer of 1967, around the time that Robin Holt died. A few weeks after Anne disappeared, that August, Fred's mother Daisy visited John and Catherine. Daisy was distraught, which was unusual for such a strong woman. Jeff Morgan read to Fred from Catherine's statement. She said that she and John had sat with Daisy in their kitchen. 'I remember John asking [Daisy] what was the matter. She told us, "Freddy's killed the girl and buried her in Kempley Woods!" She broke down and was crying. John and I were stunned.'

It emerged that Fred confessed to his father when he killed Anne. He told Walter West that he had buried her body on the edge of the woods in Fingerpost Field, up the lane from their cottage, on the way to Kempley. He revealed this to his solicitor, not the police, in a tape-recorded interview since broadcast in *Fred & Rose: The West Murders*.

Fred West: I went to my father and I told him what had happened. I asked him to go up there with me, because I couldn't go up there on me own at that time. So he walked up there with me, and we stood there talking and he said, 'Look, son, I'm your father, I'm not going to turn you in nor nothing, but if you can live with it then I'll say nothing.'

Walter must have told his wife, and Daisy blurted the secret out to John: *Freddy's killed the girl and buried her in Kempley Woods!* John told his mother not to be stupid, as if he didn't believe it. Nobody turned Fred in. If they had, Anne McFall may have been his only victim. Instead, Fred remained at large. Then he met Rose.

9
THE CODE OF SILENCE

Wednesday, 30 March 1994 • Day Thirty-five
25 Cromwell Street

'We were fucking terrified we were gonna be next,
so of course we did what we was told.'
BARRY WEST

While Fred West's parents were dead his brother John was still alive and allegations about John were coming to the attention of the police. Fred and John were close. Born a year apart, the brothers shared a bed as kids; they went on double dates as youths; and they ploughed the fields together as young men. John was the witness at Fred's first wedding, to Rena in 1962, and he witnessed his second marriage to Rose ten years later, counter-signing the register after Fred stated, untruthfully, as John knew, that he was a bachelor. Fred had never divorced Rena. He had killed her, as John may also have known. Fred said that John slept with both his wives, so the brothers kept few if any secrets from each other. In recent years, John had worked in Gloucester as a bin man and 'gulley sucker', or drain cleaner. He lived now with his second wife not far from Cromwell Street, and was a regular visitor to Fred's house.

THE FRED WEST TAPES

Many people who knew the West family before the murder investigation saw John as an even nastier character than Fred, who was at least superficially amiable. 'If anybody would have been locked up, I would have thought it would have been him,' said Alf Macklin, who knew the family from way back. 'John is a bad one, mind – a bugger.' One of the Wests' former lodgers, Gill Britt, recalled both Fred and John cornering her at 25 Cromwell Street in the 1970s when she was renting a bedsit. 'John was a regular visitor,' Gill told me for my podcast series, *Unheard: The Fred & Rose West Tapes*. 'Big, built like Brian Blessed. Very loud. Great big fat belly. Probably in his forties, I dunno. [John] pressed himself against me – back was by the fireplace wall – and put his arms on the wall, and I was squashed in the middle, pressed against me.' 'What are we going to do with this one, Fred?' John asked his brother. Gill laughed nervously. 'I can tell you that when I went upstairs to my room I was shaking. That really overstepped the mark. I feel (*sic*) quite sick, threatened, intimidated … because for that few seconds I was totally fixed to that wall.'

Now that May and Anna Marie were talking to the police, they revealed what Uncle John had done to them as children. Anna Marie said that Uncle John raped her 300 times between 1975, when she was ten, and 1981, when she ran away from home. May estimated that she was only five or six when John raped her. She recalled the day vividly. She and her siblings had been left at home in their uncle's care when John took her into the downstairs' bathroom at 25 Cromwell Street and laid her across a nappy changing board. 'Without saying anything he took my underwear off, unzipped himself and got on top of me, I felt the weight of him, wriggling against him, but he got angry, ordering me to stay still. He pressed down harder on me, lifting his revolting fat stomach out of the way as he pinned me down and carried on. The smell of stale tobacco and sweat on his clothes was overwhelming and made me want to be sick,' she wrote later in her memoir, *Love as Always, Mum xxx*. Afterwards, John tossed her a coin and told her not to tell anyone.

The allegations against John were part of a bigger picture of child abuse at 25 Cromwell Street, physical and sexual abuse that went on for years in parallel with the rape and murder of young women and girls. The details are so dreadful, and bizarre, that they read like fiction, but this is one of those true stories that is stranger than fiction.

★ ★ ★

When the West children were young they were made to sleep in the cellar, often locked in there at night, sometimes strapped to their beds. Rose was her children's gaoler, wearing the keys to the cellar around her neck. As the children grew older they were moved upstairs into the main house, their places in the cellar occupied by their younger siblings. There was a wide age range within the family, and the siblings were split into groups according to their age. They didn't all get along. There was no love lost between Anna Marie and May, for example, who viewed her older half-sister as an adult. Anna Marie moved to the upper part of the house with Mum and Dad and the lodgers in the 1970s, and she seemed to May to have had a relationship with Fred and Rose that only 'the three of them understood'. It was years before May realised that Fred and Rose, and John, were abusing Anna Marie, physically and sexually, abuse that started when Anna Marie was eight and her parents took her down to the cellar to rape her. Thereafter, rape became routine. She was abused with vibrators, and strapped to metal contraptions Fred made at work, items of torture including a frame upon which she was raped; and a device to hold a sex aid in position, then made to walk around the house. She was told that this was normal, but she mustn't speak about it. Paradoxically, Anna Marie still loved her father, as most of the kids did. However, all the kids feared Rose.

The slightest thing would set Rose off, and she would lash out violently: not just hitting and slapping but stabbing and strangling her children. She seemed to take a particular delight in hurting her stepdaughter Anna Marie, when she was not treating her as a house slave or sexual play thing, but her blood children also suffered. This led to a rift between Fred and his brother John, ironically considering what John did to Anna Marie and May. Interviewed by detectives on 30 March 1994, Fred said that he and John fell out eventually after John told other family members that Rose had been mistreating their youngest son, Barry, thus breaking the family code of silence, a code that had been part of Fred's life since childhood. Telling was the greatest sin of all in a family which had secrets to hide.

> **Fred West**: I mean, John was one of the worst for telling, I mean to this day, that's why we don't have that much to do with him, because you only got to say [something] in front of John and it's gone, it's through the whole family in minutes. He rings them all up and tells them ... That was John, he just couldn't keep his mouth shut ...
> **DC Jeff Morgan**: Hmmm ...
> **Fred West**: Barry used to annoy his mam deliberately, so she'd get after him, and she used to grab the wooden spoon and run him round the garden – right? – and slap him with it at the end. But, I mean, nothing to hurt him, just slap him, and he used to love it: his mam running after him. And John happened to come in one day just as Rose took after him down [the] patio ... And the next

THE CODE OF SILENCE

thing is John's telling everybody that he's not coming near our place because, 'Rose beats the kids with wooden spoons'. And all my sisters and that, and everybody, told them all, and my father ... that we were beating our kids with wooden spoons. [John] can't keep his mouth shut.

The wooden spoon was a large novelty spoon bearing the phrase 'The World's Biggest Stirrer'. It was no joke in Rose's hands. It was her weapon, and Barry's memory was totally different to the story his father told: 'She would use that [spoon] as a baseball bat to beat us and she broke my nose. My nose is on a slant because of the amount of times she broke it,' Barry told me years later, revealing the wretched life the children led. 'I've [also] got massive scars on the back of my head from the amount of times she split my head open with it. She broke my arm, all sorta stuff.' Sadly, these were Barry's earliest memories. 'She had intense enjoyment in beating the shit out of me ... She was just as sick as him, [but] she did most of the beating. My dad was at work most of the time. That's what people don't know: My mum was, child-abuse-wise, the main person ... My mum was a sick fuck, completely sick in the head. She beat me way more than my dad did, and enjoyed it, absolutely enjoyed it.' However, Dad could also snap. 'My dad was just a solid monster,' said Barry. 'Even on Father's Day. We all got together and we bought him a £12 Zippo lighter from Argos.' The kids had Fred's name inscribed on the cigarette lighter. 'And I remember us all giving it to him, and he was flicking it, trying to get it to work, and there was no gas in it, and he just threw it across the room. And that's how he was.'

Barry was a small person, short with olive skin and brown eyes like his mother. Her family, the Letts, were all small as were the Wests. Barry's hair was thick, dark and curly when long, like

THE FRED WEST TAPES

Fred's, but it was sometimes said within the family that Barry may not have been Fred's child at all, but the product of the incestuous relationship between Rose and her father, Bill Letts, another sinister relation. As mentioned, Bill had allegedly been abusing Rose since she was a girl. According to Fred, his father-in-law was still having sex with Rose at 25 Cromwell Street, where he sometimes stayed. One night in the late 1970s, Fred claimed that one of his daughters came downstairs complaining to her parents that Grandad Letts wanted her to get into bed with him. 'Grampy [is] going to sleep with me,' she told Rose. 'Go back to bed. He is not going to eat you, he is only going to fuck you,' Rose told the child. 'I am sure you will love that.' As Fred told this story, in written notes he made in prison in 1994, Bill didn't deny it, but complained that his grandchild was 'playing up', while Rose reasoned that her father deserved a treat in return for taking the child out, 'so she could give him her body to play with'. Fred professed to be shocked, but his shock was bogus. Incest was part of his DNA, and child abuse was as routine as mealtimes at 25 Cromwell Street, the children (some, not all) used for sexual pleasure not only by Fred and Rose but also by some of their relations and friends. One child recalls an evening when some of the kids were brought up from the cellar into the house where their parents were having a party. The kids were tied up and molested by drunken men, with their parents' encouragement. One man apparently urinated over them.

Simultaneously, young women were being brought to the house where they were abused, murdered and buried. Anna Marie was coming up for nine when Lynda Gough was murdered, the first of the nine Cromwell Street murders, the body dismembered and buried in the old inspection pit behind the property. Seven more women, some of them lodgers, disappeared over the next six years while Anna Marie was

THE CODE OF SILENCE

growing up (she left home when she was fifteen, before Heather disappeared), all probably killed in the house, and buried on the property. Anna Marie didn't see any of this activity, as she was at pains to make clear in her 1995 memoir. 'Let me say from the outset that I never knew about the bodies,' Anna Marie wrote in *Out of the Shadows*, though she conceded that at least one police officer on the investigation didn't believe her. Likewise, when they came to write books (or gave their names to books written by journalists), May and Stephen were keen to state that they had no idea people were being killed and buried in their home while they grew up.

Years later, however, one child (whom I won't identify) claimed that there were days when they were locked in a cupboard under the stairs while they heard shouting and screaming in the cellar. When they came out they saw fresh concrete had been poured in the cellar.

One of the puzzling aspects of the West case is that while the murders were being committed at Cromwell Street, the Wests also had lodgers living in the house. These were primarily young men initially, but mostly women from the mid-1970s. The police traced several of these former tenants who said that, now they were asked about it, they also remembered hearing strange and disturbing sounds emanating from the cellar. 'Stop it, Daddy!' screamed a young girl one night around 1976. This scream was heard by a lodger named Jayne Hamer, as she told the police in 1994. She didn't report it at the time, however. She said that she didn't think she would be listened to.

Gill Britt was lodging at 25 Cromwell Street in the mid-1970s when Anna Marie came to her in tears. 'Anne-Marie (*sic*) must have been about thirteen, and none of the children tended to be allowed in that part of the lodgers' house. I remember a little tap on my bedsit door. She came in, quite distressed. "Sit on my bed, Anne." Just getting myself ready to go out, you know. It was in the daytime. She was in her school uniform: navy blue, white blouse. Although I wasn't taking much notice, I did make her come and sit down. She was saying, "Look what they made me do." She mentioned Rose's name ... Pulled down her blouse ... She had very pale skin as I recall. She had black bruises all below her bra line on her chest, on her breasts ... I remember her lifting up her school skirt and these horrible black bruises were inside her thighs.' Gill told Anna Marie to put herself away (meaning cover her body up), sod Rose, and wait till she was old enough to leave home. 'When you're sixteen you can go and find your [real] mum.' Sadly, Anna Marie would never be able to find her birth mother. Rena was dead.

Fred spoke about sex constantly in front of the kids, about wanting to take his daughters' virginity, about the family tradition of incest, even sex with animals. His stated ambition – the very idea is insane – was to see Rose mounted by a bull. '[Dad] was such a disgusting man he would walk up behind my mum and put his finger up her arse, and smell it,' said Barry. Fred would then hold his fingers out to his children inviting them to also smell their mother. 'He was just vile.' Fred watched hardcore porn in front of his children, including obscene videos he made of Rose, sometimes forcing the children to watch their mother pleasuring herself, or being penetrated.

Childhood at Cromwell Street was also simply joyless. There were few ordinary comforts, such as toys to play with. Uncle John brought discarded electrical items to the house, broken televisions and radios he picked up on his bin round, which the kids turned into make-believe robots. Christmas with Fred and Rose was a very sad affair. At best, the kids were allowed to pick one item from the Argos catalogue up to the value of £10, but there were years when they received nothing. May writes that

THE CODE OF SILENCE

Rose was a good cook who made a special effort for Christmas, but Barry shuddered at the memory of his mother's sprouts. 'I put them in a tissue and then hid them in the back of a chair.' Days later Rose found them, 'and they were on the table, and she made me eat them'. Barry vomited. 'But she would put her hand over my mouth and make me swallow my own sick. That's the sort of shit I had growing up. That's the sort of Christmas I remember. I don't remember present opening.' Steve said Mum hit him at Christmas. 'Her moods didn't change … She used to hit us even at Christmas, even on Christmas Day … she used to smack you straight in the mouth.'

The West children were seen as the odd kids at school. Having been raised in poverty, Fred and Rose were parsimonious. Fred rarely opened his wallet, he stole what he wanted, and he gave his meagre wages to Rose who ran the household on a tight budget. She sent her girls to school with short hair, like boys, wearing boys' shoes because they lasted longer. To save money she made her daughters clean their hair with washing-up liquid rather than shampoo and she didn't allow the purchase of deodorant, which the girls were teased about. The West boys went to school in their sisters' hand-me-downs, allowing their hair to grow long like girls. The kids developed squints and speech defects, which can be indications of child abuse. 'When we was young, we all had speech impediments,' says Barry, who slurred the letter R so that when he said his name it sounded like Bawwy. 'I got my face punched in every day I went to school. Scared to go to school, scared to go home. You spent most of your life in-between, in the park, so I got no education.'

Just as May and Anna Marie didn't get along, Barry disliked his big brother. He didn't feel that Steve protected the younger ones, but Steve also suffered abuse. One day when Steve was about twelve, Rose ordered him to strip in the downstairs bathroom.

She then tied him to the toilet with wire, and beat him on the bottom with the buckle of her belt. 'I was covered in blood. I was in a right state.' The beating took place over the grave of Lynda Gough, now entombed under the extension, which probably excited Rose. The excuse for this eroticised attack on her son was that some of Rose's pornographic magazines were missing and she assumed (wrongly) that Steve had taken them. But anything could set her off.

Rose often lost her temper in the kitchen, irritated by something as trivial as a misplaced tea towel, the kids spilling milk, or getting in her way, causing her to fly into an uncontrollable rage, like her father when she was young. When Steve sat on a kitchen cabinet after his mother told him not to, Rose nearly killed the boy. 'She just flipped. She grabbed me by the throat and she held me by the throat with two hands ... off the ground ... I was passing out ... That was the way she was. She was fucking mad.' When he came to, Steve looked in a mirror and saw tiny blood vessels had burst, leaving red spots on his face, while the imprint of his mother's hands were around his neck. Rose gave him a note to take to school to explain the marks, saying that Steve had accidentally hanged himself.

If Rose had a knife in her hand when she lost her temper, she would fly at her kids with the blade. She nicked May repeatedly in a frenzied rage when May was around eight, or nine, jabbing at her, cutting, stabbing, nicking, screaming: 'You fucking little bitch! Do you think I won't use this on you? Do you?'

When Rose nearly cut one of Steve's fingers off, his father took him to hospital, telling the Accident and Emergency doctor that Steve had cut himself accidentally. On thirty-one occasions between 1972 and 1992 the Wests attended A&E in Gloucester, often bringing their children in with injuries. One of the boys presented with an injured finger having been 'hit with a sledgehammer'. Fred explained that he had hit his son by accident when the lad was helping him in the garden. A child presented with a lacerated hand, having supposedly put it through a window. Another hand injury was apparently caused by 'falling on a knife', while one of the girls supposedly hurt herself 'falling off a gate'. In addition, the family was treated for thrush, and one child had gonorrhoea. All this was recorded in hospital records.

Then there was school. One year Anna Marie missed sixty-eight school days, and when she did attend school her PE teacher noticed bruising on her body. 'I fell over, Miss,' said Anna Marie. A social worker nonetheless went to 25 Cromwell Street to talk to Rose, who managed to fob her off, then gave Anna Marie the beating of her life. When she was nine, Anna Marie fainted at the public swimming baths and was taken to hospital where staff observed bruises and scratches to her chest. Five years later she was treated for 'puncture wounds to both feet'.

When he was fifteen, Steve's girlfriend told his school that his parents were mistreating him, but when staff spoke to Steve he didn't feel able to break the code of silence. A few months later Fred and Rose moved him into a flat down the road, keeping a close eye on 'boy' to make sure he didn't squeal.

There were other occasions when concerned teachers and social workers tried to investigate. John Fitzgerald, a senior social worker who led an official review into the Wests' links with social services in Gloucestershire in tandem with the murder investigation, recalls: 'A paediatrician visited Cromwell Street because there were concerns being expressed from somewhere in the community about children in the West family. And she went by appointment, and when she arrived the children were neatly arranged around the house doing really interesting things, like playing the violin ... playing board games and so on, [and] she came away thinking, no, it's OK. People who injure children, murder children, torture children, they're very good at disguising what they're up to. They're a bit like a chameleon, and people around them are completely unaware of what's going on … Almost all of the child abusers I've met have some kind of innate charm, [so] Fred West, if he was confronted, would have turned on the charm in such a way that the professionals could be lulled again into a false sense of security.'

Experts at deception, the Wests continued to abuse their children behind closed doors, largely untroubled by the authorities. As the children grew up, their parents made it clear that they intended to have sex with them. While Fred would deflower his daughters, Rose would bed her sons. When Steve was about thirteen, Fred told him that he was old enough to sleep with his mother, while Barry was forced into sexual situations with his mother at an even younger age. One evening, Rose came downstairs in her nightdress and told Barry to follow her to her room. 'So I went upstairs and she said, as we was walking up the stairs, "There's a man in here and I want you to do exactly what he tells you to do, no matter what." [I] was just confused. I didn't know what she was talking about. I walk in and (sighs deeply) there was a giant black man in front of me.' This man, a regular visitor to the house, raped Barry. 'I was eight, maybe nine.' This was just the start. His abuser continued to visit the house to molest him and have sex with Rose. 'Why didn't we all run away? Let's be honest,' asked Barry. 'I suppose that's the hold he had, the power. My dad was like God. You couldn't beat him. You couldn't run away. He would find you. The truth was that if you ran [outside] and screamed "rape!" he would have been arrested. That would have been the last time you seen him. But he didn't let you think that. He made you think he would get you, no matter what, that he was really powerful, and he was strong.'

THE CODE OF SILENCE

Unlike some of the sibling relationships at 25 Cromwell Street, Barry adored his big sister, Heather, who was nine years his senior. She was naughty, and rebellious, brave enough to defy and make fun of their parents. One of Barry's few happy memories was of him and Heather 'nicking my mum's fags, and her teaching me how to smoke ... round the back of that shed.' This was the shed used as a Wendy House, near to where Heather would be buried. 'I was her favourite, I think, and we used to talk a lot ... I looked up to her ... She taught me how to be clever and get round things, and how to be naughty without being caught.' At the same time, Dad was molesting Heather. He may have even started to rape her. She never said. The others liked to think that Heather held him off, but some things were not discussed between the siblings. All agree that Heather stood up to Mum and Dad as long as she could, refusing to submit to the culture of depravity at home which, they say, she knew to be wrong. 'When it came to Heather, for some unknown fucking reason, she turned round and started to have it out with them and said, "I'm sixteen now, I'm leaving,"' said Barry. 'My Dadda turned round and said, "Absolutely no way." She started to say, "You can't keep me prisoner here forever ..." and that kind of stuff, and then it just got out of hand.'

Heather turned sixteen in October 1986. She was withdrawn, and unhappy. She had begun to rock herself back and forth, as Rose rocked herself as an abused child. Heather was also now under pressure to get a job, to pay her way as long as she stayed at home, putting her in an increasingly stressful situation. Life became more and more difficult as the months passed. Since running away from home Heather's half-sister, Anna Marie, had led a troubled life, including living on the streets when she admits she had sex with men in exchange for food and shelter, and she was estranged from Fred and Rose for years.

She got back in touch with her father and stepmother in the mid-1980s, when she became pregnant by her older boyfriend, Chris Davis, whom she then married. They had two children together. On 17 June 1987, there was a tea party at Anna Marie's house in Gloucester, a birthday party for her three-year-old eldest daughter. Fred and Rose brought their children over for this party, including Heather who was very quiet. Anna Marie noticed that Fred and Rose shadowed Heather during the day, and didn't let anyone speak to her alone. Soon after that Heather received a promise of a job at a holiday camp. It was her escape. The next day the job fell through and she was devastated. May and Heather shared a room at the time, and May says that her sister cried all night. The sisters saw each other the next morning, Friday, 19 June, before May went to school. Heather was dressed in black trousers and a pink and white T-shirt. She stayed home with their parents on a wet day. When Steve and May returned from school, their sister was gone. Dad explained brightly that Heather had got her job after all, but Mum was quiet. 'Your mother's upset about Heather going,' explained Fred, coming to May's room. It had already been cleared of her sister's possessions. He suggested that May and Steve would be happy to have more room to spread out now that Heather had left. Then May saw her mother crying. 'I don't think I'd ever seen her cry before.'

A day or two later the phone rang. Fred and Rose spoke to the caller as if it was Heather. Listening to one end of this supposed conversation, May and Steve heard Fred tell Heather off for speaking rudely to her mother. A second call with 'Heather' was overheard, Mum telling May afterwards that Heather was fine. Both calls were play-acted by Fred and Rose to deceive their children into thinking Heather was alive. In fact, her body was yards away, buried under the patio.

THE CODE OF SILENCE

Barry was not quite seven when Heather disappeared, and he became convinced that he had seen her murder. He said that he was in the cellar when he overheard a row and put his head up through the hatch to see. 'The first person to hit her was my dad. My dad back-handed her ... That landed her straight on the floor. And that was the noise which made me look ... I looked and saw her on the floor. She got back up. That's when my mum and her had a fight, basically. Heather was actually trying to fight my mum back, and that's when my dad hit her again, and that's when she fell on the floor and then they both just kept stamping on her.' A second sibling later claimed to have seen Heather's body in a dustbin the night she was killed, but sometimes they thought that this had been a dream. Barry and his sibling have also claimed that they were asked to help dig Heather's grave. 'So I actually buried my sister,' said Barry. In custody, Fred told a doctor that Heather dug her own grave, unwittingly, when she was helping him in the garden, showing how many versions of the truth there are. If any of the West children did see Heather's murder, or had any knowledge of it at the time, they didn't tell the police or social workers in 1994. If they had, they would have been uniquely valuable eye witnesses to crimes that apparently had no witnesses. These are therefore probably false memories by traumatised children, the nightmares of the tormented.

Meanwhile, the West code of silence became increasingly intense as the risk of exposure grew. 'My dad was getting more and more paranoid as the years went on, and we had an intercom system in our bedrooms [so he could listen to us],' said Barry, speaking as if he knew what had happened to Heather. 'Other than that, we were fucking terrified we were gonna be next, so of course we did what we was told, which was keep our mouths shut ... He was always threatening if we told anybody anything he would kill us. But Heather wanted to leave. He couldn't risk it. So he murdered her. That was what was going to happen to all of us when we got old enough. If we didn't turn out like him, and go with him, we was against him. And if we was against him, we would have to go in the garden – under the patio. He made us understand that.'

One day in the summer of 1992, Fred asked one of his younger daughters – a child in her early teens – to come up to the Black Magic Bar, where he had erected a video camera. When the door was shut he raped his daughter, filming the abuse. 'Stop, Dad, it hurts!' she yelled. The other children tried to intervene. Fred cursed them for interrupting. This rape was part of his lifelong policy of 'breaking in' his daughters, as he said his father had before him. The next week he did it again, and invited Rose to examine their daughter to verify that she was no longer a virgin. The day after that he took the girl to work in his van and raped her in a warehouse, telling her he would leave her alone after this. The video he made of his abuse was added to the Wests' collection of pornographic VHS tapes.

'You mustn't say anything,' Fred told his daughter, 'because I'll go to prison.'

The critical danger point came when the children approached sixteen, making them old enough to leave home. By this age they were more independent, and less willing to submit. One way to ensure their silence was to kill them, as Fred and Rose had killed Heather; another was to move them out, but keep them close, as happened with Steve. Fred and Rose felt that they could trust Anna Marie. May got an older boyfriend, Rob Williams, who moved into 25 Cromwell Street, which gave her some protection as she passed sixteen. 'Cromwell Street is the seediest place ever,' Williams told me in 1994. 'You started to get sucked in when you lived with them. You start to get

THE CODE OF SILENCE

sucked into that way of life.' He recalled that the Wests kept their curtains closed so people couldn't see into the house, the family living by electric light even in daytime. Fred didn't care about the bills. 'It still makes me laugh how they were fiddling the electric ... I remember once when all the lights went off. Rose is stood there with a lighter while Steve is fooling around with [power] cables.'

May writes that Rose seemed more subdued after Heather's disappearance, but Barry said that there were still outbursts of violence, until the younger kids turned on her. 'She beat us once, just before we got taken away, and I remember all my sisters jumping on top, and we all kind of stuck up for each other, and her beatings didn't hurt, the wooden spoon didn't hurt, and we all sort of stood up [to her] and she was tired. She was knackered,' said Barry. 'She hit us until [she] couldn't hit us anymore. And that's when she broke down. And I saw the weakness of her, and she was crying her eyes out ... she had a violent temper, but she also would break down into tears and stuff, whereas [you] never saw a weakness in my dad. You never saw him cry, or you never saw him waiver. He was always solid.' Barry contemplated killing his father to end their misery. 'I tried stabbing him when I was eleven with a screwdriver. He just laughed at me.'

One day in 1992, two neighbourhood children approached a police constable patrolling Cromwell Street, telling PC Steven Burnside that a friend of theirs was being molested by her dad, and there was pornography in their house. Three days later, on 6 August, the police raided the Wests' house. An obstreperous Rose was arrested for assault after hitting one of the officers. 'Fuck off, you bastard,' she screamed. In contrast, Fred went peacefully when he was arrested at work. He was charged with three counts of rape and one of buggery, against one of his daughters; Rose was charged with encouraging the rape of the child, and cruelty to a child. The five youngest West children were taken into emergency care, initially to Cowley Manor in Cheltenham, later to foster families in other parts of the country.

'Don't you dare say anything,' Rose warned her children in her parting words to them.

Rose became depressed after the kids were removed. She swallowed an overdose, and when she survived that she got two mongrel dogs, Benji and Oscar, for company. She beat the dogs, says Steve, just as she beat her children. 'Mum brought them up to be obedient, like she brought her kids up. If she said "sit", you sat.'

While the police searched for the videotape Fred had made of his rape of his daughter – a vital piece of evidence that was never found – the younger ones were interviewed about abuse in the house. It emerged from these interviews that Heather was missing, and Charmaine was also unaccounted for. Then one of the younger children said that Dad may have killed Heather and buried her under the patio. It was a family 'joke'. Some said that Fred started it, blurting out the story over dinner. It was hard for the police to know how seriously to take it at first. Then another child told the same story to social workers, and another. 'I turned around and said, "She's under the patio,"' said Barry. 'They said, "How do you know?" I said I saw it. "You need to look under the patio." That's what made them start digging.'

10
THE DEVIL AND HIS WIFE

Sunday, 10 April 1994 • Day Forty-six
Letterbox Field

DC Hazel Savage: Have you killed Charmaine?
Fred West: No. Not to my knowledge anyway. And that is the Gospel truth, at the moment.

Rena's remains were unearthed on Sunday morning, 10 April, three feet deep by the hedgerow in Letterbox Field, slightly higher up the field than Fred had said she would be. Nevertheless, the grave was definitely his work. It was small and square like the graves at 25 Cromwell Street, as distinctive as his signature. As with previous exhumations it wouldn't be accurate to say that a body was recovered. The grave contained a jumble of bones and, after twenty-three years in open land these bones had degraded. Once again, the legs had been removed, and there were slicing marks to the femurs. The left kneecap was missing. So were thirty-five finger and toe bones and five wrist and ankle bones. There were also unexpected items in the grave: pieces of cloth, a small chrome tube and, poignantly, a red plastic boomerang that may have been – Fred never explained – a toy Rena had bought for Charmaine.

Two days later Fred gave a detailed account of Rena's murder, one of the most lurid of his confessions. He said that he met up with his wife in the East End Tavern in Gloucester, after he came out of prison in 1971, when he said that Rena was working locally as a prostitute, which may or may not have been true. 'Rena was in the front bar with a gang [of] Irish blokes.' He hung back, ever the coward, wary of getting mixed up with 'that lot', but he managed to attract Rena's attention. 'I asked her where Charmaine was ... She wouldn't tell me ... she was well drunk.' Fred was as censorious of boozing as he was of drug taking. 'And when Rena got the drink in her, she got very loving.' They decided to drive out to the fields near his parents' home – 'our favourite spot' – on a moonlit summer night. In Fred's mind, he invariably struck by moonlight. 'I had Rolf's car.'

DC Jeff Morgan: Rolf?
Fred West: Rolf, yeah.
DC Morgan: Who's Rolf?
Fred West: Oh, he's dead now ... He was Jamaican, or something. He had a flash car. He was heavy into drugs.

Fred often referred to Rolf in later police interviews, supposedly being Rena's 'stick man' or pimp in Gloucestershire. He never gave Rolf a surname. He may not have existed. Once Fred and Rena got to Letterbox Field, he said that they made love. 'And then I lost me head with her a bit. And we had a right set-to and a right row there. And that was when she ended up getting killed against the gate. I just smashed her against the gate. Um. Then I didn't know what to do ... First time I've been ever mixed up in anything like that.' That was a lie. 'So the only thing I could think of was to bury her in the field.' The weather had been dry, so the ground was hard, which made digging difficult. Luckily, there was a mattock in the back of the car. Fred stripped his top off and hacked the grave out with that. He then used his sheath knife to dismember Rena's body. Afterwards, he washed the blood off himself in a cattle trough.

'What happened to her clothing?' asked DC Barbara Harrison, who was paired with Jeff Morgan in this interview on 12 April. Fred lit a cigarette as he had a think. 'I went and gathered all her clothes up. And tied it all up,' he replied, when he'd had time to consider the question, or make up a lie. 'Yeah, all her stuff, [and] I could see this fire in the distance all the time glowing.' He drove towards the bonfire, roaring in the night, and chucked Rena's stuff into the blaze. 'Um, so that was the end of that. Then I drove on.' He passed his parents' cottage on his way home. He would have popped in to say hello but the house lights were off so he carried on driving to Gloucester.

This confession was colourful but frustrating because it diverged from Fred's earlier interviews on the subject in a significant detail.

> **DC Jeff Morgan**: Can you tell us, Fred, why you told us originally, on the other interviews, that Charmaine was in the back of the car?
> **Fred West**: That's summat I've been trying to work out … I don't know, cos it's all mixed up.

He then went further and said that he didn't think that Charmaine was dead. 'Charmaine's in India,' he declared unexpectedly. He asked to stop the interview so he could confer with his solicitor's clerk Scott Canavan before saying any more. 'Everything he did was a game,' sighed Detective Superintendent John Bennett, who read transcripts of the interviews as they were conducted. 'He just made these things up. He was just trying to manipulate everybody.' It was also gallingly clear who was setting the agenda in the interview room.

When they resumed talking an hour later, Jeff Morgan began by saying, 'over to you Fred'. 'Right,' said Fred. 'We're going to start this interview off... I was working at [a] concrete place down Bristol Road.' So began yet another version of events leading up to the disappearance of Rena and Charmaine. Charmaine 'started playing up' after Rena went to her school to see her daughter, behind Rose's back. This upset Rose, who went to talk to Fred in prison. 'And I said, "Well, I'll sort it when I get home ... You're just going to have to try and control it till I can come home." So anyway, about a fortnight before I came home, Rena went round to see Rose.' In this version, Rena collected Charmaine from 25 Midland Road, dressed her in a sari and took her to Portsmouth, or Plymouth, Fred wasn't sure which, for a reunion with her father, apparently the aforementioned 'Billy Boy'. Then they left the UK to begin a new life somewhere in the Indian subcontinent, her natural father being Indian, Pakistani or Bangladeshi, Fred wasn't 100 per cent sure which.

DC Morgan struggled with this story. Why had Fred told the police previously that he had killed Charmaine, and buried her at 25 Midland Road? 'It's hard for me to understand [too],' replied Fred, getting upset again. 'Rena just wouldn't tell me nothing. She just kept really getting nasty and arguing ... my main argument with Rena was, "If you didn't want Charmaine, why the Hell did you leave her with me?"... That's what the big argument was, that's what we ... I ... went berserk over ... that she caused us worry, me and Rose, on taking Charmaine away, just to go and give her [to] somebody else. It just didn't make sense ... That's why I went so mad at her.'

THE DEVIL AND HIS WIFE

DC Jeff Morgan: You're actually saying [now] that Charmaine is alive?
Fred West: Yes, Charmaine is alive.
DC Morgan: Yet, you're [also] saying that you killed her. That's the problem ... why tell us that you killed her?
Fred West: I don't know. I wanted ... (becoming emotional). At one time, I just wanted to be blamed for all of it.

The next day, Wednesday, 13 April, the police started digging for Anne McFall in Fingerpost Field, encouraged by the fact that Fred had led them to approximately the right place for Rena in the adjacent field.

As the search for Anne began, back at the station Fred revealed more of his life leading up to the deaths of Rena and Charmaine. He gave the police the impression that he and Rose were both scared of Rena. 'I think that when Rena come to see Rose, I think there [might] have been odd threats chucked in, because that was the way Rena talked ... "Give me any hassle and I'll smack your fucking face in," you know, I mean that was Rena's attitude ... I think prostitution made her more like that than anything else.' The essential problem was that Rena wanted Charmaine back, but Rose didn't want to give Charmaine to her mother. When Hazel Savage asked Fred what he wanted, he spoke what sounded like the cold-blooded truth: 'I wanted rid of Rena, out of the way. That's all I wanted. Off my back ...' He complained again that Rena was a bad mother (as if Rose was better). 'Rena kept coming back and going,' he said. 'It was a nightmare.' None of them proved capable of providing a home to children. The girls 'didn't have a lot of toys,' said Fred, who couldn't even remember the kids having a Teddy bear to cuddle. Yet he clung to a sentimental final image of Charmaine, dressed in a sari standing in the kitchen at 25 Midland Road, and 'how beautiful she looked'.

> **DC Hazel Savage**: Have you killed Charmaine?
> **Fred West**: No. Not to my knowledge, anyway. And that is the Gospel truth, at the moment.

This was as clear as mud. So they went over it again. Each time Fred told his story he changed some of the details. He now spoke of taking Rena to Letterbox Field to look for badgers, absurdly. Badger-watching and lovemaking turned to violence when the subject of Charmaine came up. 'She [Rena] got nasty, and I laid into her and she laid into me. And, erm, and I smacked her up against the gate a few times. And, um, I think she caught her head off the back of the main post to the gate, and it knocked her out on to the floor. And then I just kicked her. I was kicking her on the floor. I lost it completely with her.' Did he kick his wife to death, did he strangle her, or did he stab her? The pathologist couldn't tell the police the answer because Rena's flesh had rotted, and with it any signs of her injuries. There was no forensic cause of death for any of the West victims for this same simple reason. Perhaps Fred did all these things in a frenzy of rage and hate – kicking, strangling and stabbing – hating Rena for threatening to break up his 'family of love'. He certainly lost his temper, he made that clear, but he added a lot of nonsense. 'I was in such a state. I mean, the first time I'd ever knocked anybody out, or attacked a girl. That was a very strict rule at home in the village. And if you hit a girl, like, you were in big trouble ... you were like the lowest of the low ... I've never [been] one for beating my wives up, or anything like that (laughs), or any girl for that matter.' Afterwards, he said that he toiled at his butchery by moonlight, up to his armpits in blood but hidden from the road by the corn. 'I was shaking like a leaf. The sweat was absolutely pouring off me. And I genuinely felt ill.' The police asked what he did with Rena's wedding ring.

Fred West: You very rarely see a prostitute with a wedding ring on.
DC Hazel Savage: Well, she was also your wife.
Fred West: Well, our marriage had ended … long before then, when Rose come on the scene.

* * *

Every interview led back to Fred's relationship with Rose, the Devil and his dam (wife) to borrow an old but evocative phrase. For almost seven weeks now, while Fred had been talking to the detectives at Gloucester Central Police Station, Rose had been free on bail, living in a succession of police houses, latterly in Hales Close, Cheltenham. May had kept her company, remaining loyal to Mum, whom she believed to be innocent of the murders. The police had covertly recorded 885 cassette tapes of private chat, mostly Rose talking to May. In all that time Rose had said nothing to incriminate herself, while taking every opportunity to disassociate herself from her husband.

'The fucking trouble he's caused me, May!' Rose shrieked. 'I wish I'd never met him!'

Meanwhile, the police were speaking to witnesses about Rose's violent and abusive behaviour. Nobody said that they had seen Rose murder anybody, or heard her admit to murder, but there were numerous allegations of her mistreating women and children; on her own, with Fred, and with others. One former neighbour at 25 Midland Road told the police that she came to Fred's and Rose's flat when Fred was in prison in 1971 and saw Charmaine standing on a kitchen chair with her hands tied behind her back, and Rose brandishing a wooden spoon as though she was about to thrash the child with it. There were further witness statements against Rose. John Bennett decided it was time to arrest Mrs West again, to question her about all these matters.

Barbara Harrison and another detective knocked at the Cheltenham police house at 9:25 AM on Wednesday, 20 April. Rose didn't seem surprised to see the officers again. They told her that she was being arrested, at the moment, for rape and assault, not murder. They would wait while Rose gathered together some clothes. Rose went upstairs and whispered to May to look after her wedding ring, which she was leaving in her coat pocket. May was surprised by this, as she later wrote, reminding her mother that she'd told her that she would never wear Fred's ring again. 'Her eyes flashed. "Just do as I bloody say, May! Look after it!"' Then Rose went downstairs. 'I watched from the window as she cursed and struggled as they took her away.'

'Fuck you, the lot of you!' Rose swore at the detectives as they put her into their car.

Rose was taken back to Cheltenham Police Station, where she was charged with two counts of raping a girl in the 1970s, when the victim was eleven and thirteen, along with two men (friends of the Wests); and assaulting a boy of eight, causing him actual bodily harm. Fred appeared to be shocked and surprised when he was told that Rose had been charged with abusing these children, along with two of their friends. 'It's bloody shattered me, I can't believe it,' he said.[11] Rose was remanded into custody for three days, which also gave the police an opportunity to question her about Lynda Gough, the first victim killed at 25

---

11   The rape and assault charges against Rose and the two men were later dropped.

THE DEVIL AND HIS WIFE

Cromwell Street, quizzing her about Mrs Gough's statement that she had met Rose on the doorstep wearing her daughter's clothes. Rose refused to answer questions, sticking to 'no comment'. This was no surprise to John Bennett who consulted with the Crown Prosecution Service (CPS) about the next step. Although the police had caught out Rose in some lies, the evidence that she had killed anyone was thin. Still, Bennett was certain that Rose was involved.

On Sunday evening, 24 April, Rose was told that she was jointly charged with Fred with the murder of Lynda Gough. 'I'm innocent,' she said, and nothing more. It was a major development in the investigation. When he was alone with his appropriate adult, Janet Leach, Fred expressed his dismay. 'He just said that the police were getting too close and they would find out that Rose was involved.'

★ ★ ★

The police had by now identified all but two of the nine women recovered from 25 Cromwell Street. The penultimate and most challenging identification was the so-called Dutch Girl. A nationwide review of missing women resulted in a long list of 130 candidates, whittled down to nine, one of whom was a woman named Thérèse Siegenthaler, who had not been seen since 1974 when she was twenty-one. She was not Dutch, though.

Born in Switzerland on 27 November 1952, and raised as one of five children near Berne, Thérèse Siegenthaler's parents separated when she was twelve. She came to the United Kingdom in the early 1970s. In 1974, she was studying sociology at Woolwich Polytechnic in south London, lodging not far away in Lewisham. She had a weekend job in a shoe shop in Leicester Square. Thérèse travelled around the UK extensively, often hitch-hiking to save money. She was young-looking for her age, but believed that she could look after herself. 'Thérèse was a very self-assured person physically. She was skilled at judo [and] was perhaps over-confident in her physical skills,' said her friend, Edith Simmons. Thérèse had planned a trip to Ireland in April 1974, intending to catch the ferry from Holyhead in Wales. Edith warned her friend not to hitch-hike. 'The night before she left, she stayed at my house,' Edith told the police on 15 April. 'She left about 9:00 AM, and I remember going out into the street and, again, saying for her not to hitch-hike.' The women looked forward to seeing each other in a few days. They had tickets to go to the theatre in London.

It seems that Thérèse did not heed Edith's advice, and she thumbed her way across England towards Wales, which could easily have meant passing through or near to Gloucester, depending on which roads she travelled by. One witness told the police that a Dutch hiker matching her description came to lodge at 25 Cromwell Street at this time, but Thérèse wasn't Dutch, the dates don't match, and she was most unlikely to have chosen to stay at 25 Cromwell Street when she had holiday plans and a life to get back to in London. The truth is surely that Thérèse was abducted by the Wests while thumbing a ride near Gloucester, like Caroline Owens before her, then taken back to Cromwell Street where she was raped, murdered and buried.

Edith Simmons was surprised not to receive a postcard from Ireland, and when Thérèse didn't return home Edith contacted her friend's family in Switzerland. 'Our family made inquiries, including notifying the police and the Salvation Army. My brother travelled to England,' said Thérèse's younger sister, Marrianne, 'but Thérèse was never seen again.' The murder squad now thought that Thérèse was the hitch-hiker Fred spoke of, mistaking her Swiss-German accent for Dutch, and that she was the victim buried opposite Shirley Hubbard in the cellar of 25 Cromwell Street. It was up to Dr David Whittaker to prove her identity, and he was waiting for her dental records to arrive from Switzerland.

★ ★ ★

The key to prosecuting Fred and Rose on joint murder charges seemed to lie in their shared sexual activities, which included a passion for bondage, a proclivity for child abuse, and the willingness to abduct women whom they raped and abused to death, the ultimate culmination of their sadistic sex games. The Wests' sex life was therefore of great interest to the police, every aspect of it, including Rose's prostitution which seemed to have begun early in her relationship with Fred, or even before she met him.

'I never knew,' Rose's mother told me, when I went to see Daisy Letts in the spring of 1994, looking for answers. 'Are you trying to say Rosie was a prostitute when she went to school?' That was, in fact, what one of Daisy's sons had told me. Daisy reacted with incredulity to the suggestion that her home had been 'a prostitute's home'. 'Whatever happened, happened after Rosie left our home,' she said.

Daisy Letts was a timid little woman who lived alone in a bungalow in Herefordshire, her husband, Rose's father, Bill, having died of lung cancer in 1979 aged fifty-eight. He had abused his wife to the end. Daisy seemed elderly at seventy-five, but she would live to celebrate her 100th birthday. Despite all the evidence, she wanted to give me the impression that Rose came from a good home – 'Nothing abnormal about home life at all' – but in the next breath she lamented 'all the miserable years' she had spent with Rose's father, a 'tyrant' who abused them as relentlessly as Rose abused her children, which was surely what set her on that crooked path. 'He was anything but normal,' Daisy said of her late husband. 'Yes, he was very violent [and] I would say he was sadistic, because he seemed to enjoy making you unhappy.' That also described Rose.

Daisy told me that she never discussed sex with Rose, not even to tell her daughter the facts of life, but somebody initiated Rose into sex early on, and that person was surely her father. By the account of her younger brother, Graham, whom I spoke to at this time, Rose started to abuse him when they were kids, and there was a suggestion that she was selling her body as a teenager. Daisy refused to engage with this though. 'The only thing funny in the family was Dad's violence,' she insisted to me. Rose was slow and childish. Then she met that 'jabbering' liar Fred, who Daisy considered to be insane. That's when Rose went bad. They tried to break the pair up, but even though Daisy saw that her daughter was unhappy with Fred at times, noticing that her eyes were red from crying, Rose stayed with Fred. She walked out on him once, when Heather was small, coming home to her parents in Bishop's Cleeve. Fred came after her. Her parents told her not to go back to him. 'She turned to her father while Fred stood at the back door and said, "You don't know him," she said, "you don't know him, there's nothing he wouldn't do, including murder."' Daisy didn't take this outburst seriously, though Rose had spoken the truth. 'I just thought she was sort of highly strung.' This was around the time that Charmaine disappeared. Daisy seemed barely to have noticed Charmaine's absence, referring vaguely to 'when that little girl went back to what'sname'. When Heather disappeared sixteen years later, Daisy paid a little more attention. She asked Rose if she had heard from Heather, but she was easily fobbed off when Rose said that Heather had gone off 'with her cronies'. No one in the family was suspicious enough to contact the police.

THE DEVIL AND HIS WIFE

Life had been hard for Daisy. Her marriage had been Hell. She described her husband as a 'Heller'. She had not been able to cope at times, suffered a nervous breakdown and underwent electric shock treatment. The murder investigation hit her 'like a bomb ... Can you imagine what a shock it was? Can you imagine seeing in the paper that a garden was going to be dug up, and realising it was where she lived? It was terrible.' Daisy admitted to me that she had considered killing herself. She started to cry, then stopped herself and made us tea. Suddenly, she turned and asked me: 'How did they kill them? I was told there was threads of ropes in some of the graves. [One of my daughters] said there was orgies going on where they sacrifice victims.' I said that Rose was probably fully involved, but the details were so disturbing that I didn't want to tell her more. 'How could she? How could she?' Daisy asked me in an insistent whisper, her eyes widening with horror. 'Isn't it dreadful?' Then she went back to making the tea.

At this time, during the investigation, I was talking to other members of Rose's family, and to Fred's family. It seemed to me that Daisy wasn't the only one struggling with history. The families didn't want to admit to secrets going back generations that explained how Fred and Rose evolved into people capable of rape and murder. Rose's dad was a violent sadist, and Rose became that and more. It was likely that Bill Letts also corrupted her sexually, just as Fred may have been corrupted by his parents. The families didn't want to talk about that. If Daisy had known that Bill was having sex with her daughter, she kept it to herself.

One time when we spoke Daisy hinted to me that she was avoiding the truth. I had called her on the phone to check a fact about Rose's background for the book I was then writing about the murder case. 'I don't mind you telephoning,' she told me, saying that the initial shock of the investigation had abated slightly. Then she said: 'I think as honest as you might like to be, sometimes you do think you are absolutely telling the truth, but afterwards you think it might not be right what you said.'

Rose must have been corrupted in her childhood for her to put up with Fred's aberrant sexual behaviour when they met. She was very young when she joined Fred in his depraved world of pornography, bondage, prostitution and group sex. Fred told the police that he and Rose had their first 'gang bang' with local men of Jamaican background around the time they were living at 25 Midland Road. She was only sixteen then, about to turn seventeen. The men she was introduced to were often Fred's mates from the building trade. 'There was about three or four different Jamaicans,' he told the police. 'There's probably about a dozen of them [that have] been tried out, like, to make sure they don't say nothing.' Rose had to sleep with these men. She also advertised for clients in contact magazines, and she owned all the paraphernalia of a prostitute by the time she lived at 25 Cromwell Street, including a red light. The children had to answer the phone for her and take bookings for 'Mandy', Mum's working name. For a time 'Mandy' also kept a prostitute's flat in Stroud Road. Despite what Daisy Letts said, the whole family knew that Rose was a prostitute, and had been for years. That wouldn't matter so much, except that she involved the children.

Anna Marie was now talking to the police and the story she told was appalling. Having been raped and molested by Fred and Rose from the age of eight, her stepmother fondling and taunting her while her father abused her, Anna Marie further said that when she was twelve she was drawn into her mother's sex work. She was taken to pubs to meet men, and introduced to Rose's clients at 25 Cromwell Street. Anna Marie had to have sex with these men, too. 'Sometimes I had to go first, sometimes second,' she later wrote, 'but she was always there, watching.'

THE DEVIL AND HIS WIFE

Likewise, Barry West said that he was made to submit to a man who came to the house for sex with his mother. 'She got paid extra.' Before she started to reply to all police questions with 'no comment', Rose told the police that clients paid Fred, making him her stick man, but she was sometimes paid direct. One punter infuriated her by writing a cheque, instead of giving her cash. 'Look, what this bastard's give me!' she complained to Fred. They got into a row with the man who, Fred said, got his own back by telling the police that the Wests were showing the children pornographic films, which he denied. The children say that it happened all the time. Other punters paid the Wests in kind. Arthur Dobbs, a married man in his forties, visited 25 Cromwell Street around 1985 after seeing a photograph of 'Mandy' in a contact magazine. They went up to her bedroom. 'Mr West came in, followed us in,' said Dobbs. 'He told me to get undressed.' Dobbs did so, then had sex with Rose. Dobbs returned four times a week after that, initially paying £10 for sex. After a while he serviced Fred's van in lieu of payment. One day Rose told Dobbs that Fred was having sex with one of their daughters. Dobbs claimed that he tipped off social services. If true, this was another missed opportunity to stop the Wests.

As Dobbs' story showed, money wasn't the only motive for Rose prostituting herself. It was part of the Wests' way of life, exciting for Fred, the voyeur, maybe also for Rose, and part of their twisted idea of a 'family of love', whereby children were prostituted and Rose became pregnant by her clients, though all her children, regardless of their biological father, were registered under Fred's surname. Three of the younger girls had dark skin, the result of Rose's relationships with black men, but Fred saw them all as his own, calling them 'our love children'. 'I was their father, and that was the end of the story,' Fred told the police, suggesting that pregnancy increased Rose's sex drive.

THE FRED WEST TAPES

'When Rose was pregnant, she was always extra sexy for some reason.' There may indeed have been a link between Rose's pregnancies, her libido, and the attacks and killings. Fred told Caroline Owens, when they assaulted her in 1972, that Rose had a 'bun in the oven'; she was in fact pregnant with Stephen. She was still pregnant with Stephen when Lynda Gough was killed in 1973; and she was pregnant with Louise when Shirley Robinson was murdered five years later. Or maybe it was a coincidence.

One man became especially intimate with Fred and Rose. He was a Gloucester man of Caribbean background, older than Fred, who had a *ménage à trois* with the Wests for years, or as Fred put it all three of them 'mucked about' together. 'You know, we go out in the fields and Rose would run about naked, and we were naked as well ... carry on amongst ourselves and have a bloody good time,' he told the police. This man became 'part of us'.

> **DC Jeff Morgan**: Rose liked him a lot, did she, from a sexual point of view?
> **Fred West**: Yes, if I was there. She was fine with him. I mean ... She would do it ... as a turn-on for me, and herself, but that's all it was. And once anybody started getting serious Rose stopped it ... Rose is very suspicious of people.

★ ★ ★

By this stage in the investigation, 25 Cromwell Street had been searched exhaustively, revealing further evidence of the Wests' exotic sex life, including a drawer loaded with large dildos and vibrators. One enormous flesh-coloured vibrator was kept in a wooden box that had originally contained a bottle of whisky. The vibrator was approximately the same size as the whisky

THE DEVIL AND HIS WIFE

bottle. Strangest of all were large glass sweet jars – Roses brand, naturally – containing dirty underwear.

> **DC Hazel Savage**: Whose are they, then?
> **Fred West**: Rose's.
> **DC Savage**: Why are they in a jar?
> **Fred West**: Erm, well there's quite a good reason for that ... She used to wear them with different blokes and then when they become soiled then she chuck them in there.

Customarily, Rose didn't wear knickers. 'She never had underwear on,' says former lodger Gill Britt. 'Sometimes she'd come in and talk to you and sit there on the washing machine with her leg cocked up on the side with no knickers on, and you just pretended you didn't notice ... vile, vile, vile.' Rose put knickers on for her assignations as a prostitute, took them off when she came home from having sex, and put them back on for her next date with that same man. Hazel Savage informed Fred that Rose's used knickers had been sent to the police laboratory and they were indeed 'thickly stained with semen'. She asked why Rose didn't wash them. Fred laughed at a naïve question. He explained that he filmed Rose putting her knickers on and taking them off when she came home. 'And if I felt like it, when she stripped off, I used to put her on the bed and make love to her.' The dirty knickers turned him on. The knickers were labelled with a date and a number referring to the punter, and the times Rose had sex with that man. The police had found knickers with the number ten. 'That was ten times she wore [them].' This was recorded in a ledger, as were the details of Rose's menstrual cycle. When an affair ran its course, the Wests had another bizarre habit, one so odd that even the police sounded surprised by it. Fred explained that he and Rose took her stained knickers to the country, 'up on the hills', where they burned them in a can. They put the burnt remains in a blue pot, a souvenir from Prinknash Abbey, the lid sealed with superglue. The pot was on the mantelpiece at home.

> **DC Hazel Savage**: What did you want to keep the ashes for?
> **Fred West**: Well, just for years to come, like.
> **DC Savage**: To do what with?
> **Fred West**: As souvenirs of our sex life.

Close inspection revealed that some of these knickers dated back to 1985. Considering the absence of clothing in the graves, the detectives wondered whether these could be the remains of the victims' underwear. DNA evidence was still relatively new in 1994, and it did not play a part in the West investigation, but Savage noted that the knickers appeared too small for Rose, who gained weight in mid-life. Fred said that he didn't know what size underwear his wife wore.

> **DC Hazel Savage**: The date on these, one pair, is 21 June '85. And that's ... Well, it's months, wasn't it, before ... Heather disappeared.
> **Fred West**: No, it's nothing to do with Heather at all. Nothing at all ...

Perhaps the knickers belonged to someone the police hadn't yet found. Detectives were almost certain that there were more victims, though they didn't have many names, other than Mary Bastholm, the waitress who disappeared from a Gloucester bus stop in 1968. The police had not forgotten Mary, and there was mounting evidence that she could be a thirteenth victim. A witness had told them that Fred was a regular in the Pop-in café where Mary worked. Another witness, Vincent Oakes, a former neighbour of the Bastholm family, gave a statement saying that he had seen Mary in a parked car around the corner from her house, with an older man, on four or five occasions leading up to her disappearance. Oakes got the impression that Mary didn't want her parents to know about this man. He was ninety-nine per cent sure that the man was Fred West. 'Rubbish,' said Fred, which generally meant the opposite. 'I never seen the girl in my life.'

> **DC Hazel Savage**: Where is she now, Fred?
> **Fred West**: You ask me, I don't know.
> **DC Savage**: I am asking you.
> **Fred West**: Well, I don't know. I certainly haven't seen her. And that is it, I have never seen her, I've never known the girl, never spoken to the girl in my life.

Mary was a teenager Fred probably knew, of the age group he targeted, who disappeared from a bus stop he was familiar with, all of which was his *modus operandi*, and remarkably like what had happened to Lucy Partington. 'It may not be how you see it, but the truth is that those [two] people were last seen at bus stops, and there are a lot of similarities,' DC Savage told him. 'And you have made certain admissions about what you've done with those other people, and here we are on a night in Gloucester, in the winter, this girl disappears off the face of the Earth from an area that you knew.'

> **Fred West**: I'm telling you, I know nothing at all about Mary. Nothing.

THE FRED WEST TAPES

DC Hazel Savage: I don't believe you, Fred.
Fred West: Well, that's up to you, Hazel.

Savage tried to appeal to Fred's primitive sense of doing the right thing. 'She should be recovered like the rest of them, and the decent thing done with her remains, and I think, Fred, that you can give us that answer.' This made Fred cross. He protested that he wasn't in a 'counting match', trying to break the record number of victims for serial murder. He could not help them with Mary Bastholm, 'cos I know nothing about it'. Savage suggested that there may be something about Mary's death that Fred felt unable to admit to. 'There is only one that is difficult for me to talk about, or two … one is my daughter,' he replied, becoming more emotional, 'and the other one's Anne [McFall].'

When the detectives had left the room, however, Fred told Janet Leach another story. He did know what had happened to Mary Bastholm. He told Leach that he picked Mary up that winter night, in 1968, but he didn't kill her. The murder was committed by Rose, his brother John and other men he didn't name. There was, he suggested, a whole gang of people involved in these crimes.

11
PLAN B

Tuesday, 26 April 1994 • Day Sixty-two
25 Midland Road, Gloucester

> 'I have not ... told you the whole truth
> about these matters.'
>
> FRED WEST

The police began to dig at 25 Midland Road on Tuesday, 26 April, looking for Charmaine West, the little girl nobody had seen since 1971, when, aged eight, her Gloucester junior school, St James's, was told that she had 'moved to London' with her mother. The school accepted this explanation. That afternoon, detectives sat down with Fred to go through the events leading up to Charmaine's disappearance, trying to find the missing pieces of the puzzle that made up the picture of her short life. This meant going back to Fred's first marriage in Glasgow, where officers had been interviewing witnesses. I was also in Scotland to research this part of the story, meeting the same people.

After Fred's unsuccessful attempt to abort Rena's baby, Charmaine was born in Coatbridge, Scotland, in May 1963, Coatbridge being Rena's home town. The identity of Charmaine's biological father was never established, and she was given Fred's surname. Fred, Rena and the baby then moved to a tenement in Savoy Street, Glasgow, where Anna Marie was born the following year, after which the family moved to Maclellan Street in the Kinning Park area of the city. During this time Rena made two new friends, Isabella 'Isa' McNeill and Anne McFall, young women who worked together in a knitwear factory. Isa was twenty and Anne was seventeen. Anne was girlishly pretty with long dark hair which, fatally, was Fred's type.

The three young women hung out together at the Wests' flat. Then Isa moved into the flat to help look after the West children, as their 'nanny', which is when she said that she discovered Fred was a 'Jekyll and Hyde' type of character who abused his wife and the children. The kids were penned in bunk beds like animals, Fred having fixed mesh across the bunks to stop them crawling out. 'It was like a gaol,' Isa told me when I found her in Scotland. 'The only time they got out was when he went to work in the ice cream van.' Fred also tried to restrict Rena's freedom. 'Fred would not let her out of his sight,' said Isa. 'I think he was scared in case she would move, leave him.' Rena complained to her friend that her sex life with Fred was bad. '[When] he had sex he took it whether she wanted it or not,' explained Isa. 'It was quick ... He beat her up after sex, or any time if he was in a bad mood.'

Isa told the police the same story, which was related to Fred in custody in Gloucester. He totally rejected what Isa said.

Fred West: She just made that lot up. That's rubbish, absolute rubbish. I was never capable of hitting Rena anyway. Because anybody would tell you Rena could look after herself.

Unhappy in her marriage, Rena began an affair with a married neighbour, John McLachlan. 'Up in Glasgow he [Fred] was

PLAN B

knocking everybody off,' John told me when I visited him in his flat in a Glasgow tower block. He was now in his late fifties, a heavy smoker covered in tattoos and he looked unwell. 'Rena said, "What's good for the goose is good for the gander."' The relationship was serious enough for Rena to allow McLachlan to tattoo his name on her hand, and she added her name to his arm. McLachlan showed me his arms. The tattoos had faded and stretched with time but it was still possible to read Rena's name on his mottled skin. 'I scored out "Fred" and put "John" on [her hand],' he said. 'I did it with a sewing needle in a cork [and] black India ink.'

'What did Fred say?' I asked.

'Fred was not too fucking pleased!'

One evening, Fred followed John and Rena into Kinning Park. McLachlan ran off when he saw Fred, but when he heard Rena screaming he came back. 'He was laying into her, [so I] kicked the shit out of him.' As a result, Fred developed a hatred of McLachlan. 'Bastard!' he exclaimed, when his rival's name was mentioned by Hazel Savage in the interview room in Gloucester, one of the rare times he showed vehement dislike of another man. 'That's all I can say about him.' He portrayed McLachlan as a sinister figure, the head of the Skulls motorcycle gang. McLachlan, who had worked as a bus driver, remembered Fred as an abusive coward who mistreated his family. 'He used to slap Charmaine around the back of the head in Glasgow, because she asked for an ice cream ... He was a vicious man.' He also sexually abused Rena. 'She said that he tried to tie her wrists quite a few times.'

After Harry Feeney was killed in 1965, apparently run down by Fred in his ice cream van, Fred fled to England, taking the children with him, but his mother didn't want Charmaine living in Much Marcle because of her dark skin, so Fred put the kids into care. Borrowing money from his family, he rented a caravan at the Willows site on Sandhurst Lane, Gloucester, a site used by gypsy families, and got a job driving for a local slaughter company. Despite all that had happened in Glasgow, Rena decided to try again with Fred, and Anne McFall and Isa McNeill elected to accompany her to England. None of them had much of a life in Scotland. Anne in particular, having had a very rough time, hoped to make a new start down south. Ever the bullshitter, Fred talked about them all living together in a lovely big house in Gloucestershire. Anne desperately wanted to believe it.

The women took a coach to Gloucester in February 1966. 'Fred got us from the [coach] station, picked us up in an abattoir van full of bones and cow hides,' Isa recalled. '[It] smelt really bad.' Fred then drove them home, not to a lovely house but to his filthy little caravan on a gypsy site. Even Fred knew that this was a mistake. 'There were [six] of us in there, in the 'van. It was too crowded,' he told the police. It was also boring for the Scotswomen marooned in a field without work, or money. Fred 'paid' Isa and Anne in cigarettes to mind his kids. 'We just sat around in the caravan [all day].' When he came home from the slaughter house, in a bad mood, covered in blood, Fred beat Rena and he mistreated Charmaine. 'He lost his temper at the least wee thing,' said Isa, who noticed that Anna Marie didn't get hit as often as her half-sister. 'He didn't have much time for Charmaine.'

Rena soon decided that she wanted to go back to Scotland, but she had no money for the fare, so she wrote to friends for help. In April, her lover John McLachlan and his pal, John Trotter, drove south to Rena's rescue, arranging to meet her at the caravan when Fred was at work. McLachlan arrived early. To his surprise, Fred was still at home. He slapped Rena when she told him that she was leaving him. Isa said she was going,

PLAN B

too. Fred refused to let Rena take the children, clinging on to Charmaine as if she was his treasure. McLachlan punched Fred, but he still held on to the screaming child. So Rena climbed into McLachlan's car. 'I'll kill you if you show your face again,' Fred threatened them. A crowd had gathered, attracted by the screaming and yelling. 'A few other people came out of the caravans, friends of Freddy West, and tried to intervene,' said McLachlan. Somebody must have called the police, because a constable rode up on his bicycle. Then Anne McFall announced that she was going to stay with Fred. 'I think she was infatuated with him,' said Isa, who had suspected that something was secretly brewing between Fred and her friend.

Rena was beside herself. 'Something might happen to [the kids]!' she told McLachlan as they drove away. 'He might lose his rag.'

'We'll get the weans another time.'

It wasn't long before her concern for her children brought Rena back. She was at the site in the summer of 1966, shortly after which Fred towed his caravan to the Watermead Caravan Park, behind the Flying Machine pub on the other side of Gloucester. This was probably an attempt to avoid Rena, or the hire purchase company he owed money to, or the authorities, maybe all three. Fred was forever getting on the wrong side of people. Social workers had become concerned about the welfare of his children. The investigation team had found a report of the children being seen, in 1966, in a 'deplorable state' without shoes to wear. The report noted that the girls were in and out of care, sometimes living with foster families, while Rena came and went.

She was back again in October. Fred temporarily moved Anne out of his caravan to stay with a friend, apparently trying to hide his girlfriend from his wife. When Rena discovered that Anne was still on the scene, she broke into the place where Anne was staying and stole an iron, cash and cigarettes. Then she fled back to Scotland. A young WPC, none other than Hazel Savage, was dispatched to arrest Rena, and bring her back to Gloucestershire for a court appearance, which was Savage's first contact with the West family. Rena told Savage that she had stolen the items to spite Fred, who had another woman. The case came to court in November 1966. 'Mrs West's husband, Mr Frederick West, tanker driver, told the court that the woman he was living with was still in Gloucester, but he intended to pay her fare back to Scotland immediately,' reported the *Citizen*. Rena was convicted of housebreaking and theft and put on probation for three years. Her criminal record was now almost a page long, including convictions for theft and soliciting.

Like Rose, Rena was a woman who seemed willing to accommodate Fred's sexual appetites, at least to some extent. While she complained to friends about their sex life, and said that he beat her and tried to tie her up, the police also had a witness who said that Rena posed for pornographic pictures taken by Fred. 'I remember one day when both Fred and Rena visited me they showed me a set of large black and white photographs of Rena in various sexually explicit poses. Both of them seemed quite excited about them,' Rena's friend Margaret Clarke told detectives, Clarke being the same woman who stood lookout while Fred tried to abort Charmaine. Clarke also told the police that when she visited Fred's caravan she saw Fred rubbing six-year-old Charmaine – who was naked – against his groin. 'He made some comment to the fact that she enjoyed it, and that if she carried on she would come.'

★ ★ ★

Suddenly, Anne McFall vanished. Shortly after her disappearance Fred moved to a third caravan site, Lake House, at Bishop's

PLAN B

Cleeve, then to a flat in Cheltenham. When a social worker visited him here in February, 1970, Fred said that his children were being looked after by an ex-girlfriend from Scotland, by which he seemed to mean Anne. But where was Anne? Meanwhile, Rena was still trying to get her girls back. That February, Charmaine and Anna Marie were placed in foster care with a Gloucestershire family who recalled Rena coming to see the girls. Fred arrived at the house and the couple had a blazing row. Fred remembered the incident and told Hazel Savage that he had been upset with Rena because she wanted to take Charmaine out, but not Anna Marie. 'I mean, Anna Marie was a complete failure as far as she was concerned,' he said. 'Never should have happened.'

> **DC Hazel Savage**: Because she never took her away from school, did she ... she only took Charmaine ...?
> **Fred West**: I mean, she'd go and give Charmaine things, wouldn't give Anna nothing. That used to bloody hurt me, she doing things like that ... she did not want to know Anna Marie.

Before the police could develop a smidgeon of sympathy for Fred, a nasty grin crept across his face. Savage noticed his smile and remarked upon it, realising something new about Fred and his attitude to the investigation.

> **DC Hazel Savage**: You're enjoying it, aren't you?
> **Fred West**: Yeah, why not?
> **DC Savage**: I don't know. I don't understand it.
> **Fred West**: You will in the end.
> **DC Savage**: Will I? When will I understand it?
> **Fred West**: I don't know. At the end (laughing). Whenever that is ...

That evening, Rose was charged with the murder of Carol Ann Cooper, the Worcester teenager who disappeared in November 1973; Rose having previously been charged with the murder of the Gloucester seamstress Lynda Gough, who disappeared in April 1973. Two days later, Rose was charged with the murder of Lucy Partington, the university student who disappeared from a Cheltenham bus stop in December 1973. That was three murder charges she faced jointly with Fred, the three killings having taken place within eight months – a frenzy of murder.

'I'm innocent,' said Rose.

On Thursday night, Fred met with his solicitor and defence counsel to discuss their strategy now that he and Rose faced joint murder charges. Fred seemed discomposed by this development. He told his legal team that he had taken all the blame for the murders originally in an attempt to keep Rose out of it. His lawyers said that they would try to reverse what he had said, if he wished to change his story. Meanwhile, Howard Ogden advised Fred not to answer further police questions, which didn't sit well with Fred who thought that he could still talk his way out of trouble – showing what a weak grasp he had on reality.

Following this confab, Ogden alerted Detective Superintendent John Bennett that Fred might have something new and significant to say to the police. Senior officers waited in nervous expectation as Fred was brought back into the interview room just after 9:30 AM on Friday, 29 April. Ogden handed a new note to the officers. It read:

> *I have not, and still [can] not, told (sic) you the whole truth about these matters. The reason for this is that from the very first day of this inquiry my main concern has been to protect other person or persons, and there is nothing else I wish to say at this time.*

PLAN B

While this fell short of an admission that Rose was involved, it seemed to indicate that Fred was reassessing his position *vis-à-vis* Rose, that he might even be starting to turn against his wife. This became Fred's Plan B, as Ogden says. Hazel Savage was keen to know more. 'Now what on earth am I supposed to understand from that [note]? What does that mean?' she asked Fred.

> **Fred West**: Means what it says, don't it …?
> **DC Savage**: Who are these people who you're trying to protect, Fred?
> **Fred West**: No comment.

Savage confronted Fred with evidence that Rose had been seeing women behind his back. They had witnesses who spoke about how consensual lesbian sex often took a rough turn, one woman saying that Rose had forced a vibrator into her until she bled. 'It would seem as if she is, under your very nose, sexually assaulting women,' Savage told Fred. 'You are not alone in this whole saga … I could understand if it was very difficult for you to tell us if Rose was involved. We're not stupid, this is your wife you're talking about, somebody you've learnt over the years to trust, and who you've modelled to a way of thinking. I know that, and you know I know that, don't you? Hmm?' Fred made no reply. 'You've done everything together. Every single thing. She's been your "cow", she's been your "bitch" … You're nodding.'

> **Fred West**: Yeah …
> **DC Hazel Savage**: And suddenly, here come the police. Here come all these witnesses and the whole private thing … that you loved and cherished for all these years of marriage, since Rose was sixteen, suddenly has been

blown open publicly for the world to see. And that's very difficult to come to terms with, that's upsetting, isn't it? Your very innermost feelings are made public ... And it's becoming more and more obvious daily, that these things weren't down to you alone.

The pressure intensified when Rose was charged with a fourth murder, that of Thérèse Siegenthaler, the Swiss hitch-hiker who went missing in 1974, her remains having now been positively identified by the forensic dentist Dr David Whittaker.

'I'm innocent,' was Rose's response.

Seeing how sensitive Fred was to any suggestion that Rose might have acted behind his back, the police asked him about letters they had found between Rose and a female lover in Swindon, whom she met via a contact magazine the year after Siegenthaler's disappearance. Fred knew about the affair, to the extent that he drove Rose to Swindon to meet her girlfriend, and he picked her up afterwards, but he didn't seem happy to be reminded of it. 'No comment on it,' he said tersely.

The next day, Rose was charged with the murder of Shirley Hubbard, the teenager in the mask. Her identity had been proven finally by Dr Whittaker, whose working method included comparing her reconstructed skull to a photograph of Shirley as a bridesmaid, grinning for the camera. Shirley Hubbard disappeared a year before Rose met her Swindon lover. It had been an exceptionally busy time in the lives of the Wests, with victims being abducted, murdered and buried every few months, while Rose was dating, working as a prostitute, and raising a large family.

That evening a police officer digging beneath the kitchen at 25 Midland Road uncovered a child's skull. John Bennett announced the news the next day, Thursday 5 May, while

PLAN B

Professor Bernard Knight carefully excavated the small skeleton, the little bones mixed with coal, evidence of the old coal cellar in which the body was dumped in 1971.

Just after 2:00 PM, Fred was brought back into the interview room.

> **DC Darren Law**: I don't [know] if you're already aware or not, Fred, there's been a find at Midland Road.
> **Fred West**: Ah, yes … I'm glad you found her … it must be, um, Charmaine.

Contrary to his cock-and-bull stories about Charmaine going abroad, his stepdaughter had never left 25 Midland Road, and the police now knew that she had been buried naked, which indicated that the crime had a sexual element. The job of identifying her remains, and working out what exactly had been done to her, was even harder this time because the corpse had seemingly been disturbed by subsequent building work, as Fred had said. However, it looked like Charmaine may have been cut up and violated like all the others. Professor Knight could not say for certain, but once again body parts were missing, and the bones were not in the correct anatomical order. Hazel Savage seemed to struggle to contain her emotions as she confronted Fred with these grim facts.

> **DC Hazel Savage**: You always made a big fuss about saying that she would be perfect, because she was a little kid, a little girl. She's not, Fred.
> **Fred West**: Pardon?
> **DC Savage**: She's not perfect.
> **Fred West**: (sniffing)
> **DC Savage**: She didn't remove her own bones. She's not

in one perfect skeleton. A child ... a little kiddie. This is a kiddie that you loved and wanted to keep, and wanted to keep for Rose.

Fred West: (silence)

DC Savage: It looks, Fred, as if Charmaine's been stuffed into that hole. It's a hole that is the same depth and width [as] the others that have been dug, and it looks as if she's been stuffed into there ... And there are odd bits of bone which are separate ... Who took the bits off that little kid?

Fred West: No comment (crying).

DC Savage: Somebody must've done. This kiddie that you've always told us you loved as your own. 'There was never any difference in our family,' you said. [Despite who the biological father was]. 'They took my name and they were my children.' Now, suddenly, she's stuffed in this hole. You've told us about it before, but you're now saying, 'I don't know who took the bits off her' ... What's the matter, Fred? You're upset.

Fred West: No, I'm all right.

DC Savage: Well, you're not alright, are you? You're crying.

With all but one of the victims, Anne McFall, now recovered, the police had less reason to handle Fred as gently as they had earlier in the investigation.

DC Hazel Savage: Had something awful happened to her body while she was alive? Had this little kid been tortured in any way? Had this little child been subject to any terrible beatings? Had this little child been tied up for kinky sex? ... This is an eight-year-old girl. This child that was your daughter. Fred, did that happen?

PLAN B

> **Fred West**: She was my daughter ...
> **DC Savage**: Well, she's dead. She's stuffed in a hole. She's been cut, or damaged in some way. She's not complete.

Fred sniffed, snivelled and mumbled incoherently. Savage reminded him of Charmaine's baptism, and when he had told the police that he loved the child as his own. 'How could you live with yourself, Fred?' Rather than face up to Charmaine's murder, Fred's febrile mind jumped ahead to her funeral. 'Charmaine will be buried ... by Heather. Nobody else is having her,' he spluttered. 'She's mine.' It was not seemingly the killing that upset him as much as the prospect that he might be denied the bones of his murdered children. He turned to his appropriate adult and cried: 'They can't take Heather away from me, can they, Janet? ... Charmaine, I mean.'

Janet Leach tried to reassure him, but Savage had had enough. 'Are we talking about sex involving young children ... bondage involving young children?' she asked him.

Fred wouldn't answer. 'I've just got the fear they're going to take Charmaine away from me,' he muttered. 'I'm the only dad she's had.'

The police told Fred that they also now knew that Charmaine had sustained a broken collarbone in life, which would have been a painful injury for the little girl. Fred tried to explain this away by saying that Charmaine had fallen out of her bunk bed – the one he penned her in – after Rena put whisky in her bottle. 'I wouldn't hurt her,' he said. 'I never even smacked a child.' There was further evidence that Charmaine had been consistently abused and neglected, including a note on her medical records that she had scabies. She also had enlarged glands, a small detail but one that added to the bigger picture. Some facts were too stark to be brushed aside. Professor Knight thought that Charmaine's body might have been cut in two. Both kneecaps were missing, as was part of her breastbone, twenty-one wrist and ankle bones (out of thirty) and forty-seven finger and toe bones (out of seventy-six). The professor found no evidence that Charmaine's corpse – or any of the bodies – had been moved after death, whereby body parts could have been lost in transit. There was no evidence either that animals had preyed upon the remains. The professor also said that it was very unlikely that the missing bones had rotted away to nothing. The only tenable explanation left for the missing bones in all twelve murders was that body parts had been deliberately removed in life, or just after death, an horrific scenario either way. The weight of evidence was that Fred did this, Fred who learnt to cut up a pig as a child. If Fred and Rose murdered together, Fred was probably the butcher.

'I thought the world of them [children],' Fred snivelled, referring to Charmaine and Anna Marie. 'I wanted them with me ... I didn't want Rena to take them to Scotland or nothing ... I absolutely thought the world of them both.' Yet when he and Rose had custody of the children they mistreated them. There was mounting evidence of sadistic child abuse over years that ended with their stepchild dead, aged eight, by far the youngest of the murder victims; and their eldest daughter dead at sixteen. The more the police investigated this dreadful case, the more they saw that Fred and Rose were partners in physical and sexual abuse, with Fred probably responsible for the disposal of the remains, and Fred and Rose had covered up for each other. Fred in particular had done everything he could to protect Rose from the police. There was now a faint hope, however, that Fred might change his story and turn against his wife.

12
TOUGH COPS WANT ANSWERS

Wednesday, 11 May 1994 • Day Seventy-seven
Gloucester Central Police Station

'You are a man obsessed by sex.'
DETECTIVE INSPECTOR TONY JAMES

The police were frustrated. For the past month a team of officers had been digging in Fingerpost Field, where Fred told them he had a 'feeling' Anne McFall was buried. The excavation had grown to the size of a swimming pool without any sign of Anne, and the cost of the operation was becoming enormous. 'They haven't found anything yet,' DC Darren Law told Fred on 11 May, asking him if he might come back to the scene to guide them further. Fred had been out to the fields twice now, and he wasn't keen to return. 'I don't feel like I'll find more up there anyway,' he said. After some further chatter he deigned to look at an Ordnance Survey map of the crime scene – which he couldn't read – and he took a glance at some police photos. These reminded him of happier days. 'It just had a peaceful, romantic feeling,' he said of his old 'love spot', where he took Anne to look for badgers, but he didn't think the police would find Anne there.

THE FRED WEST TAPES

This was becoming too absurd. Detective Superintendent John Bennett decided that it was time to make some changes in the interview room. The appropriate adult Janet Leach was told that she was no longer required full time, though she might be asked back. Bennett had thought for some time that Leach had grown too close to Fred, who despite his appalling crimes and vile ideas could appear charming when he wanted to be. There was a rumour that Leach had become emotionally involved with the prisoner, which she denied. Bennett feared she may have developed Stockholm syndrome, a psychological condition coined in 1973 after hostages in a bank robbery developed sympathy for their captors. Leach signed an agreement with the police, dated 24 March, that everything she had heard in the interview room would remain confidential, and the next day a new appropriate adult took her place. She was invited back, briefly, but let go for good in early May. She went down to the cells to say goodbye to Fred, who didn't attempt to charm the new appropriate adults, all of them male.

The interviewing officers were also changed. Genial Jeff Morgan, amiable Barbara Harrison and young Darren Law were all given a break. Dealing with Fred over the past weeks had been a fascinating if 'surreal' experience for Law. 'You are there, face to face, with a man who is telling you how he's killed a lot of women, basically,' he reflected in the Netflix series, *Fred & Rose West: A British Horror Story*. Fred was affable and talkative, and the full horror of what he said in the interview room only sunk in later. 'I do recall driving home and thinking I cannot believe this is going on, you know, in Gloucester of all places. I just can't believe this is happening.' Hazel Savage was also stood down. Savage had played a bigger role in the investigation than any of her colleagues. Although she was direct with Fred to the point of bluntness, it was clear that he

TOUGH COPS WANT ANSWERS

not only respected her but also liked her. He even tried to flirt with her at times. 'When I first met you, you gotta be about the beautifulest woman in Gloucestershire, weren't you?' he told the detective one day.

'Alright, let's stop the rubbish, Fred.'

In place of these familiar faces entered two new detectives. In a movie, this might be thought of as the familiar 'good cop/bad cop' routine, though everybody on the team was doing their job as directed by the senior investigating officer. The new officers were not 'bad' but they were less willing to tolerate Fred's evasions. Detective Constable Stephen Harris, forty-one, brought a solemn demeanour to the interview room, questioning Fred in a gloomy Welsh accent. He was partnered by the taciturn Detective Inspector Tony James, forty-four, one of the officers who had served the search warrant on Rose in February. Harris and James made no attempt to befriend Fred, and the atmosphere in the interview room chilled to zero as they went directly to the horror of the case, demanding straight answers.

The new officers showed Fred anatomical charts of his victims, with the missing body parts marked in red. They began with Juanita Mott. 'And missing is the upper part of the breastbone, the first lumbar,[12] the eleventh thoracic;[13] the fourth, fifth, sixth cervical vertebra; the right first rib; both patellas (kneecaps); fifteen carpals[14] out of a possible sixteen; six tarsals[15] out of possible forty; fifty-eight finger and toe bones out of a possible seventy-six. A total of eighty-eight missing bones from those remains,' Detective Inspector James told Fred, identifying

---

12   Lower part of the spine.

13   Part of the spine.

14   Wrist bones.

15   Ankle bones.

the missing bones by their anatomical names. 'Have you any explanation for all those missing bones?'

'None whatsoever, sir.'

The searchers had been thorough. Earth had been sieved to make sure that even the tiniest bones were not overlooked in the recovery process. The police had been meticulous enough to recover individual fingernails, yet in many cases no corresponding fingers. The implication was that fingernails had been pulled out, and fingers cut off. Fred didn't engage with this. He told Janet Leach, however, whom he continued to see privately as a friend, that fingers were removed to foil identification. That wasn't entirely convincing because toes were missing, too, and the police don't take toe-prints. Torture was the most likely explanation for the missing digits.

The next chart related to Shirley Robinson.

> **DI Tony James**: Missing from this body: both patellae (kneecaps); the seventh vertical cervical vertebra; the first and second thoracic vertebra; both twelfth ribs; all carpal and tarsal bones, except [two] at the ankle: twenty-eight out of a possible thirty; forty-two finger and toe bones out of a possible seventy-six ... Can you explain where seventy-seven [missing] bones are?
> **Fred West**: No idea (emotional). Shirley was expecting a baby as well ... So, the baby was with her, was it?
> **DI James**: The remains of a foetus have been recovered [near] the remains of Shirley Robinson.

The inspector itemised ninety-six bones missing from Alison Chambers, the care home runaway initially misdescribed as 'Shirley's mate'. He offered to show Fred the chart of his daughter Heather's skeleton, again with numerous missing body parts. Fred refused to look. He was sobbing now. Howard Ogden asked Fred if he wanted a break. 'I'm alright,' said Fred. So, James carried on, itemising Heather's missing bones: fifteen wrist and ankle bones, twenty-two finger and toe bones (though again some detached fingernails had been recovered) and the right kneecap. Fred had kneecapped his daughter.

> **DI Tony James**: Have you kept these [body parts] for some reason?
> **Fred West**: I don't know where they are.
> **DI James**: I understand you're into keeping souvenirs. Mention has been made of knickers that have been burnt and kept in jars.
> **Fred West**: That wasn't my idea.
> **DI James**: Sorry, what wasn't?

The officers were sharp, well-prepared and quick to pounce on any slip of the tongue. Fred lit a cigarette and sucked on it, preferring not to explain himself further.

James continued in the same careful manner, enumerating every body part missing from each victim. Fred muttered that he had no explanation for any of it.

> **DI Tony James**: Are these people still alive when you remove [the body parts]?
> **Fred West**: No comment on that.

Nor did Fred want to explain the grotesque mask wound around Shirley Hubbard's skull. These were facts so stark that he could not bat them away with evasions and lies, so he didn't say anything. Fred's silence was not such a problem for the police because he had previously confessed to killing eleven of the twelve victims, and he had shown the police where the bodies were buried, so he was sure to be convicted. The team believed that Fred and Rose were in it together, however, and Rose had admitted nothing and there was no forensic evidence linking her to the murders (other than the fact that nine bodies were found under her house and garden, which required some explaining), so prosecuting her would be a challenge.

There was, though, circumstantial evidence tying Fred and Rose as a couple to the crimes. The statement given by the Wests' former nanny, Caroline Owens, was vital in this respect, showing the Wests acting together in abducting and attacking a woman. DI James now revealed that the police had another witness who helped bolster a joint case against Fred and Rose.

> **DI Tony James**: I want to talk [to you] about a statement of evidence we've received from a lady called Elizabeth Agius ... Does the name mean anything to you? You're shaking your head ...
> **Fred West**: No, never heard of her.

The detective reminded Fred that Elizabeth Agius had been his neighbour at Midland Road, when her maiden name was McCall. She was known to her friends as Liz. 'Oh yeah ... Liz,' Fred remembered now. 'She lived in the flat next door, top flat.' Liz was a nineteen-year-old unmarried mother of two living at 24 Midland Road in 1971. One day when she was struggling with her pram on the front steps Fred lent her a hand. ('I don't like to see anybody struggle,' he told the officers.) Fred invited Liz in for a cup of tea, and introduced her to Rose. Liz agreed to babysit for her neighbours, so they could go out for the evening. When they returned, she asked if they had been anywhere special. 'No, we only went around looking for young girls,' replied Fred, explaining that he and Rose often cruised around looking for teenagers, to get them into prostitution. They sometimes drove as far as Bristol or even further to London looking for 'young runaways', ideally virgins aged fifteen to seventeen. It worked better if Rose was in the car, because girls felt safer accepting a lift from a couple.

What did Fred have to say to that?

Fred West: Utter lies, sir, I never said nothing like that, never dealt with anything like that in my life.
DI Tony James: Fifteen to seventeen is the age group of some of these girls, Mr West.

Liz Agius told the police that Fred had made a pass at her, saying that he wanted to tie her up. Rose tried to talk her into a threesome. When she refused, she was drugged and woke up in bed with Fred and Rose anyway.

Fred West: Can't you see where she got it from?

Fred suggested that Liz was spinning a story to sell to the newspapers. In fact, she had contacted the *Sun* before talking to the police, and was being paid for two television interviews. Many people who had known the Wests were in this position, which could be used in court to suggest that their stories had been exaggerated for gain, if not invented. That was a problem for a later date.

Tony James reminded Fred that several of the victims had disappeared from the streets, hitching or waiting for buses, which tallied with what Liz Agius said he told her. There was more. Liz said that Fred got so hot under the collar that he snapped a pair of handcuffs on her, as a prelude to wanting to have sex with her, and he became so jealous of the man who became her husband that he threatened to kill him and bury him in the cellar. Despite all this, Liz Agius remained friends with the Wests and later visited 25 Cromwell Street, where Fred showed her his new cellar which, he said, he might convert into his 'torture chamber'.

All lies and rubbish, according to Fred.

DI Tony James: And the business about you wanting to tie her up?
Fred West: I have never tied a girl up in my life.
DI James: That's coincidence that we found items of bondage with these remains … is it?
Fred West: Definitely. Must be.

Although he had seemed unsettled initially by these two tough detectives, Fred had quickly regained his composure, sounding surprisingly confident now, even a little off-hand with James and Harris.

The cops increased the pressure. DI James suggested to Fred that he was 'a man obsessed by sex' and the crimes were the result of his warped sex drive.

DI Tony James: See, the whole theme that seems to be running through this is one of a sexual nature. That you're a man obsessed by sex. And what Liz Agius is saying seems consistent with what other people have said …
Fred West: No.

Having boasted of his sexual appetite and countless lovers, Fred did another U-turn and started to present himself to the

TOUGH COPS WANT ANSWERS

police as a man of mild sexual appetites, as he suggested to the Birmingham psychologist in 1992, when he claimed to be impotent. DC Harris wondered if that might be a motive for attacking women.

> **DC Stephen Harris**: Would you describe yourself as being sexually inadequate?
> **Fred West**: Yes ...
> **DC Harris**: Have there ever been occasions where you've been with a woman and not been able to get an erection?
> **Fred West**: Oh yeah. I thought all men got that problem ...
> **DC Harris**: What happens to [you] when you can't manage an erection? Do you get angry?
> **Fred West**: No. I'm not an angry person.

Having been confronted with the evidence of Caroline Owens, May West and Liz Agius, Fred was informed that his eldest daughter, Anna Marie, had also given the police a statement about sexual abuse she suffered at the hands of her father and stepmother at 25 Cromwell Street. She said that she had been tied up, beaten and raped, escaping her abusers only when she ran away from home aged fifteen.

> **DI Tony James**: What do you say about that?
> **Fred West**: No comment, sir. Definitely not.

Furthermore, Anna Marie, Caroline Owens and Liz Agius all talked about the Wests putting them into bondage, or wanting to tie them up. Surely they couldn't all be lying. Furthermore, Anna Marie said that she had sticky parcel tape put over her mouth like Caroline Owens and several of the women who were found dead.

> **DI Tony James**: So no one could hear them screaming?
> **Fred West**: No comment, sir.
> **DI James**: Is that what the mask was for, that we found on Shirley Hubbard, the fifteen-year-old?
> **Fred West**: No comment, sir.

The police had interviewed yet another witness, a former Cromwell Street neighbour named Kathryn Halliday, who was now in her late thirties. In 1988, after splitting up with her husband, Kathryn rented a room at 11 Cromwell Street. When she had a plumbing problem, the landlord sent Fred round to fix her leak. Fred got chatting to Kathryn and was intrigued to discover that she was in a lesbian relationship. 'If you see my missus, she will sort you out,' he told her. Kathryn Halliday went to 25 Cromwell Street, where Rose virtually dragged her upstairs for sex, while Fred watched, before joining in briefly. Despite this rough first encounter, Kathryn returned to the house for regular sex sessions with Rose, visiting 25 Cromwell Street almost daily after the West children had gone to school. Sometimes Fred was there. He showed her pornographic videos, 'with bondage and sadism', as a precursor to sex with Rose, occasionally leading to a threesome.

> **DI Tony James**: She says that during one of the sessions she had with you in bed, she was tied to the bed. She said, 'I can't remember exactly how it happened, but I suddenly found myself tied by both arms and legs to each corner of the bed. There then followed a conversation where Fred and Rose were threatening to leave me tied there all night …'

TOUGH COPS WANT ANSWERS

She says there was a wardrobe in the room and whips were hung on the wall. One was an ordinary bullwhip, and the other a cat-'o-nine-tails. Do you have those items?
Fred West: No comment, sir ...

Although the police found two whips and a rice flail at 25 Cromwell Street in 1992 during the child abuse inquiry, when that inquiry ended these items, along with sex toys, rubber clothing and pornography, had been offered back to the Wests. Rose said she didn't want the items back, so the police destroyed the lot. As a result, much evidence was now unfortunately missing.

James continued to read from Kathryn Halliday's statement:

DI James: 'They showed me a catalogue of latex and rubber clothing, which showed people wearing these suits and masks and hoods ... Some of these covered the whole head, and [had] eye and nose holes, but some had none ... Fred went to the wardrobe and took out a suitcase. It contained some of these suits and hoods. They were all black, and I can remember picking up the top one, which smelt sweaty and had obviously been worn.' Have you ever had hoods and clothing like this?
Fred West: Never, sir.

Ultimately, Kathryn Halliday was bound, gagged and blindfolded during sex, then smothered with a pillow (as Caroline Owens was smothered). 'It got more and more violent,' she said. 'They wanted me to do more and more all the time. They wanted to go beyond limits. They pushed me beyond my personal limits, and when they began to hurt me badly I began to ease off going there because of the physical pain that they were causing me ... Rose West wanted me to do things to her that were very, very aggressive, i.e. with the dildos ... They told me that even if I couldn't take those dildos then, when they were first using them, they would soon make me able to take them.' After one of these sadistic sessions, she noticed that her stomach had been cut with a knife. Kathryn stopped seeing the Wests and moved away from Cromwell Street. She felt lucky to have escaped. Fred appeared wholly unmoved by her story.

The detectives fired further questions at him. Did he abuse Anna Marie and 'encourage her to go with other men' as she told the police? 'That's disgusting,' replied Fred.

> **DI Tony James**: Is it correct that you had sex with Anne-Marie (*sic*)?
> **Fred West**: No comment, sir.
> **DI James**: Do you find that 'disgusting'?
> **Fred West**: No comment, sir.
> **DI James**: Did you have sex with any of your victims after you killed them?
> **Fred West**: No comment, sir.
> **DC Stephen Harris**: What would you say to the suggestion that you kept your victims alive in your cellar, after you had abducted them, and they were used down there for your sexual gratification, [or] were they kept for your wife's sexual gratification?
> **Fred West**: No comment, sir...
> **DC Harris**: Were those girls subdued and tortured in your basement?
> **Fred West**: No comment, sir.

Fred was also asked if he had suspended victims from the joists in his cellar, where he had drilled four holes.

TOUGH COPS WANT ANSWERS

> **Fred West**: There was only two holes ... put up for the children to [swing] on.

There were in fact four.

> **DC Stephen Harris**: Were any of your victims hung up on those beams?
> **Fred West**: No comment, sir.

The detectives made it plain that they feared that Fred was capable of almost any atrocity, with a final round of questions based on what witnesses had told them, and their own supposition. Were the Wests into witchcraft and witches' covens, for instance? From the start there had been a suggestion of ritualism about the Cromwell Street crimes, and a workmate of Fred's said that he spoke about witches. No, said Fred, claiming not to know that there was a 'sexual side in witchcraft'. Did Fred perform abortions, as more than one witness claimed, describing his dirty abortion kit including a nasty implement with a corkscrew end. He denied it, though it was almost certainly true. Did the Wests collect videos of humans having sex with animals? Fred refused to answer that, which was also probably true. Did the Wests have a kink about fascists and domination? 'What's fascists?' asked a bewildered Fred. Told that fascists were like Nazis, he said: 'I'm Conservative and I vote Conservative.' Did the Wests make 'snuff videos'? It was explained that 'snuff videos' were films of people being killed.

> **DI Tony James**: People have been killed in your house, haven't they, Mr West ... Did you video any of this?
> **Fred West**: No comment, sir.

THE FRED WEST TAPES

The police tried the same strategy with Rose, asking her provocative rapid-fire questions in an attempt to break down her barriers. 'Was [victim's name] tied up in your house in Cromwell Street?' she was asked, as reported by Gordon Burn in his book, *Happy Like Murderers*. 'Was she taken down to the basement and held there as a prisoner? ... Did you tie her up? ... Did you tie her hands with rope? ... Were you present when she was being tied up? ... Did you gag her? ... Did you put cloth around her face, or over her eyes? ... Was she tortured while she was still alive? ... Was she cut at all while she was still alive? ... Did you take part in cutting her head off? ... Did you cut off her legs? ... Were you forced to do any of these things? ... Did you cut her fingers? ... Did you cut off her toes? ... Did you assist in the disposal of any parts of her body?' Rose continued to answer 'no comment', apparently unfazed by the scenarios presented to her, possibly because none of it was new to her. She had lived this life with Fred.

Likewise, Fred kept his cool under fire. After forty-one minutes, the detectives had used up all their ammunition for now. 'OK, it's twenty-five minutes past six [in the evening],' said DC Harris. 'We'll conclude this interview now.'

In the morning, Fred was even less co-operative. 'I have lied throughout the statements,' he said. He now claimed that he was not involved in any murders. In which case, the police implored him to tell them who was responsible. 'My life means nothing to you, but it means a lot to me,' said Fred mysteriously. Asked if he was frightened of someone, Fred said, 'You've only got to look at that,' pointing to police illustrations of the skeletons. He wasn't so much scared for himself, he said, as for his surviving children. 'I can't do anything at the moment. It's too dangerous to try.' Then he started to play the victim, saying that 'nobody spares a thought for what I've lost in this. I've lost more than anybody else.' He turned to Howard Ogden and asked his solicitor to end the interview because he had nothing more to say.

★ ★ ★

Later that day, Friday, 13 May, Fred was moved to prison for the first time since his arrest in February. He was driven to HMP Winson Green in Birmingham, where he was admitted as a prisoner of 'exceptional risk' who might try to harm himself. For this reason, he was kept under observation in the Health Care Centre on his first night.

In the morning, Fred had his mugshot photograph taken with his prison number, WN 3617. He stared glumly into the camera, agape and puffy-eyed, looking depressed and sinister. He was also interviewed by a doctor, the prison staff keen to know how he was feeling. He would be interviewed regularly by doctors in the months ahead to ascertain and monitor his mental state. 'He was very polite to me, and whatever I asked he did,' said one of the Winson Green doctors who saw Fred frequently. Did these prison doctors think that Fred was mad? 'I didn't do his personality analysis, [but he wasn't] mad in the sense of being schizophrenic, he was not mad in the sense of depression, depressive psychosis, certainly not,' says one. 'He was not psychotic … Mr West was not deluded in any sense … He was lucid.' Anybody who had listened to or read the transcripts of Fred's police interviews – peppered with outlandish stories, fantastical claims and visions of ghosts – may have been surprised to hear this.

Apparently sane, Fred was escorted to D-Wing, where he was given his own cell on D3 landing, an exclusive high-security enclave of no more than ten inmates, including the most dangerous men in Winson Green. At least three members of prison staff had to be present when a D3 inmate was unlocked. As a remand prisoner (Category A), who had not been convicted, Fred enjoyed comforts and privileges on the wing. He wrote to his family and Janet Leach asking them for tobacco, lined paper, batteries for his Walkman, and puzzle books, all of which he was allowed. He used a *Fun Fax* dictionary to solve puzzles. He also did light prison work to help pass the time – sewing buttons on shirts. He was let out of his cell for meals, exercise and 'association' with other inmates, during which time he made a friend. 'I got to know Fred well,' said the inmate who became his prison pal (his name is redacted in his statements in prison files), 'neither of us were trouble makers.' Inmates and staff treated Fred as a celebrity, said the friend; fellow prisoners nicknaming him Digger. Fred worried that he received favouritism from the screws, whispering to his friend that they were 'conspiring against him.' Like Rose, Fred was suspicious to the point of paranoia. 'Things like the staff used to spend a lot of time talking to him, they used to call him by his first name, rather than his surname,' said his friend. 'He used to be given more food than the other prisoners. We discussed all these things during the exercise periods and we both thought the prison staff were softening him up in order that he would open up about the Gloucester murders, and the staff would put statements in about him.'

After a couple of days, Fred received the first of a series of visits from Howard Ogden who had permission to tape-record his interviews with his client as he prepared for the trial that was looming. Fred's manner with Ogden was always different in private. He became coarser, and said things that he didn't say to the police, though that didn't necessarily mean that what he told Ogden was true. Significantly, he spoke about Rose in an increasingly negative way, unlike anything he had said in the interview room. 'Rose fucking ruled me,' he growled to Ogden. He talked about her promiscuity and sexual appetite, 'that started from the fucking day we met. When she was coming to the caravan seeing me [in 1969] she'd been fucked before she come to see me.' He described Rose's sexual interest in women, and how she would pick up men in front of him when they were out, seeming to gloat over the details. 'She'd either fuck off with somebody else, [or] be fucked in the car park right by the side of me … I thought, fuck me, this woman never changes.' He also started to allude to other people being involved in the murders, including his brother John, who was arrested that week regarding allegations of raping his nieces.

Meanwhile, Rose was being charged with more murders: Shirley Robinson, Alison Chambers and, on 26 May, Heather. Her response remained the same. She made no comment to police questions and said 'I'm innocent' when charged. Fred and Rose were now jointly charged with nine murders, all the recovered victims save Rena. Although Rose had known Rena, and had a motive for seeing her dead, there was no evidence that she was involved in this crime.

★ ★ ★

Of the twelve victims Fred had identified to the police, one body was yet to be recovered. The police had been working in Fingerpost Field for seven weeks, creating a 600-square-metre archaeological dig. On rainy days, the excavation turned into a muddy pond. After a few sunny days, the earth dried hard and officers had to chip at the soil with pickaxes. Meanwhile, a village of police tents and portable cabins had grown up around the pit, the police watched by reporters, photographers and TV camera crews lounging in cars parked on the lane. The police contemplated giving up. On 7 June, Det. Supt. John Bennett told the waiting journalists that this phase of the investigation might soon be over, which the press turned into a story about wasted public money. This upset Bennett, a man with an iron sense of discipline and good order, who had put his heart into the investigation and found dealing with the unruly media one of the most challenging aspects of the job. The SIO decided to knock off early for once. He was in his car on his way home, feeling very weary, when he received a pager message from colleagues to come back to Fingerpost Field. Just as they were about to give up the police had uncovered something at the edge of the search area, near a coppice. It was a skull.

Watched by the team, Professor Bernard Knight climbed down into the hole. The bones he found were broken and brown after years in open country. Still, the story of Anne McFall's last moments was revealed to the pathologist. She had been dismembered, her legs cut off, with familiar slicing marks to the femurs. She had apparently been tied up with dressing gown cord, which was still wrapped around what had been her wrists and body. She had been buried naked, covered in a quilt or curtain. A cardigan was in a plastic bag, which Fred had dumped with her. Again, several body parts were missing: the right twelfth rib; the outer left shin; four wrist and ankle bones; and thirty-six finger and toe bones. It seemed that Fred had cut fingers and toes off his victims from the start, if Anne was his first victim. Finally, there were the remains of Anne's unborn baby, a foetus of six to seven months gestation. In murdering the mother, Fred had also killed their baby. It was an almost unthinkable horror, and a crime he committed years before he met Rose. This proved one thing: Fred was capable of killing alone. Was the police case that Fred and Rose acted together in the crimes committed at 25 Cromwell Street still viable?

13

ROSE DON'T WANT ME

Thursday, 30 June 1994 • Day 127
Gloucester Magistrates' Court

'I should go to Hell for what I've done.'
FRED WEST

For the first time since their arrest in February Fred and Rose were about to see each other again. It was a beautiful warm summer's day, the last day of June. The world looked radiant, even dingy old Gloucester where the press had gathered at the magistrates' court. This was for a brief and simple remand hearing, where a magistrate would decide whether the Wests could continue to be held in custody, pending a trial, or whether they should be released on bail. Such matters are usually of little interest, and there was no chance of the Wests being bailed, but the court swarmed with people this summer morning. Photographers and TV crews staked out the front and back entrances, to make sure that they didn't miss the prison vans. Reporters including myself queued for the few available seats inside, along with members of the West family and the public. Detective Superintendent John Bennett marched over the road from police headquarters with some of his senior officers to watch the drama of the reunion.

Fred and Rose were brought into court separately, Fred first. He looked pale and tired after four months in custody, dressed in a blue jacket and sweater, swaying slightly as he stood in the dock, mouth agape. Rose squeezed into the dock beside him, a heavyset woman in a tight space, separated from her husband by three officers, everybody squashed. 'She dumps herself in the box and stares straight at me,' recalled the magistrate, Lloyd Parry, who by coincidence formerly owned a house overlooking 25 Cromwell Street, where he had often seen Fred working. 'She was just as if she had come straight out of Sainsbury's, plonked her shopping down and her handbag, sat there with her arms folded.' Fred and Rose confirmed their names, ages and address to Parry who read out nine joint murder charges. In addition, Fred was charged with killing Rena and Charmaine, making eleven counts of murder in his case. He hadn't been charged yet with Anne McFall's murder. Rose additionally faced two charges of rape and one of assault.

Fred was primarily interested in Rose. He touched her neck at the start of the hearing, but she didn't respond. He glanced around the court room in confusion, making eye contact with his son, Steve, who nodded back at his dad. Meanwhile, Rose behaved like a woman on a bus who pretends that the nasty looking man next to her doesn't exist. At the end of the hearing, after the Wests had been remanded into custody for a month, Fred again tried to talk to Rose, but the dock officers stopped him and Rose evinced no desire whatsoever to communicate. 'I don't think Fred heard a word I said,' said Parry. 'He was totally and utterly discombobulated by Rose blanking him.'

Fred's solicitor saw this meeting as being highly significant. 'That was a very telling moment,' said Howard Ogden. Up to now, Fred had believed that Rose would stand by him, while he would do everything possible to protect her. That had been their pact. She had now made it public that the pact was broken. 'That was a turning point,' said Ogden.

While Fred was in Gloucester for his remand appearance, the police embarked on a final round of interviews, conducted by DCs Stephen Harris and Nick Barnes. The officers were puzzling over the last months of Anne McFall's life, when she was living with Fred in Gloucester. They had established that Anne was visited by a child care officer, Mr Edwards, shortly before she died. He took notes which the officers read to Fred. 'I visited with a health visitor student and saw Anne [McFall] and Charmaine and Anna Marie,' Edwards wrote on 14 April 1967, having visited Fred at the Watermead caravan site in Brockworth. 'The caravan is [in] rather a poor state, and seemed to have deteriorated since I saw it at Sandhurst [Lane]. The children are obviously sleeping in the same room as their father and Annie [McFall].' Three months later, on 25 July 1967, Edwards noted that a probation officer named Lombard had been back to the caravan. 'Miss Lombard is extremely worried about these children who are being looked after by Annie McFall, who is now expecting Mr. West's baby in three months' time ... Every so often, their mother [Rena] visits from Glasgow and takes over the care of the children who are now thoroughly confused.' The police believed that Fred killed Anne a few days after this.

'I never touched Anne at all. No way,' Fred told the detectives, insisting that Rena killed Anne. There was no evidence of that, while the police had witnesses who said that Fred physically abused Anne.

DC Nick Barnes: These statements paint a picture of you beating up [women] ...

THE FRED WEST TAPES

> **Fred West**: But I've never beat anybody up [in] my life! I'm an absolute coward, if you want to know. I wouldn't attack anybody ... Not even a woman.

In addition, members of Fred's family knew that he'd killed Anne, as Barnes reminded him. 'Freddy's killed the girl and buried her in Kempley Woods,' his mother Daisy told his brother John and his wife in August 1967. John refused to discuss the matter with his mother at the time and a few months later, in February 1968, Daisy West died of a heart attack. While she was suffering from bronchitis, and she was obese, Fred's mother was only forty-six. Perhaps discovering that her son was a murderer – and the stress of covering this up – exerted a fatal strain on her heart.

Nonetheless, Fred insisted that he hadn't killed Anne. 'I have not got no violence in me,' he protested, the double negative serving to highlight the absurdity of his lie. He started to play the victim again, muttering that 'somebody else' was involved. 'My ex-wife, my daughter ... two unborn children. How much more do I need to go? ... And you think I don't want to know what happened to them?'

He then made some disparaging remarks about Rose, mild criticism but nonetheless remarkable for an uxorious husband who had gone out of his way to protect his wife. Recalling Rose when they met, Fred said: 'She had a glum look on her face. You know? Rose never smiled. Well, she don't now ... Rose didn't look at you, she looked through you. [Her] eyes are so cold looking at you.' He suggested that the first he knew of the murders was when he was told about them at 25 Cromwell Street on 24 February. He could only be referring to one person.

ROSE DON'T WANT ME

> **DC Nick Barnes**: I shall ask you a direct question: is Rose West the person that told you about where these bodies were buried?
>
> **Fred West**: I've got no comment [but] I didn't have nothing to do with it.
>
> **DC Stephen Harris**: Would it be fair to say you have everything to do with it?

Fred said that he couldn't tell the police the whole truth 'because I'm protecting somebody', as he had written in his recent note. 'And I am still protecting somebody ... I can't say it no plainer than that, can I?'

While he was now implying that Rose was involved, Fred was also saying that his earlier confessions were false. DC Barnes suggested to Fred that Anne McFall was the reason.

> **DC Nick Barnes**: You will not accept responsibility for Anne McFall, and it is because of that that you are now distancing yourself from the eleven. Because if you did the eleven, and buried them, you must have done Annie McFall, and you can't face that. That's the truth of the matter. That's the whole reason now why we have these retractions ... you can't face that you killed and buried Anna (*sic*) McFall.
>
> **Fred West**: I have no comment.

Barnes reminded Fred of the similarities between the twelve murders. All the victims were female. They had all been cut up and buried in the same way. 'Surely that's an MO in itself.' Fred seemed confused. 'Do you understand what we mean when we say MO?' Fred did not. The detective explained that MO stood for *modus operandi* – a pattern of behaviour.

Furthermore, the victims were known to Fred, three of whom he made pregnant, two being his children; and they were all buried in places associated with Fred. Who else would think to bury Anne McFall near Moorcourt Cottage 'in the middle of nowhere'?

'That's not nowhere!' protested Fred.

'You put her there, because it was an area you knew,' Barnes persisted. 'Who else would have dug it?' Fred made no comment. 'There isn't any other person that we know of that had contact with Anne McFall in 1967, and had contact with Heather in 1987, other than you! You're the common factor.'

Fred sounded defeated finally. 'The only thing I done wrong [was] trying to sort it out myself,' he muttered. 'I made a mess of it, trying to guess what happened.' The officers stopped the tape machine just after 3:30 PM. This was the last of 142 police interviews, 110 hours of tape having been recorded since February. That afternoon they charged Fred with Anne McFall's murder, and sent him back to HMP Winson Green to await a committal hearing before a magistrate who would decide whether to send Fred and Rose for trial.

Three days later when Howard Ogden visited his client in Birmingham, Fred angrily denounced his wife. Talking in his machine-gun voice, laced with obscenities, he described Rose as a woman of boundless depravity who was habitually cruel, even to animals (banging cats against walls, he now said). He suggested that Rose and others killed the Cromwell Street victims, and more women in the gaps in the timeline of murders. He spoke about the other murders taking place at a farm which Rose had access to. Fred expressed his surprise and upset now that Rose had turned against him. 'You know what Rose is doing now? Distancing me and her,' he complained. 'See, I'm beginning to wonder, did Rose have any love towards me at all? Or was I

ROSE DON'T WANT ME

somebody there to use all the time? I was easy touch, and do as I told, and not interfere.'

Ogden tried to get Fred to focus on his defence. Despite having confessed at various times to eleven of the twelve killings, he now seemed intent on pleading not guilty to all charges, though getting him to agree on what he saw as 'the truth' – a coherent defence that he would stick to – was like trying to nail jelly to a wall. Almost every time they spoke, Fred changed his mind. 'What is your defence?' Ogden asked, frustrated. If he pleaded not guilty, he and Rose would be pitted against each other at trial, which probably wouldn't end well for either of them. 'This is a classic cut-throat defence where each blames the other and the jury sits and listens and says, well, they are as bad as each other.'

Fred told Ogden that Rose informed him about the murders on the evening of 24 February, after the police arrived at the house with the search warrant and he had gone to the station to talk to Hazel Savage. When he told Rose that they had nothing to worry about, she told him that they most certainly did. Fred claimed that he took a deep breath before asking his wife what the fuck she meant. She said Heather was buried in their back garden. Fred told Ogden that he almost died when he heard this, as if it was news to him, and had to sit down. He asked his wife to explain herself, and she said that their daughter was buried near the garden fence. Fred swore with surprise. 'It seemed as though my whole life stopped there,' he told Ogden, in a tape-recorded interview later broadcast in *Fred & Rose: The West Murders*. He claimed to have decided there and then that he would have to take the blame for his wife, which he said he always did. He asked Rose to tell him more and Rose said that their daughter was dismembered. Fred sniffed back tears. He asked why she had cut Heather up. Rose said to fit her in the dustbin.

THE FRED WEST TAPES

'Her daughter, in a dustbin!' exclaimed Fred, as if shocked to his core by the idea, though this was of course what Fred himself had done, with or without Rose's assistance.

He asked Rose if that was all. No, she said, there were several more bodies, maybe nine in total. She told him about the ones buried in their cellar. 'Well, fuck me, thou ain't done bad,' Fred told his wife, by his account. Then she told him about Charmaine, revealing that she was at 25 Midland Road. Fred hoped Charmaine wasn't cut up, not a child. No, she said, Charmaine wasn't cut up.

Fred went on and on like this, telling the story in dialogue as if Rose had committed all the murders and he knew nothing about it until the police were at their door, as big a lie as ever crossed his lips.

He then said that Rose told him about Lynda Gough, and how she stole and wore the dead girl's clothes. Rose said that she washed them first. Fred cursed with amazement, wondering at how low his wife could go. He asked Rose where Lynda was buried, and she told him in the old car inspection pit behind the house. She said that was the first murder at 25 Cromwell Street, which Fred said was true. When he asked his wife why she had killed Lynda Gough, Rose said she 'fancied her'. Fred said Rose sometimes got carried away with a girl. He saw that once. She hurt the girl so badly, 'did so much damage to her', that she had to kill her.

Still, he didn't rule himself out of all blame. 'Fuck me,' he said in a moment of clarity, 'I should go to Hell for what I've done.'

★ ★ ★

The next day, Fred and Rose were back at the magistrates' court for another routine remand hearing where she blanked him again. Afterwards, the prison officers on escort duty almost put

ROSE DON'T WANT ME

Fred into Rose's van by mistake, giving Fred and the screws a big laugh, their hilarity captured by a press photographer. When the picture was published, the governor of HMP Winson Green received letters of complaint from members of the public. The governor seemed irritated by this. Having Fred in custody was a headache for the governor, and it was about to get worse.

After the hearing, Fred had another meeting with Howard Ogden. It didn't go well. 'He gave me, I would say, the seventh version of "the truth" in Winson Green prison when I couldn't [go along with this any longer],' says Ogden. 'It must have shown in my face.' Fred was equally unhappy with his solicitor, complaining about him in a 30 July letter to his probation officer. When Ogden came back to Winson Green two days later, Fred refused to leave his cell, telling the officer who came to fetch him that he didn't want to see Ogden again. When the officer came back fifteen minutes later to ask if he was sure, Fred became 'even more upset and was crying'. The screw left Fred sobbing on his bed, watched by a colleague, while he summoned one of the prison doctors. 'I was asked to see him because he had become tearful following a disagreement with his solicitor and staff on the wing were concerned about his mental health,' said Dr James McMaster. 'He said that he was upset due to a disagreement with [Ogden] … He feels uncertain how to deal with the court case.' Fred muttered to the doctor about how it had been his intention to protect his wife, even if it meant serving a life sentence, but now he seemed unsure that Rose was worth his sacrifice. Fred was put on Special Watch, checked every fifteen minutes to make sure he didn't try to kill himself.

A few days later it was reported that Ogden was offering to sell interview tapes and other information about Fred to the media for £1 million. Ogden admitted trying to do a deal, though he said that he wasn't looking for as much as a million pounds, and argued that he had done nothing improper. 'I am doing what West wants me to do,' he told the Press Association. 'He wants people to know his story and he wants me to tell it. It has been no secret for weeks now that the story is for sale, and I have engaged an agent to handle the deal.' He claimed that he and Fred had discussed, in a light-hearted way, the casting of a feature film of the murder case. Fred no longer saw the joke. He changed his representation and his new solicitors obtained a High Court order stopping Ogden, who had to return his tapes, letters and other items. The Law Society later suspended him for unbecoming conduct. 'I felt the reason he has sacked his solicitor was because he wanted to go back to the beginning and start again developing a new story, which he did,' Fred's probation officer noted on 3 August. 'While he rambles at length, he is now clearly suggesting that Rose ... probably did all the murders.'

Fred wrote to his former appropriate adult, Janet Leach, asking her to visit him. When she came to Winson Green he told her that the murders were primarily committed by three people: Rose, her father, Bill Letts; and Fred's brother, John. There were other male members of the murder gang, but he didn't name them. (While there is evidence of several men being involved in sexual assaults with the Wests at Cromwell Street, there is no proof of a murder gang as such.) He said that ritual killing took place in a barn, on a farm, where girls were slaughtered like pigs. He intimated that victims were tortured, their fingernails (the missing fingernails) burnt. Fred didn't deny that he took part in this, but he said that the murders were mostly down to Rose who became violent during assaults, beating girls up and forcing objects inside them with catastrophic results. The dead were 'Rose's mistakes'. He claimed that some victims killed at the farm were brought back to 25 Cromwell Street by John West on his dustcart for burial (a scenario ruled out by Professor Knight who believed that all the victims found at the house were killed at the house).

Fred told Leach that 'the farm' was near Berkeley, southwest of Gloucester. It may have been abandoned, judging by his description. It may have been fiction, the make believe of a maniac who had grown up on a farm. Fred never mentioned the farm to the police. He said that up to twenty additional victims were buried at the farm, and elsewhere. The other crimes spanned three decades. Mary Bastholm was a victim, supposedly killed by Rose and John back in 1968. Another woman was killed by Fred and Rose in Birmingham as recently as 1992–93, buried near to where he had been staying at the time; and two more bodies were hidden in Fingerpost Field.

This confession was as vague as it was sensational. Apart from Mary Bastholm, Fred did not name any additional victims, and he failed to identify the farm, or the precise location of any graves. Fred talked so much, it was hard for Leach to remember everything he said, and almost impossible to know what, if anything, he told her was true. Fred also told Leach that he made stories up when talking to her, Ogden and his son, Steve, to see what leaked to the press, because he was fed up with people making money from him. He asked if she was shocked by what he had told her. She was shocked, but she tried not to show it. She promised to keep what he told her secret.

Fred was thinner and more haggard-looking after seven months in custody. His fingers were stained yellow from smoking. He complained of arthritis, diminished eyesight and deafness, and as a result he had been given a hearing aid and new glasses. As summer shaded into autumn, some of Fred's visitors observed that he was deteriorating mentally as well. 'He talked at length about his childhood and younger years. Seemed more depressed, more likely to cry for no apparent reason and more into a Mills & Boon vision of the world. I think his personality grows ever more fragile,' his probation officer noted on 28 September, the day before Fred's fifty-third birthday. This astute probation worker wasn't dazzled or confused by Fred, as some people were. 'During interviews he rambles somewhat, usually talking about his early life, childhood loves and relationships. He tells stories in great detail, elaborating on exact locations, car number plates, etc. I tend to let him ramble because it gives me an opportunity to listen to him,' the officer wrote after a meeting in October. While what Fred said was often misleading, the officer recognised that the way in which he spoke was revealing. 'My gut feeling is that he is becoming more depressed and more fragile. I feel that he rushes more easily to tears and his professed view of the world is ever more Mills & Boon – a world in which he is ever the stereotypic gentleman, opening car doors for young ladies, helping them courteously, making love but never having sex. In his early country years he relates to his "friends" the badgers and foxes ... my main worry [is] that Fred will escape into total fantasy before I can put together a balanced view of him and events.'

Fred's attitude to Rose fluctuated between heartbreak and loathing. When his eldest son, Steve, visited Fred that month, he said that his dad told him he was considering committing suicide to protect Rose, as if he still loved her. 'He is always in tears when I see him,' Steve told me in November, having just visited both his father and mother. Rose told Steve that she couldn't bear to look at Fred any more. 'She says it turns her stomach every time she stands by him in the court. Sad really. I never expected Mum to say that of Dad.' However, Fred spoke with Steve in the same contradictory way as he spoke to the police and Janet Leach. One minute he denied any involvement in the murders, the next he spoke about further crimes he had committed at 'the farm'. 'He said [he] could make as much noise as he [wanted] there ... because it was in the middle of nowhere.' Yet he seemed intent on pleading not guilty. It made no sense.

Meanwhile, Fred was trying to improve his literacy. 'He is writing a book. Each chapter is dedicated to women,' Steve told me. 'He is writing about Anna (*sic*) McFall at the moment ... He has just started it.' Anne had loomed large in Fred's mind since Rose turned against him, as if he wanted to reassign his affections to someone who could not let him down. 'I was loved by an angel, Anna, I met Anna in Glasgow ...' Fred began his memoirs,[16] which came to be known by that name. He wrote in a child's hand, his spelling and grammar atrocious, but it was just about possible to follow the story. Like his police interviews, *I Was Loved By An Angel* is a mash-up of fact and fiction. He described Anne McFall as 'a happy and joyful young lady' who was 'more of a mother' to his girls than Rena. Anne came to Fred one night wearing a negligée. He described their first night of lovemaking in the purple prose of romantic fiction, 'like heaven it was'. Afterwards, he serenaded her, singing and playing his acoustic guitar. Further blissful nights followed, kissing and cuddling by moonlight, after which Anne slept with her head resting on his chest. All Rena wanted was to 'be a prostitute', he wrote, while Anne wanted to 'be my wife and mother of my children'. After Fred and Anne moved to the Brockworth caravan site, they got into the habit of sitting on an old air raid shelter in the evening looking at the lights of Gloucester. 'We were standing on top of the world.' They

---

[16] Anna being Fred's name for Anne McFall. I have made light corrections to make quotations comprehensible.

planned a life together, hoping to marry and have a child. Fred didn't just love Anne. 'I worship her,' he wrote, using the verb he had once applied to Rose. 'She was my angel. Rena could be the Devil ... at last I would be getting married for love.' Having a baby with Anne would be 'the most wonderful thing in the world.' Fred wrote about shopping with Anne for maternity dresses, but no more after that. He didn't attempt to describe when, how or why she died.

Instead, he switched to writing about Shirley Robinson, another extramarital affair whereby he got a woman pregnant then killed her. Fred claimed that Rose's father introduced him to Shirley, when Bill Letts was proprietor of the Green Lantern café, portraying his father-in-law as a sexual predator. Fred offered Shirley a room at 25 Cromwell Street and made her pregnant, as she requested, telling her to keep this secret. 'I said Rose is the boss over me and the house, so don't trust Rose. She can be violent.' He claimed to be humiliated by Rose's infidelities, and appalled by her brutality. 'I couldn't believe how hard Rose could be to me, she had no heart and was so cold. To get a kiss off Rose was so rare ... all she wanted to do was to slap you in the face and you slap her in the face.' As with Anne McFall, this chapter ended before Shirley's death.

Death was on Fred's mind as he scribbled in his cell (DC-8). Rose's birthday was approaching and Fred wrote her a love letter that was part last will and testament:

To Rose West, Stephen, May and Mo,[17]
Well Rose it is your birthday on 29/11/94 and you will be 41 and still beautiful and [you] still love me and I love you. We will always be in love. The most wonderful thing in my life

---

17 Fred's nickname for his daughter Tara.

ROSE DON'T WANT ME

is when I met you. Our love was special to us. So love keep your promises to me, you know what they are. Where we are put together for ever and ever, it is up to you. Lay Heather by us. We loved Heather. I would love for Charmaine to be by Heather with Rena. Well, Rose, you will always be Mrs West all over the world. That is wonderful to me and you. I have not got you a present, but all I have is my life. I will give it for (sic) you my darling. When you are ready, come to me. I will be waiting for you.

IN
LOVEING MEMORY
Fred West
Rose West
REST IN PIECE WEAR NO
SHADOW FALLS IN PERFECT
PIECE HE WAITS FOR ROSE
[H]IS WIFE

He drew a tombstone around these last words as if this was the inscription he wanted to have carved into their gravestone, but he didn't send the letter. Thirteen days later, Fred wrote to his wife again. 'To Rose, as in life as in death our love will never die ... the world knows you are my wife and I am your husband, and always will be. You will become a widow. I love you darling ...' He didn't send that letter either. The next day Fred and Rose saw each other again briefly at Gloucester Magistrates' Court. Again, she ignored him. They were scheduled to meet next at the committal hearing in February 1995, by which time Fred would have to decide what his plea would be when they came to trial.

When Janet Leach saw Fred on 16 December she said that

he seemed 'fine', but she misread him, as did the staff at HMP Winson Green. Despite years of abuse, Anna Marie remained devoted to her father. She said that he treated her more like a girlfriend. The link between father and daughter was strange but strong and she understood him. She had been visiting him in prison and talking to him by phone. He had spoken to Anna Marie about wanting to 'finish it myself', and about his funeral arrangements, telling his daughter that 'Rose don't want to know me no more'. He asked for a lock of his daughter's hair. She was concerned about him. 'I've got to go now, my angel,' he told her at the end of their last phone call before Christmas, blowing a kiss down the line. It sounded like the last goodbye.

Around the same time Fred told his probation officer that his case was a 'mess' and he complained to one of the prison doctors of having trouble sleeping, and being worried about Rose. John Bennett had been concerned about Fred's well-being since his transfer to Winson Green. He had been assured by the governor that prison staff would watch Fred closely. Aside from the day he was admitted, and the upset over Howard Ogden, the staff felt that Fred was doing well. 'F. West was a model prisoner. He never gave us any bother, and discipline and behaviour-wise he gave no cause for concern,' wrote a senior officer. Dr James McMaster saw Fred before Christmas and said that he 'did not appear to be a danger to himself'.

Janet Leach was meant to pay Fred a Christmas visit, but she rang the prison to say that the weather was too bad to travel to Birmingham. Fred had previously complained that his family weren't coming to see him enough. Now Leach wasn't coming either. Above all, Fred had lost Rose. On Boxing Day he was seen crying in his cell and didn't come out for exercise for two days. However, Fred bade the staff a friendly 'Good morning' when he was unlocked for breakfast at 7:30 AM on Sunday, 1 January 1995. He was seen by a doctor as a matter of routine at 9:30 AM, when he appeared 'normal and had no problems or complaints', but his inmate friend noticed that something was off. 'On that Sunday, Fred didn't seem his usual self.' Fred showed no interest in prison gossip when his friend tried to chat to him in the yard, talking instead of the old days in Much Marcle. Fred also complained of the cold. It was snowing in Birmingham on New Year's Day. He said that he wanted to go back to his cell.

Fred was let out again to collect his lunch at 11:30 AM, joking with the officer who served him that the chicken legs on the hot plate were so puny that they looked more like pigeon legs. The other choice was pork. Staff ate their lunch in their room while the inmates were locked in their cells to eat. When an officer came to DC-8 to unlock Fred, just before 1:00 PM, his door was jammed. A second officer came to his colleague's aid, and together they forced the door. 'As we got it open I saw a body hanging down just on the other side,' said the second officer. Fred was hanging by a ligature at the end of a seven-foot rope, made of strips of green bed sheets which he had stitched together, using the sewing kit the prison had provided him with for sewing buttons on shirts, then threaded through the ventilation grille over his cell door, having stood on a bag of shirts to hang himself. It would have taken weeks to make the rope. Fred had planned his death.

'His feet were off the ground, his head was to one side with saliva coming out of his mouth, his lips were blue. I put my arms around his legs,' said a third officer who arrived almost immediately. 'Someone undid the ligature and West slumped forward over my right shoulder ... I got him on to the bed ...

THE FRED WEST TAPES

There was no pulse but he was warm. [I] extended his airway by tilting his head back ... his tongue was yellow and swollen ... I remember saying, "I can't get any air into him."' The three officers tried to revive him with chest compressions while shouting for more help. There were soon five officers crowded into the cell. Then a nurse arrived. 'I went straight to the cell and saw West lying flat on the bed. Cardiac massage was being given by one of the prison officers ... and mouth-to-mouth resuscitation,' the nurse said, '[but] initial observation indicated that he was already deceased. His skin was greyish, lips blue, and feeling for a pulse there was none. There was no sign of any breathing.'

'There's nothing more we can do,' she said.

They sealed the cell and waited for the prison doctor, who pronounced Fred dead at 1:40 PM. The cell was then searched, officers going through Fred's belongings. Like many prisoners he had an eclectic collection of bits and pieces in his cell. Along with a lock of hair, a photograph album, a packet of Benson & Hedges cigarettes, Friday's *Sun*, a hidden piece of razor, and a pork chop in a plastic bag, were 'miscellaneous personal papers' including several notes Fred had written to Rose. This last one was printed:

TO
ROSE WEST
HAPPY NEW YEAR
DARLING ALL
MY LOVE.
FRED WEST
ALL MY LOVE
FOR EVER AND
EVER

ROSE DON'T WANT ME

He had also left graffiti on the cell walls, writing: 'Freddy, the mass murderer from Gloucester.' It was his epitaph. He seemed to believe that he had achieved something by destroying people's lives.

14

THE DEPTHS OF HUMAN DEPRAVITY

New Year's Day, 1995
HMP Winson Green

> 'Fred West is dead and I've got to take the responsibility for what he done.'
> ROSE WEST

When John Bennett arrived in Birmingham – having dashed across the country from his home in Gloucestershire, where he had been cooking the family lunch on New Year's Day – he found Fred West dead on a trolley in the mortuary in Newton Street. Rigor mortis had started to set in, and as the detective superintendent looked down at the face of his nemesis the tightening muscles in Fred's face appeared to curl his dead lips into a smile, 'that sickeningly smug grin that was his trademark'. In addition to this Joker-like grimace there were bits of tissue paper stuck to his lips, tissue the prison officers had put on his face before attempting resuscitation, not wanting to exchange bodily fluids with him. Fred had seldom looked so weird.

THE FRED WEST TAPES

Bennett attended the post-mortem that evening, which was conducted by the regional Home Office pathologist Peter Acland. He examined Fred's body for signs of foul play (there were none), and as per routine he cut the skull open and pulled his brain out to look it over for scarring, or other signs of obvious damage. Dr Acland then sliced through the brain to see if there was anything abnormal inside. Part of the family folklore was that Fred suffered brain damage as a youth in a motorcycle accident, and after falling from a fire escape. The West family GP supported this theory when Fred came to court in 1961 charged with incest, suggesting that Fred might possibly be epileptic as a result of his head injuries. It might also be presumed that the brain of a man as aberrant at Fred West *should* look unusual, but Dr Acland saw nothing peculiar when he held Fred's brain in his hands. This didn't rule out brain damage, just that there was nothing wrong to the naked eye. He put the pieces of brain into a plastic bag, which in turn was placed in Fred's stomach cavity with other organs that had been removed for examination, all routine stuff. The pathologist was in no doubt that Fred killed himself by hanging, which would be the verdict at the inquest.

Fred's death dominated the news. I worked on the front page story at the *Daily Mirror* in London, having moved across from the *Sunday Mirror*. Sunday, 1 January 1995 was by coincidence my first day in my new job. As I wrote my copy I wondered why Fred had killed himself, and what his death meant for the case that had become a significant part of my life with my book, *Fred & Rose*, half-written. I shared in the widespread surprise that the highest profile remand prisoner in the UK had managed to kill himself before his trial. What had gone wrong?

Almost everybody who dealt with Fred at HMP Winson Green gave a statement and aside from the probation officer and

THE DEPTHS OF HUMAN DEPRAVITY

his inmate friend they all stated that he appeared to be normal leading up to his death. The prison governor wrote that Fred gave him and his staff 'no cause for concern ... In fact he was an exceptionally polite, courteous and cheerful prisoner'. He seemed happy playing pool and sewing buttons on shirts. 'I was very surprised that he hanged himself.' As to why he did it, it seemed that Fred killed himself because he was in despair about his case, also possibly to help Rose, despite turning against her in recent months. Inconsistency was one of Fred's characteristics. He may have thought that the charges against Rose would be dropped if he was dead. That was her hope. 'I think there was a sense of relief,' says her solicitor, Leo Goatley, who visited Rose in prison that afternoon after the news broke. Far from being grief-stricken, Rose reacted as if she had been handed a Get Out of Gaol Free card. 'Certainly no feelings of loss, sorrow, bereavement ... On the contrary, I think that she glowed with a certain relief.'

The impact on the West children was complex. May was driving when she heard the news on the car radio. She pulled over and wept 'uncontrollably'. Her half-sister Anna Marie wept 'hysterically', and after downing pills and drink she had to have her stomach pumped. Fred was a beast, but he was their father. Barry West saw the suicide as the coward's way out. 'He got away with murdering all them people and my sister, and abusing me and my sisters,' he told me. 'I'm completely disgusted my dad killed himself.' Reaction varied among the victims' families. Some relatives like Juanita Mott's sister Belinda were angry. Others saw Fred's suicide as justice, even a relief. Lucy Partington's sister Marian heard the news after returning from a New Year's Eve party. 'People [asked] didn't I feel cheated? But that didn't seem to come into it really,' Marian told me. 'My initial thought, I remember feeling, was that it was a sort of divine justice. Good, I won't have to look at him now. I won't have to see him [in court].'

News of Fred's death overshadowed the announcement that DC Hazel Savage had been recognised with an MBE in the new year's honours list. Gloucestershire police trumpeted the award with a press release: 'Welcoming the award the Chief Constable of Gloucestershire, Mr Tony Butler, said "Hazel Savage has [had] an exceptional police career [and] I can speak for the whole Constabulary when I say this award is richly deserved ..."' The chief constable almost choked on his words a week later when it was reported in a newspaper that Savage had met with a literary agent in recent months to discuss writing about the case in a book. When tackled by her bosses, she admitted the story was essentially true but said that she had not divulged any private information, she hadn't received any money, and she had written to the agent to say that she didn't want to go ahead. Nevertheless, this undermined the integrity of the police questioning when Fred accused people around him of profiting from his story and the detectives in the room – including Savage – expressed shock at such an idea (as we read in chapter eight). Savage was taken off the inquiry, and found guilty of discreditable conduct.

While John Bennett felt let down by Hazel Savage, 'a huge embarrassment', he soon faced bigger problems. 'When Fred killed himself the clamour from some quarters, including the Lord Chief Justice, [was] that [Rose] should be released,' he says, 'the CPS didn't think there was any evidence against her.' The matter was decided at the committal hearing in February, by which time Rose had been charged with a tenth murder. Late in the day, Dr David Whittaker had been provided with a high-quality photograph of Charmaine showing her baby teeth, which she was in the process of shedding when she died. The photo was dated 29 April 1971. By comparing her teeth in the photograph

THE DEPTHS OF HUMAN DEPRAVITY

with the teeth in her skull, Whittaker calculated that Charmaine died no more than three months after the photo was taken. Fred was in prison nearly all that time, which put Rose in the frame for the murder. In which case, Fred would have merely disposed of the body. Personally, I was never entirely convinced by this.

Rose's barrister Sasha Wass tried to 'stay' the prosecution at the committal by arguing that the case had taken too long to come to court, it had been prejudiced by the press, and there was a lack of direct evidence against her client. The magistrate ruled however that Rose would stand trial. The popular press billed it with typical but unnecessary hyperbole as 'the trial of the century'.

* * *

'I make it clear from the outset that there is no direct evidence of anyone – Frederick West or Rosemary West – killing any of these girls. Nobody says, "I saw Frederick stab" or "I saw Rosemary strangle,"' the prosecutor, Brian Leveson QC, said in his opening speech at Winchester Crown Court on 6 October 1995. Rose was pleading not guilty to ten murder charges. 'The evidence is circumstantial,' explained Leveson, which Richard Ferguson QC, defending, translated for the jury as meaning 'speculative'. The seven-week trial was intense and fascinating, partly because the outcome was uncertain.

Rose had gained weight in custody. Her skin was sallow, her face was jowly. She dressed conservatively for court, usually wearing a white blouse with a long plain skirt and a yellow metal cross on a chain for luck. Her short dark hair flopped over her large spectacles. She showed almost no emotion as over sixty witnesses gave evidence against her, including Caroline Owens who told the court that she was speaking for the women who had not lived, as she had, to tell their tale.

THE FRED WEST TAPES

The evidence of Anna Marie was harrowing, as she described being raped and abused by Fred and Rose as a child. Although she had remained close to her father, she had no love for Rose and believed that it was her duty to tell the court what she knew. Everybody in court seemed to hold their breath as she revealed her extraordinary story. 'I was screaming and crying, and Rosemary sat on my face and my father was forcing my legs open,' she said of the first time, speaking slowly and quietly. 'I had my hands bound and I was gagged.' Her father made her pregnant when she was fifteen, an ectopic pregnancy which she miscarried. Despite all this, she said that she loved her father. She was so mixed up as a kid that she used to tell Fred that she would marry him. 'I would have done everything for both Rosemary and my father,' she said, looking across the court at Rose. As she spoke, Anna Marie fingered a locket. It contained the ashes of her dead sister Charmaine.

The jury was shown crime scene photographs, including grotesque pictures of human remains; belts, straps and cords used to bind the victims, and gags to stop them screaming, as Brian Leveson argued. Up in the public gallery, the seats arranged like circle seats in a theatre, families of the victims were not prepared for everything they saw and heard from the well of the court below. 'You listen. You know what's going on, and you can hear the gasps of other people listening,' recalls Juanita Mott's sister Belinda in *Fred & Rose West: A British Horror Story*. 'Me, personally, I couldn't take it all in ... It was just how? How can they do it. How? Or why.' A jury visit to 25 Cromwell Street was arranged, the jury transported from Winchester by coach to Gloucester, their progress tracked by a helicopter hired to capture aerial shots for the TV news. This 'view' helped bring home to the jurors how small the murder house was. Extracts from Rose's police interviews were read, interviews in which she said that Heather telephoned home after her disappearance, which was impossible; as was her claim that she last saw Rena after she came to collect Charmaine from Midland Road. Such slips were rare, however. Rose had been much more careful in what she said to the police than Fred. At the end of the prosecution case, having attended court every day, I was in no doubt that Rose was a dreadful person, and that she was a liar. But where was the evidence that she had murdered anyone?

Rose insisted on going into the witness box in her defence. Questioned gently at first by her QC, she emphasised how young she was when she met Fred. 'He promised me the world. He promised me everything, and because I was so young I suppose I fell for his lies.' She wanted a home and family, and Fred offered her that life. 'I was in love with him at that time.' She denied any knowledge of the murders, saying that Fred sent her out of the house to have sex with other men and she didn't know what he did when she was absent. She now saw Fred as the Devil. 'I know it might sound daft, but I saw him with horns and complete with a Satanic grin, because he never looked sorry for what he did or anything.' The exaggerated way in which she spoke rang false, as did her tone of injured innocence.

> **Rose West**: It is all very well for somebody to say I said this, and I said something else now, because I am the one in the spotlight. Fred West is dead and I've got to take responsibility for what he done ...
> **Brian Leveson QC**: What is happening, Mrs West, is this: it is not everybody dumping everything on you; it is you dumping everything on Fred West. Is it not?
> **Rose West**: Fred is responsible for these murders, sir, it wasn't me.

THE FRED WEST TAPES

Rose knew what Fred had said in his police interviews, and she insisted that some of the tapes were played to the jury, despite being warned by her team that there might be repercussions. Fred's spirit had hovered over the trial from the start, his name mentioned in virtually every exchange, but now his gruff voice was heard in court, describing Heather's murder, and insisting that Rose knew nothing about this or any of the murders.

> **Fred West**: I mean, the thing I'd like to stress ... Rose knew nothing at all ... Rose used to say, 'Christ, I wish we'd try and get in contact and find out where Heather is.' Although they didn't get on, she still loved her ... she hasn't done nothing ...
> **DC Hazel Savage**: Have you told anybody outside your family at all?
> **Fred West**: Nobody whatsoever, never, nobody, it's been kept in me all that time.

The jury heard what Fred and Rose wanted them to hear. However, the prosecution was then allowed to play extracts from other interviews to rebut this evidence, extracts which showed Fred to be an unreliable witness. Having discussed this with her family, Brian Leveson had the jury listen to Fred's account of dating Lucy Partington in Cheltenham, when in reality she was away at university in Exeter, as an example of the lies he sometimes told. Leveson also called rebuttal witnesses who said that Fred had given them versions of events completely different to what he told the police. The star witness in this respect was the former appropriate adult, Janet Leach. She said that Fred told her within days of his arrest that Rose was involved in the murders, and the Wests had a pact: '[He said] he would take the blame for everything, and that he

THE DEPTHS OF HUMAN DEPRAVITY

would sort everything out.' This sounded like the truth at last, but there was a problem.

During the trial, several prosecution witnesses admitted to having been paid or promised money by newspapers and television companies, which was used by the defence to suggest that they may have exaggerated their evidence. Janet Leach denied on oath to Brian Leveson that she had made a media deal, as she had previously assured the police that she was an untainted witness. During cross-examination, Leach had a funny turn. She took ill and was driven to hospital where, the court heard, she could neither speak nor move her legs. When she returned to court four days later in a wheelchair, escorted by a doctor, Leach was confronted with evidence she had not told the truth. She had a deal with Mirror Group Newspapers, my newspaper group, giving the *Daily Mirror* an option on a book. The deal was worth a notional £100,000, and an advance of £7,500 had been paid to her partner. The deal had been done in secret by a colleague of mine. I knew nothing about it. Leach tried to deny it at first when she was asked about it in court, but grudgingly admitted it when Ferguson produced a letter of agreement she had signed with the *Mirror*.

> **Richard Ferguson QC**: You were ... asked [by Brian Leveson], 'Have you spoken to them about it?' referring to the press, and you said, 'No.' That just was not true, was it?
> **Janet Leach**: No.

Other witnesses had taken money from the press, but they didn't try to hide the fact in court. 'Let us not mince words,' the judge, Justice Sir Charles Mantell, told the jury, 'she lied to you.' For a moment the case teetered. There was mention of the jury being discharged, which could mean a retrial, something that nobody wanted. The police feared it might not be possible. The judge held steady. After closing speeches, he sent the jury out on 20 November, the twenty-ninth court day, after a summing-up during which he told the jurors, among other things, that when they considered what Fred West said in his police interviews it wasn't a choice between truth and lies. 'There is the possibility of what he said being a halfway house.' The deliberations of juries are always mysterious, and this jury was being asked to make sense of subtle circumstantial evidence that was meant to prove, as Brian Leveson said, that Fred and Rose were 'in it together'. Privately, Leveson wasn't certain that he had done enough. 'You're thinking, is there some point I've missed? What are the jury thinking about?' he reflects in *Fred & Rose West: A British Horror Story*. 'It was by no means a given that Rosemary West would be convicted.' The only person who seemed confident was Rose. She thought that she would get off. The tension as we waited for the verdicts was so thick that you could hardly breathe.

After a long and nervous wait we were called back into court. The jury found Rose guilty of all ten murders. The verdicts were unanimous. Justice Mantell lost no time in handing down a life sentence, later changed to a rare whole life sentence, meaning that Rose would never be released. Two charges of rape and two of indecent assault would remain on file. Rose showed no emotion in the dock but she sobbed down in the cells after sentencing. Later she expressed anger, still insisting that she was innocent. Leo Goatley applied for leave to appeal. When this application was refused, Rose told Goatley that she didn't want to pursue it further. 'I've decided I'm gonna spend the rest of my life in prison,' she said.

'Does that mean you are admitting to any of this?'

THE DEPTHS OF HUMAN DEPRAVITY

'Oh no.'

She has never changed her story.

★ ★ ★

A few months later John West stood trial in Bristol for rape and indecent assault. The victims were his nieces Anna Marie and May. Normally, rape victims are not identified in public, but Anna Marie waived her anonymity, as she had at Rose's trial, to give evidence against her uncle; May later wrote about her uncle raping her. The night before the jury was sent out, on 28 November 1996, evidently believing that he would be convicted, John West committed suicide. Like his brother, he chose to hang himself rather than suffer a prison sentence. He hanged himself at home in his garage. Like Fred, he took many secrets with him.

Meanwhile, Rose was moved around high security prisons, spending time in HMP Durham at the start of her life sentence, where she struck up a brief friendship with Myra Hindley. She forged a more lasting relationship with a prison visitor who she came to call Mum, a vicar's wife who became like a second mother to her, and prefers not to be named. 'Mum' took Rose at face value when she described herself as a victim of two men: '[Fred] was an inhuman monster [but] she had a hideous time with her father [too]. What life has she ever had?' asks Mum. 'I am not her judge. She was judged, she was tried, and went to prison forever. That's between her and God.' The women kept in touch by telephone after Rose was moved to her next prison. 'People say, "What do you talk about?" We talk politics, we talk about the planet, we talk God, we talk about knitting, sewing, *Strictly Come Dancing*,' says Mum. 'All she wants is to get on with her life sentence, and occupy herself the best way she can ... she just wants peace.'

THE FRED WEST TAPES

The pacific woman whom Mum describes – quietly sewing in her cell, asking Mum to phone in her *Strictly* vote – is not the person her children knew. The children who survived 25 Cromwell Street were scarred by the experience, few more badly damaged than the youngest boy. Along with four of his siblings, Barry West was taken into care in 1992, when Fred and Rose were arrested for child abuse. Barry, who had just turned twelve, was allowed to choose a new name (which I shall not reveal), and a court order was made protecting the identity of Barry and his siblings until they reached adulthood. Barry was sent to live with foster parents in Kent, Dave and Brenda Foreman, who had experience of dealing with challenging children. 'He was a likeable lad. The thing is he got these problems,' Dave sighs. 'A very, very tragic case, the worst one I dealt with all the time I was fostering.' The Foremans noticed that Barry hardly seemed to sleep, too traumatised to close his eyes at night. Like his father, he was dishonest. When Dave and Brenda bought him a bike, he sold it for cash telling them that it had been stolen. Another time he stole £1,000 that Dave had at home for his business. One morning the Foremans woke to discover that Barry and another foster child had driven their car into the garden wall. Barry was also volatile, the sort of person who could turn nasty in a snap. One night their adult daughter, Trace, found Barry sitting alone in the dark with a knife, 'and of course I was frightened.' Barry started to abuse substances. 'I was sniffing petrol. I was having bad night terrors ... I was drinking,' he admitted. 'I set the bedroom on fire.' Around the time that Fred and Rose were arrested, Barry threatened to set himself on fire. As a result he was locked up in a psychiatric unit under the Mental Health Act. 'That was the first time.'

Like his dad and older brother, Barry did building work in adult life, but he spent a lot of time in hospital, often sectioned

THE DEPTHS OF HUMAN DEPRAVITY

under the Mental Health Act. 'I was head-butting the walls. I was dissociating. I was just going mad ... I kept seeing my sister killed, and getting raped. It's such an overwhelming feeling, it makes you flip out.' He was diagnosed with Dissociation Identity Disorder, a split personality where he would inhabit different characters, and talk about himself in the third person. 'When I dissociate, I scream at the sky.' He was haunted by his past, and who his parents were. 'Like father like son. I hate that expression. It makes me feel sick, because I am the complete opposite of my father.' However, he could be aggressive and abusive like Fred, and like his dad he was often in trouble with the police for petty offences. 'I've been to prison a few times, yeah – burglary, car crime, theft.' When he wanted money in 2002, Barry sold an interview to the *News of the World*, in which he claimed to have witnessed Heather's murder. If that was a figment of his imagination, he convinced himself that it was true.

Barry's girlfriend contacted me out of the blue in 2010, asking if I would help him tell his story. I had just finished writing a biography of Paul McCartney and was absorbed in planning another book, so the West case seemed far behind me, and when we spoke by phone Barry decided that he wasn't ready to go ahead. I told him that he could get back in touch again in the future if he wanted to, not expecting to hear from him again. Eight years later he sent me a message via my website. 'I did witness Heather being murdered,' he insisted when we spoke this time, sensing correctly that I didn't believe him on that point. His story of abuse and suffering convinced me as being authentic, however. 'I got raped a couple of times by my mum's punters, because she was a prostitute ... I witnessed a lot of horrendous things.' Our conversation then took a bizarre turn: 'He got beaten up and bullied. Then at home he got abused and raped.' He? I realised that Barry was talking about himself in the third person, which was a facet of his split personality. Barry told me that he had been in and out of psychiatric hospitals and revealed that he was in a psychiatric unit now, speaking to me on a mobile phone. In normal circumstances, I would have ended the conversation there. One of the first lessons I learned as a young journalist was to be wary of crazy people coming to you with stories, they can't be relied upon and are almost always trouble, but Barry's circumstances were exceptional. 'I am Fred and Rose West's son, so I have mental health problems,' he told me, 'they fucked me up.' This made sense and it seemed like a story worth telling. The West children were victims. Their experiences were important, complex and little understood. In the years since the murder case not much had been heard of any of them, save Steve West who was jailed in 2004 for having sex with a fourteen-year-old girl, whom he made pregnant when he was thirty-one, thus extending the family history of sexual abuse into the next generation. Barry felt that Steve had let them all down.

On a freezing day in April 2018, during the cold snap known as the Beast from the East, I visited Barry in a psychiatric hospital in Kent. He was on a secure ward with a heavy locked door, but he was allowed visitors. After I was buzzed in, the security door shut behind me with a clunk. Once inside, the ward was overheated and stuffy. Barry was thirty-seven years old, small and dark with his mother's sullen demeanour. I spent an hour talking with him that afternoon, at the end of which I remarked that I had not seen him smile. He said he had nothing to smile about. He admitted to having a criminal record (his convictions were fairly minor and they were spent), and a history of drug abuse, which he claimed to have conquered. He assured me that he was feeling better and that he was keen to make a new start. I said that there was nothing I could do

THE DEPTHS OF HUMAN DEPRAVITY

while he was in hospital, but once he was discharged, and well, we might be able to arrange a television interview as part of a documentary to mark twenty-five years since the start of the West investigation. I was also planning to update my book.

Several months later, after he had been discharged, I met Barry on the south coast of England where the authorities had provided him with a flat. He lived on benefits, spending empty days smoking and chatting up women on Facebook. He had an ex-partner and a child somewhere, but he told me that he didn't see his child. 'Life has kicked me so hard so many times I am literally immune to pain now. I get kicked in the bollocks almost every day. I'm not bothered any more,' he told me. 'I just want a little tiny bite of life before I go. It's like there's this big cake in the middle of the table and everyone is having a go on it, and I am trying to get in to get a slice before I pop my clogs. That hasn't happened yet. I've been close, but it hasn't happened yet. Who knows this time I might get my slice ... I seriously believe I will meet a nice person, go back to work [and] be happy.'

I took the project to an independent television production company and arranged for Barry to be paid for his contribution to a documentary, which gave him the money he wanted. I would conduct the interview as the producer, and he agreed that I could write about him. His would be one of several voices in the documentary, but an important one because he had never spoken on TV. Lawyers were consulted and psychiatric support was provided. We did everything we could to look after Barry, abiding by Ofcom rules that regulate the television industry. Barry thanked me, but he became erratic as filming approached.

When I came to his flat to pick him up for the interview, he threw a tantrum and pelted me with crisp packets. I calmed him down and got him into the hire car. We were due to film in a hotel the following day. We had dinner that evening in the hotel restaurant. When Barry saw the menu, he asked me if he could order steak and chips. When I said yes he was as pleased as a child. I noticed that he clasped his steak knife with his fist. His handwriting was also that of a child's. These were things that he had never learned to do properly. While there was a childlike quality to Barry, he could turn nasty, and even in a good mood he was not easy company. Midway through dinner he abruptly left the table. I assumed that he had gone to bed and so ordered dessert, relieved to have some time to myself. The cameraman was due to arrive and I was looking forward to having a chat with him over coffee. Then I heard Barry yelling in the lobby. He was having a row with the manager, who had refused to give him a key card to get back into his room. In the few hours we had been at the hotel, Barry had managed to lose his key card several times and he had been wandering the corridors trying random doors. As I arrived in the lobby, Barry was shouting racial insults at the manager. He then threw a card at him. The manager told Barry to leave the hotel, and picked up the phone to call the police.

'Please don't,' I said, intervening. 'I'll look after my friend.'

Barry was freaking out. 'Do you know who I am?' he screamed at the manager, loud enough for everyone in the lobby to hear. 'I am Fred West's son!'

I couldn't believe it. 'Please calm down,' I told him. I promised the manager that I would take charge of my friend, if he let him stay, and escorted him to his bedroom. I slept that night in the room across the hall, wondering if I should cancel the interview.

Next day was equally fraught. Barry disappeared mid-morning when we were due to start filming, he simply ran off, at which point I almost washed my hands of the project, thinking how foolish I was to have allowed myself to get involved with this man. Barry reappeared suddenly an hour later, apologised to me

THE DEPTHS OF HUMAN DEPRAVITY

(which was rare) and said that he was ready. We had agreed to film him in silhouette, and we would disguise his voice, so he wouldn't be recognised when the documentary was broadcast. When we got him seated in the hotel meeting room – which we had blacked out as a temporary studio, the lights and cameras were adjusted and the director of photography was happy – Barry answered my questions about his childhood, including being raped by Rose's punter. He talked about his love for Heather and the culture of secrecy at 25 Cromwell Street. He admitted to mental health issues, and a drug problem. He became emotional as he recalled the cruelty he suffered. It was the small details, like Rose forcing him to eat her sprouts until he was sick, that upset him most. He wept. After a break to smoke a cigarette and compose himself, he said that he thought his mother was the driving force in the murders, but ultimately Fred and Rose were as bad as each other. 'To me they were the Devil and the Devil's wife ... People often ask me, were they mad or were they evil? I haven't made up my mind yet. Maybe a bit of both.'

Barry crashed out in his room after his interview, and I stayed on for a second night in the hotel to make sure that he was alright. I was asleep when I heard knocking on my door. It was Barry, dressed, unsmiling, staring at me. At times like this Barry's resemblance to Fred and Rose could be unnerving.

'Can you drive me home, mate?' he asked.

'When?'

'Now.'

'It's the middle of the night.'

'It's twelve.'

'It's dark out.'

It took him a moment to realise that it was twelve midnight, not twelve noon.

'Can I get a drink then, mate?' he asked me.

THE FRED WEST TAPES

I took Barry down to the hotel bar where, to our surprise, a masked ball was concluding. Tipsy men and women in evening dress and Venetian masks were lurching about, laughing and flirting with each other. I made my way through this inebriated crowd to the bar to buy Barry a glass of orange pop – like his father, he didn't drink alcohol – while he waited for me on a sofa, sitting between two women wearing snap-on bird masks. Barry stared ahead in bewilderment as if he had woken up in Hell.

When morning came, I drove Barry home. Being with him all weekend I discovered that he had been lying about his drug use. He promised me when we embarked on the film that he had quit drugs, and our documentary would help him finance a new start in life, but he finally admitted that he was using heroin daily. He said that he only felt well enough to function when he had heroin. The rest of the time he was as sick as a dog. I told him that he now had an opportunity to turn his life around. He was out of hospital, as he wanted. He had made money from the documentary, which is why he approached me. 'You need to stop using drugs and start again. It's not too late,' I said as I drove him along the coast to his flat. He looked away sadly across the sea, as if I would never understand.

In the new year, I contacted Barry to tell him that editing was finished. He was still worried that people might recognise him. I offered to show him the finished film in advance on a laptop to reassure him that he was in silhouette, his voice changed, as we had agreed. He didn't want to see it. Meanwhile, transmission of the documentary was scheduled. I had written an article for the *Radio Times*, and some of the contributors were appearing on breakfast TV to talk about the programme, which was listed in the newspapers and was being trailed on TV leading up to a 9:00 PM broadcast.

On the afternoon of transmission day, as I worked at my desk,

THE DEPTHS OF HUMAN DEPRAVITY

I received a dramatic phone call. Barry had suddenly withdrawn from our film. Although he had signed a contract and release form, and been paid, he didn't want the broadcaster to transmit his interview. Due to his fragile mental state the broadcaster acquiesced. This all happened hours before the film was due to be shown. A repeat programme was shown instead at 9:00 PM. Our film was then re-edited to remove Barry's contribution – cutting about six minutes in a forty-five minute documentary – before being transmitted a couple of weeks later. Despite Barry's absence, it rated highly.

The sad coda to this story came during the Covid pandemic. Barry went into rehab in Scotland where he was weaned off heroin, not for the first time. He then returned to Kent, where he slipped back into his old ways and was admitted to a psychiatric unit. After being discharged in February 2020, he was provided with a flat at a 'supported living' facility in Maidstone known as the Beeches. A team of professionals supported Barry. They found him challenging. He had been addicted to heroin for years and despite numerous overdoses, and cures, he didn't seem to want to quit drugs. He complained of chronic shoulder and neck pain, probably psychosomatic pain, and believed that opioids were the only answer. When doctors didn't provide the drugs he craved he became angry. He was considered a danger to himself and to others. When he was admitted to hospital in April 2020 with an overdose he told the staff that he was in so much pain he 'didn't find life worth living'. A doctor noted that Barry kept a 'suicide bag' with a rope to hang himself. He had also become dependent on a system which he resented. 'I'm so institutionalised, it's ridiculous,' he once told me, admitting that he preferred life in hospital, where he was given drugs and had routine, though when he was there he wanted to leave. I realised belatedly that the reason I found Barry relatively OK to deal with when we first met was that he was in hospital on medication. His behaviour deteriorated after discharge.

Eighteen months after I last had contact with Barry, on 27 August 2020, he went to Chatham to score drugs before returning to Maidstone. The next morning a member of staff came to his flat to give Barry his medication and found him dead, slumped over a coffee table. He was forty. The police found no evidence of an intruder, or suicide. Barry had died after his lungs filled with vomit. A cocktail of drugs was in his system: prescription drugs including buprenorphine and codeine, also traces of morphine and cocaine. The details were revealed at his inquest. Although he had talked of suicide, he had recently assured his psychiatrist that he was not feeling suicidal. The coroner concluded that Barry was frustrated by his inability to get doctors to prescribe the opioids he wanted, so he probably went out to buy them on the street, then overdosed accidentally.

Barry West's death was recorded as misadventure, but he was another victim of Fred and Rose West, the little boy that Rose chased with her wooden spoon, the son Fred mocked in his police interviews.

> **Fred West**: Oh, he's a complete bloody head case, Barry is.
> **DC Jeff Morgan**: Is he?
> **Fred West**: Yes … Barry's been always the backward one of the family, like.
> **DC Morgan**: Yeah…
> **Fred West**: I think social services have got one load of problems with him.

It was characteristic of Fred and Rose to speak about people with the detachment of psychopaths. They cared nothing for

THE DEPTHS OF HUMAN DEPRAVITY

the women they murdered. Likewise, they seemed unable to empathise with their children. When Fred spoke about 'our family of love' it was a fantasy and a lie, like saying that he made love to the women he raped. Rose may have been the only person he ever loved, as much as he could feel love. 'I don't believe he was capable of loving anyone,' Rose told Winchester Crown Court, though their letters were filled with mutual declarations of love. She was the one person in the world willing to share his depravities, even to exceed him in cruelty, and he held her in awe for that.

Fred West has been dead for over thirty years, but his widow lives on in prison in her seventies. Rose has never responded to invitations to discuss the murder case. She has ignored letters from her former solicitor, who now believes her to be guilty, and she has never engaged with the police, or me. May stayed loyal to her mother for years, but gradually she started to see that Rose was a lying manipulator, quick to play the victim but unable to face what she had done. Rose shows no inclination to help the families who continue to look for explanations. After years of soul-searching, Lucy Partington's sister Marian wrote to Rose in 2004, a generous letter that she didn't post for another four years, wondering if she was doing the right thing. Marian wrote that she had felt a rage against Rose at times, but that had passed and she had tried to forgive her. 'Please know that I do not feel any hostility towards you, just a sadness, a deep sadness that all this has happened ...' She received a curt reply from prison staff:

> *Dear Marian Partington,*
> *Mrs West has received your letter and asked me to relay a message on her behalf, and asks that you please cease all correspondence. She does not wish to receive any further letters from you. Any further letters will be kept in security.*

THE FRED WEST TAPES

There is a heartlessness to this note that speaks volumes about Rose West's mentality. It shows her to be a woman who is cowardly and too emotionally crippled to engage with her past and the people she has wronged.

★ ★ ★

One of the questions always asked about the Wests is how many more victims they might have killed, as if twelve isn't enough. From the moment the police found Heather West under the patio at 25 Cromwell Street, Fred insisted that there were no more victims. He said it time and again. 'That's it … There is nobody else … There ain't no more …'

Then there were more, and more. There may well have been victims beyond the twelve the police recovered. Fred made wild statements in private about how many people were killed, but it is likely that there was at least a thirteenth victim: Mary Bastholm, last seen at a Gloucester bus stop in 1968. The Bastholm family have looked for answers for years. Her parents are long dead. Her brother, Peter, died in 2020, not knowing what had happened to his sister. His widow, Denise, was left to carry the flame. In 2021, I was part of a documentary team that worked with Gloucestershire police to excavate the basement of what had been the Pop-in café, where Mary worked, after a cadaver dog indicated that a body might be buried there. The café was closed, and the basement was dug up by the police, reopening the West case after more than a quarter of a century. Mary's remains weren't in the café, but the fact that she has never been found indicates that Fred probably had another hiding place somewhere. I know of only one other named individual who might be added to this list. An American teenager named Donna Lynn Moore, or similar, was seen at 25 Cromwell Street in 1973. She has never been traced, despite every effort by the

THE DEPTHS OF HUMAN DEPRAVITY

police, but neither has her family been located, suggesting that the information may be incorrect.

There were missed opportunities to stop the Wests, as I have highlighted in this book. The authorities failed Charmaine, whose disappearance from school in 1971 was not investigated when it should have been. Caroline Owens' rape was mishandled the following year. The police had regular contact with the Wests, without realising what was really going on. It wasn't until 1992 that they looked into allegations of child abuse. The Wests got away with that, the third time Fred had walked free from court after being charged with sexual offences. Finally, Hazel Savage noticed that a family member was missing and the police got a search warrant to look under the patio. By that time, Fred and Rose had been abusing and killing for three decades. It would be comforting to imagine that systems can be put in place to detect such offenders sooner, but the authorities are not entirely to blame. Fred's parents knew that he was a killer from the start, and his mother shared that knowledge with at least two other members of the family. No one thought to tell the police. Only half of the twelve murder victims were reported as missing. Also, people as depraved as Fred and Rose are hard to catch. Fred was an expert at deception, who took pride in his wickedness. He was 'Freddy the mass murderer from Gloucester', the chuckling fiend of the interview room who admitted that he was enjoying himself.

The horrific crimes that constitute the West case plumb the depths of human depravity, as Brian Leveson told the jury at Rose West's trial. 'We have been forced to consider what human beings can do to one another.' Everybody involved in this case, including Sir Brian, the West children and myself, have been affected by the experience. A window opened for us into a dark world that seems barely credible, yet is real.

THE FRED WEST TAPES

The darkness seeps in and becomes part of you. It is part of me now as I write these last words, as if Fred infected me thirty years ago. The moment I heard his voice on tape, I was captivated by the banal horror of the man; his chatty account of rape and killing revealed something about crime that I hadn't understood before then. To people like Fred and Rose, rape and murder is normal. Moreover, it is fun. The crueller and weirder the act the more thrilling they find it. In writing this book I have studied Fred's interviews in detail, as you have. We have seen his lies, of course. He spent his life burbling ridiculous and often obscene falsehoods, but we have also seen the truth growing, like weeds, between the cracks in his lies, as he revealed himself despite himself. Many people will write Fred and Rose off as 'monsters'. I try not to use that word. It is too easy. I avoid 'evil', too, as evil is associated with the Bible, and that sort of morality doesn't work for me. Some readers may reject the suggestion that Fred was to some extent mad, thinking that is a cop-out, but it seems to me (as it did to others) that he was not entirely sane, to put it mildly. He was a conundrum, a man who was stupid and cunning, simultaneously charming and wicked. He was conscious enough of what he did to hide his crimes, but he lived much of his life in a delusional fantasy world. He was a filthy beast, rapist and killer, who presented himself as a lover, Good Samaritan and family man. Together with Rose he broke all the rules of society. After he was caught, he twisted and turned in the interview room like the Devil, if the Devil was real and lived for a time in Gloucester.

ACKNOWLEDGEMENTS

In addition to studying police interviews with Fred West, and those conducted with Rose West, I undertook extensive research into the murder case as it unfolded in 1994–95, both as a reporter and as an author writing my first book, *Fred & Rose* (Warner Books, 1995 [now Sphere]). I attended Rose West's committal hearing and murder trial, where a lot of information was revealed, including witness statements.

In 2018–20, I did further research to update *Fred & Rose*, which is when I met Barry West. Between 2019 and 2021, I produced three television documentaries on the Wests for ITV. In updating my book, and making these films, I caught up with several people I hadn't spoken to for years, including John Bennett, Leo Goatley, Professor Bernard Knight, Howard Ogden, Derek and Wendy Thomson, Sasha Wass KC, Steve West and Dr David Whittaker. I met John Fitzgerald, who led the investigation into links between the Wests and social services; former lodger Gill Britt; Lynda Gough's mother, June;

Belinda and Mary Ann, sisters of Juanita Mott; and Marian Partington, sister of Lucy Partington. Around this same time, I made the podcast series, *Unheard: The Fred & Rose West Tapes* (Somethin' Else, 2019). The tapes referred to in that title are my archive of interview tapes, not the police interview tapes in this book. Recently, I was Senior Producer on *Fred & Rose West: A British Horror Story* (Blink Films for Netflix, 2025), a project I masterminded, which gave me an opportunity to talk with Sir Brian Leveson. In preparation for this book, I spoke to more people, including Dr Peter Acland, Dave Foreman and family, Jean Korbi, Lloyd Parry and the family of the late Harry Feeney. I have studied prison files relating to Fred West in the National Archives; I consulted newspaper articles and documentary films, including *Fred & Rose: The West Murders* (DMP for Channel 5, 2001); and I referred to the following books:

Bennett, John with Graham Gardner, *The Cromwell Street Murders: The Detective's Story,* Sutton Publishing, 2005

Britton, Paul, *The Jigsaw Man*, Penguin, 2023

Burn, Gordon, *Happy Like Murderers*, Faber & Faber, 1998

Goatley, Leo, *Understanding Fred & Rose West: Noose, Lamella and the Gilded Cage,* The Book Guild Ltd, 2019

O'Hagan, Andrew, *The Missing*, Picador, 1995

Partington, Marian, *If You Sit Very Still*, Jessica Kingsley Publishers, 2016

Roberts (formerly Owens), Caroline, *The Lost Girl*, Metro, 2004

Wansell, Geoffrey, *An Evil Love: The Life of Frederick West,* Headline, 1997 (Updated edition)

West, Anne Marie (*sic*) with Virginia Hill, *Out of the Shadows*, Simon & Schuster, 1995

West, Mae (*sic*) with Neil McKay, *Love as Always, Mum xxx*, Seven Dials, 2018

ACKNOWLEDGEMENTS

West, Stephen and Mae, *Inside 25 Cromwell St.*, Peter Grose Ltd. with the *News of the World*, 1995

My thanks to Gordon Wise at Curtis Brown; to Ciara Lloyd and her team at Bonnier Books; and to Dan Chambers and his colleagues at Blink Films.

SOURCE NOTES

Fred West is abbreviated in the following notes to FW, Rose West to RW. The RW trial refers to Rose West's murder trial at Winchester Crown Court, October–November 1995. With a few exceptions, police interviews are identified by the date and sometimes by the time that they commenced. The catalogue system – FW1, FW2, etc. – is mine, and differentiates between multiple interviews on the same day. Where interviews have previously been published or broadcast, I have cited the relevant book or documentary. Several police interviews were played and/or read in court.

Epigraph 'You're enjoying it ...': police interview 26.4.94 (FW85). Also, *An Evil Love* (Wansell).

CHAPTER 1 – HEATHER UNDER THE PATIO
Epigraph 'You're digging ... it': police interview 24.2.94 (FW1). NB: broadcast in *Fred & Rose: The West Murders* (DMP for Channel 5, 2001), and *Fred & Rose West: A British Horror Story* (Blink Films for Netflix, 2025).

THE FRED WEST TAPES

FW first attends Gloucester Central Police Station: Gloucestershire police timeline.

Hazel Savage/FW 'First of all … patio back': interview 24.2.94 (FW1).

Savage's career: *Gloucestershire Constabulary Cromwell St. Investigation Media Information Pack 1* (1995), henceforth Media Pack 1 (see also Media Pack 2).

RW 'This is stupid': *Inside 25 Cromwell St.* (Stephen and Mae West).

Derek Thomson 'Rose rang me … spoke to him': to author.

'Here's the first … removed': police video in *Fred & Rose West: A British Horror Story* (Netflix, 2025).

Terry Onions/RW 'Right then, Mrs West … aren't you?': interview 24.2.94 (RW trial evidence).

Three paving stones up, etc: Rob Williams to author (NB: Williams was May's live-in boyfriend, and was reporting his conversations with the West children to me).

RW 'kill that bitch …': *Inside 25 Cromwell St.* (Stephen and Mae West).

RW 'He told me to …': interview 4:35 PM, 25.2.94 (RW trial evidence).

FW 'Can we go to the police station?': Media Pack 2.

Howard Ogden/FW 'Keep your gob shut … told them!': to author.

Janet Leach background: author notes/her evidence in court.

FW 'Right, what happened … to Barry': interview 4:57 PM, 25.2.94 (RW trial evidence).

Barry West 'My first memories …': and all subsequent quotes to author.

FW 'So that was … I'm finished': interview 4:57 PM, 25.2.94 (RW trial evidence).

FW 'cracking … crack': undated interview quoted in *An Evil Love* (Wansell) and *Happy Like Murderers* (Burn).

SOURCE NOTES

Ogden '[As] we were gathering ... group hug': to author.

Onions/RW 'I'm telling you ... He's finished': interview 4:35 PM, 25.2.94 (RW trial evidence).

CHAPTER 2 – SHIRLEY AND 'SHIRLEY'S MATE'

Epigraph 'Anyone can say ... mother': FW police interview 26.2.94 (FW3). Also, *Happy Like Murderers* (Burn).

FW 'She contacts me ... to you': interview 26.2.94, *The Cromwell Street Murders* (Bennett).

Diazepam: interview 26.2.94 (FW3), also Scott Canavan in *Fred & Rose: The West Murders* (Channel 5, 2001).

FW 'thick as two short planks': interview 3.3.94 (FW10). Also, *An Evil Love* (Wansell).

Ogden '[Fred] sought to ... experience': to author.

Onions/RW 'You've been in custody ... want to go': interview 11:52 AM, 26.2.94 (RW trial evidence).

RW named the man she claimed to be with the night Heather was murdered under cross-examination at trial, 1.11.95.

John Bennett 'a control freak': Bennett to author.

Bernard Knight's background: to author, and his trial evidence.

Knight/Bennett 'I remember ... one body': to author.

Forensic evidence: RW trial and committal evidence 10.2.95.

FW/Savage 'When I walked ... No': interview 26.2.94 (FW3). Also quoted in *Happy Like Murderers* (Burn); *Fred & Rose: The West Murders* (Channel 5, 2001); and *Fred & Rose West: A British Horror Story* (Netflix, 2025).

Savage 'I did try ... got this right': interview 26.2.94 (FW3).

Family tree: RW trial admissions.

Savage/FW 'You told me ... cow [and] bitch': interview 26.2.94

THE FRED WEST TAPES

(FW3). Also, *Happy Like Murderers* (Burn).

RW note, 'I, Rosemary West ... Mrs R.P. West': *An Evil Love* (Wansell).

Old cow: *Inside 25 Cromwell St.* (Stephen and Mae West).

RW childhood: author's notes, interviews with Daisy Letts.

Daisy Letts 'We were so ... think about it': to author.

FW 'Her father ... dozen times': *Fred & Rose: The West Murders* (Channel 5, 2001).

RW rape claims: her trial evidence, 30.10.95.

May West on her mother: her book, *Love as Always, Mum xxx*.

FW 'And she said ... ruin my jobs': interview 10.3.94 (FW25).

RW 'This man started ... me out': *Inside 25 Cromwell St.* (Stephen and Mae West).

RW 'He said you ... knife us': her trial evidence, 30.10.95.

FW 'She said her ... I'll take Fred': interview 26.2.94 (FW3).

Onions/RW 'Who's the controller ... lots of ways': interview 8:29 PM, 26.2.94, RW trial evidence.

Onions/RW 'Has he ever ... twisted it': interview 11:52 AM, 26.2.94 (RW trial evidence).

FW 'I mean, that is ... of life': interview 24.2.94 (FW1).

Barry West 'That's what people ... psycho': to author.

RW hit officer: police source.

Savage/FW 'In another part ... the problem': interview 26.2.94 (FW4) partially read in RW trial, 3.11.95.

Savage/FW/Ogden/Darren Law 'I understand ... That's it': interview 26.2.94 (FW5).

FW 'bright moonlit night ... help with it': interview 26.2.94, *Fred & Rose: The West Murders* (Channel 5, 2001).

SOURCE NOTES

CHAPTER 3 – A PASSION FOR BONDAGE

Epigraph 'We weren't living a straight sex life': police interview, 2.3.94 (FW9).

FW 'ripped': interview 12:02 PM, 27.2.94 (FW6). Also, *Happy Like Murderers* (Burn).

Bennett decided FW was a psychopath: to author.

Shirley Robinson background: witness statements read at RW trial, including the 3.3.94 statement of her mother, Christa Carling (*née* Lewezki), ('I took ill …'); also Crescent School staff member ('extremely withdrawn and sullen').

£7-a-week: statement of lodger Claire Rigby, RW committal, 8.2.95.

Mortgage: *An Evil Love* (Wansell).

Shirley Robinson recorded as six weeks pregnant: RW trial, Admission 23.

FW 'It was quite … pregnant': interview 9.3.94 (FW22).

FW/Ogden 'I turned round … was it': interview 27.2.94 (FW6).

FW at crime scene 'Right, Fred … nothing else': police video 27.2.94, *Fred & Rose West: A British Horror Story* (Netflix, 2025).

RW/Onions/Neville Smurthwaite 'She was pregnant … No': interview 11:48 AM, 27.2.94 (RW trial evidence).

FW 'I got raided … raided, raided': interview 2.3.94 (FW9).

FW 'occasional shandy': interview 12.5.94 (FW98).

RW/Smurthwaite 'I didn't want … thought about it': interview 11:48 AM, 27.2.94 (RW trial evidence).

RW said at her trial that FW 'threatened to kill me': her evidence, 31.10.95.

Bailed, and bugged: RW trial evidence (admissions).

FW 'I think Rose knew … strangled her': 28.2.94 interview read in RW trial, 3.11.95.

THE FRED WEST TAPES

FW 'Shirley is going to be my next wife': evidence of Anna Marie Davis, RW trial, 18.10.95.

Bennett 'These interviews are crap!' and Savage outburst: his book, *The Cromwell Street Murders*.

FW/Savage 'Yeah, that was ... loose': interview 1.3.94 (FW7).

Paul Britton background: his book, *The Jigsaw Man* (quoted).

Bennett 'He was what ... properly': to author.

1992–93 child abuse case: The Queen vs. Frederick West and Rosemary Pauline West, indictment, Gloucester Crown Court, National Archives HO336/689.

Bennett 'There are several ... this inquiry': *The Jigsaw Man* (Britton).

Britton 'You should ... sure of it': *The Jigsaw Man*.

FW 'I didn't know her ... head forward': interview 1.3.94 (FW7)

Savage/Law/FW/Leach 'Most people ... Yes, please': interview 1.3.94 (FW8).

FW 'weren't living a straight sex life': interview 2.3.94 (FW9).

FW 'I felt right weird ... a question': interview 2.3.94 (FW9).

Bennett 'West's face ... of him': his book, *The Cromwell Street Murders*.

FW/Savage 'hero ... my family': interview 3.3.94 (FW10).

Custody arrangements: HM Prison Service correspondence, National Archives (HO336/684); and author's interviews including Ogden ('I've got this, Fred.')

Leach 'After only two ... tell the police': her 22.9.95 police statement, broadcast in *Fred & Rose West Reopened* (Blink Films for ITV, 2021); and her trial evidence, 7.11.95.

CHAPTER 4 – FRED'S EARLY LIFE

Epigraph 'Whatever you enjoy ... doing it': police interview 14.3.94 (FW30).

SOURCE NOTES

Britton 'Let Mr West talk': *The Cromwell Street Murders* (Bennett).

FW 'Well, I was born ... I'm the eldest': interview 3.3.94 (FW10).

FW/Savage 'And we were ... Yeah': interview 3.3.94 (FW11).

Savage/FW 'So, who was ... the boss': interview 3.3.94 (FW12).

FW 'a pillar of steel': interview 30.3.94 (FW67).

FW 'And she used ... judge nobody': interview 14.3.94 (FW30). Also, *Happy Like Murderers* (Burn); and *An Evil Love* (Wansell).

FW 'And we used ... squirrels': interview 3.3.94 (FW11).

Slaughtered like pigs: Leach police statement 22.9.95; and *Daily Mirror*, 23.11.95

FW 'I've always loved Gloucester': interview 3.3.94 (FW11).

Population of Gloucester still only 92,000 in 1990: *Hansard* 29.1.92. It has since expanded but remains one of Britain's smallest cities.

FW 'Yeah, they were ... black': interview 3.3.94 (FW11).

April 1961 theft conviction (stealing from shops): *Citizen* 21.4.61; and Hill to author.

October 1961 theft conviction (stealing from work): *Citizen*, 16.10.61.

FW 'a massive thing': interview 3.3.94 (FW11).

FW 'when they opened ... and all off': interview 21.4.94 (FW75).

FW 'I was splattered ... twelve months': interview 3.3.94 (FW11).

Bennett 'I don't know if ... have said': to author.

Doug West 'out near a week': to author.

FW 'I called her ... disorderly': interview 3.3.94 (FW12a).

Savage/FW 'Well, I mean ... over them?': interview 3.3.94 (FW12). Also, *Happy Like Murderers* (Burn).

FW 'in the navy': interview 3.3.94 (FW12).

Savage/FW 'You're a man's man ... complied': interview 3.3.94 (FW12).

THE FRED WEST TAPES

Whips at 25 Cromwell Street: RW trial (admissions).

FW/Savage 'She thinks ... change it': interview 3.3.94 (FW12).

FW 'Welcome home ... level': interview 3.3.94 (FW12a).

FW/Barbara Harrison 'Mother was very ... you know?': interview 14.3.94 (FW30).

FW 'one massive ... in a field': interview 16.3.94 (FW36).

Kitty West dialogue 'I'm pregnant ...' recalled by Jean Korbi to author (quoted).

FW 'Yes, of course ...': Ledbury *Reporter*, 23.6.61.

FW 'Well, doesn't everyone ...': *Fred & Rose* (Sounes).

Court report 'took the blame ... refused to do so': Ledbury *Reporter*, 10.11.61.

Suggestion of brain damage: 1961 court evidence of the family GP, Dr Brian Hardy; author's 1994 interview with the GP.

Anna Marie West 'Fred was abused ... father': her book *Out of the Shadows*. Also Leach's statement 22.9.95.

May West 'He [Fred] said ... father had done': her book *Inside 25 Cromwell St*.

Jean Korbi '[Fred] was still ... after him': and all subsequent quotes to author.

Girlfriend raped: witness Mrs 'B', giving evidence at RW trial, 1.11.95.

FW 'I went in ... on the run': interview 3.3.94 (FW12a).

Margaret Clarke 'told Fred that ... unsuccessful': her court evidence, RW trial, 2.11.95.

FW 'It was just a ...': interview 14.3.94 (FW30).

Fred + Rena tattoo: prison file, National Archives HO 336/684.

FW 'Mam went mad ... Leave!': interview 3.3.94 (FW12a).

FW 'There was an almighty ... run for it': interview 3.3.94 (FW12b).

Isabel Kirby (*née* Corbett) 'I had seen ... plain evil': to author.

SOURCE NOTES

FW 'I backed over ... four': interview 7:05 PM, 3.3.94 (FW12b). Further background: FW to probation officer HMP Winson Green, National Archives (HO336/686).

CHAPTER 5 – NINE MORE (APPROX.)

Epigraph 'I don't think any ... mind': police interview 4.3.94 (RW trial evidence).

FW/Jeff Morgan 'She's now ... big fat girl ... ring a bell': interview 3.3.94 (FW13). Also, *An Evil Love* (Wansell).

Lynda Gough background: RW trial evidence, 11.10.95.

FW 'wouldn't have thought so': interview 3.3.94 (FW13).

June Gough 'I immediately noticed ... you are wearing!': her evidence in RW trial, 11.10.95.

FW/Savage 'interviewed ... home a few times ... underneath it': interview 4.3.94 (FW14).

Leach/FW/Canavan dialogue: recalled by Leach and Canavan in archive in *Fred & Rose West: A British Horror Story* (Netflix, 2025).

Ogden 'He'd seek ... expletive': to author.

'9 more' note: Media Pack 2.

Bennett 'It's like ... a kind': to author.

Savage/FW 'Who's that ... is it?': interview 4.3.94 (RW trial evidence).

Gough/Ben Stanniland/David Evans: RW trial evidence of Stanniland and Evans, 12.10.95; also Stanniland's statement read at committal, 8.2.95.

Stanniland 'the reaction was ... the door': his evidence at RW trial, 12.10.95.

Savage/FW/Law/Ogden 'So that ... knocking off': interview 4.3.94 (RW trial evidence).

Lucy Partington background: RW trial evidence and Marian Partington to author.

THE FRED WEST TAPES

Marian Partington 'It was quite … to that place': to author for my podcast series, *Unheard* (Somethin' Else, 2019).

Partington 'She was renowned … sensible': her book, *If You Sit Very Still*.

FW 'It's just that … yeah, yeah': interview 4.3.94 (RW trial evidence).

Partington 'They said that … was Lucy': to author for *Unheard* (Somethin' Else, 2019).

FW 'Rose was there … someone': interview 26.3.94 (FW61).

RW 1969 letter: RW trial evidence.

Partington 'Her sexual status was innocent': her book, *If You Sit Very Still*.

FW 'come the loving … nasty … Nobody at all': interview 4.3.94 (RW trial evidence).

Head clearance: RW trial 6.10.95.

FW 'That line there … second girl': FW on police videotape, 4.3.94.

Police source 'He would say … character': to author.

RW 'a cold, wet, damp cave': RW trial evidence, 30.11.95.

FW 'That's the girl in the fireplace': interview 11.3.94 (FW27).

FW told police he cut heads off over holes: *An Evil Love* (Wansell).

'Murder squad detectives are searching …': *Sunday Mirror*, 5.3.94.

FW's convictions: RW trial evidence (admissions).

FW/Morgan 'What happened … I couldn't touch … do it now': interview 5.3.94 (FW15).

5.3.94 field trip: Media Packs.

Police 'The area that … tree': police video, *Fred & Rose West: A British Horror Story* (Netflix, 2025).

FW/Ogden 'Rena come fucking … man': *Fred & Rose: The West Murders* (Channel 5, 2001).

SOURCE NOTES

FW/Harrison/Morgan 'I said to her …100 per cent … for the dustman': police interview 9:22 PM, 4.3.94 (RW trial evidence).

Bennett 'Questions were coming … then on' and clash with Ogden: his book, *The Cromwell Street Murders*.

Bennett 'I make no … getting out': to author.

Major Incident Room: Media Packs.

Partington description: 1973 missing poster.

Partington forensic evidence: RW trial (admissions); and committal hearing 6.2.95.

Partington 'There were many … of others': to author for *Unheard* (Somethin' Else, 2019).

Dropped kitchen knife: RW trial evidence (admissions). Also, FW to police: 11:33 AM, 8.3.94 (FW18).

Partington 'That's what … the long haul': to author.

Girl from Newent (Juanita Mott) forensic evidence: RW trial evidence (admissions).

FW/Morgan 'She was by that motor … dustman': interview 6.3.94 (FW16). Also, *An Evil Love* (Wansell).

Mott background: RW trial evidence; author's conversations with sisters.

Belinda Moore (*née* Mott, later Allsopp) 'My mother was … local authority': police statement 7.3.94: RW trial evidence.

Belinda 'I think my sister … nothing has come up': to author.

Mott conviction: *Happy Like Murderers* (Burn); and *An Evil Love* (Wansell).

Jenny Fraser-Holland (later Baldwin) 'She left … out of character …': her evidence, RW trial 12.10.94.

Belinda/RW dialogue: to author for *Unheard* (Somethin' Else, 2019).

THE FRED WEST TAPES

CHAPTER 6 – EVIDENCE OF TORTURE

Epigraph 'I don't believe in suffering': police interview 11.3.94 (FW27).

Lynda Gough's remains: RW trial evidence (admissions).

FW said he flushed Gough's underwear: interview 25.3.94 (FW58).

June Gough 'Lynda had left ... you see': RW trial evidence, 11.10.95.

Lynda's note: RW trial evidence (admissions).

June Gough 'Perhaps I've ... that house': to author.

FW 'Nobody'd ever find me': recalled by Leach in archive, *Fred & Rose: The West Murders* (Channel 5, 2001).

Morgan/FW/Harrison 'Right [I] would ... find Anne': interview 7.3.94 (FW17).

Robinson shared bedroom with Wests: RW trial evidence 13.10.95.

Robinson became 'part of the West family': RW trial evidence of lodger Liz Brewer, 12.10.95.

Savage/FW 'Well, why ... and Charmaine': interview 8.3.94 (FW18).

Thefts: FW previous.

FW/Savage '[That] all started ... isn't it?': interview 8.3.94 (FW19); partly read in RW trial, 3.11.24.

Sex and the Vampire: Gloucester *Citizen*, 13.1.73.

Savage/FW '[There was] a missing girl ... Cooper is fifteen': interview 8.3.94 (FW21).

Colin Cooper quoted from 1994 police statement: read at RW trial, 12.10.95.

Andrew Jones quoted from his 1973 police statement: RW trial, 12.10.95.

FW re Lulu 'a gang bang job': interview 9.3.94 (FW22).

FW 'No way I ... can you?': interview 10.3.94 (FW25).

SOURCE NOTES

FW 'They always used ... just went': interview 13.4.94 (FW72).

FW 'And then Margaret ... got him': interview 10.3.94 (FW24).

Allegation RW mistreated Steven McAvoy: Anna Marie West in her book, *Out of the Shadows*.

FW 'When the officer ... nothing happened': interview 21.3.94 (FW50).

FW on Margaret McAvoy 'Only me, up the wall': interview 21.3.94 (FW50).

Harrison/FW 'She's alright ... anything': interview 10.3.94 (FW24).

FW 'apart from Anne ... I'm concerned': interview 10.3.94 (FW25).

FW/Savage 'I'm getting the ... tape off': interview 10.3.94 (FW26).

FW/Savage 'The thing is ... torture anybody': interview 11.3.94 (FW27).

CHAPTER 7 – SEARCHING EVERYWHERE

Epigraph 'I shall always protest ... fucking nick': police surveillance tape, *Fred & Rose West: A British Horror Story* (Netflix, 2025).

May West 'The pressure ... his father': her book, *Inside 25 Cromwell St*.

Moving police houses: Gloucestershire Police timeline.

RW dialogue in houses: police surveillance tape in public domain: *Fred & Rose: The West Murders* (Channel 5, 2001); *Fred & Rose West: A British Horror Story* (Netflix, 2025); and *Love as Always, Mum xxx* (Mae [May] West).

Murder squad numbers: Media Pack 2.

Morgan/FW 'There are people ... worshipped each other': interview 14.3.94 (FW28). Also, *Happy Like Murderers* (Burn).

'Kiss an Angel Good Mornin'' by Ben Peters (Ben Peters Music, 1971).

FW 'I'm an absolute ... know': interview 12.5.94 (FW99).

THE FRED WEST TAPES

FW 'I had too many ... the heart': interview 14.3.94 (FW28).

FW wanted to artificially inseminate Anne McFall: *An Evil Love* (Wansell).

FW 'Whatever May says ... pervert': interview 14.3.94 (FW31).

FW/Savage 'That's her eyes ... photograph of Heather': interview 16.3.94 (FW32).

FW 'schoolgirl look ... big girl': interview 16.3.94 (FW34).

'[Rose] made me ... like a child': RW trial witness Jane Bayle, 13.10.95.

FW 'she had very soft ... I'm driving!': interview 16.3.94 (FW33).

FW 'She wasn't that ... a few spots': interview 17.3.94 (FW40).

FW 'a very young look to her': interview 18.3.94 (FW42).

Savage/FW 'You've told him ... before': interview 4:35 PM 16.3.94 (FW36); partly quoted in *Happy Like Murderers* (Burn).

Britton 'When you carve ... early life': his book, *The Jigsaw Man*.

Jeffrey Dahmer and cannibalism: Mailonline, 5.10.22.

Bennett 'Now, what a ... ridiculous': to author.

Public concerned FW may have buried bodies on their property: interview 14.3.94 (FW29).

FW/Savage 'And patios ... endless': interview 14.3.94 (FW31).

Ninety-six locations: revealed as part of Operation Tryfan, 2021 (*Fred & Rose West Reopened*, Blink Films for ITV).

Morgan/FW 'So, we've got ... them [all]': interview 18.3.94 (FW46).

Bennett 'I never ... anything': to author.

FW 'I been there': interview 18.3.94 (FW44).

FW 'stringy hair ... the time': interview 18.3.94 (FW45).

Alison Chambers' background: RW trial evidence and committal hearing.

SOURCE NOTES

Dezra Chambers '[Alison] rebelled ... come home': *Fred & Rose West: A British Horror Story* (Netflix, 2025).

Enfys Davies 'Alison was very ... attraction was': 29.3.94 statement read in RW trial.

Former JBH resident 'Alison was a ... her that': to author.

Chambers letter 'I am at present ... feet': read in legal argument, RW trial, 13.10.95.

Shoulder to cry on: evidence of anonymised victim 'Miss A' in RW trial, 16.10.95.

Social worker report: interview 4:10 PM, 14.3.94 (FW30).

FW 'Because most ... you know': police interview 26.3.94 (FW61).

Shirley Hubbard background: RW trial evidence (12.10.95) including statements by Glenys Lloyd, Linda Hubbard and Daniel Davies (quoted).

David Whittaker 'There was an ... hundreds still': to author.

FW/Morgan 'She was going ... helping others': interview 18.3.94 (FW45).

Bennett's clockwise deduction: his book, *The Cromwell Street Murders*.

Trip to allotment and 25 Midland Road: interview 20.3.94 (FW47).

Savage/FW 'Fred, do you ... Charmaine is': 20.3.94 police video, *Fred & Rose West: A British Horror Story* (Netflix, 2025).

FW/Savage 'on a tip ... at Much Marcle': interview 20.3.94 (FW47).

Savage reads 'If anyone thinks ... do not': interview 10.3.94 (FW26).

Savage/FW 'Back in 1968 ... went missing': interview 20.3.94 (FW48).

Denise Bastholm 'It was a place ... bus stop': to author.

Leo Goatley 'There was clearly ... somebody else [involved]': to author. Also, his book, *Understanding Fred & Rose West: Noose, Lamella and the Gilded Cage*.

FW/Savage 'What do you … believe it': interview 20.3.94 (FW48).

CHAPTER 8 – OUR FAMILY OF LOVE

Epigraph 'We don't want … truth': police interview 22.3.94 (FW54).

May West 'dirty, thieving … man': her book *Love as Always, Mum xxx*.

FW drilled hole in bedroom door: RW trial evidence. Information in May statements repeated in her books, *Inside 25 Cromwell St.* and *Love as Always, Mum xxx*. Quoted.

Savage/FW 'What about that … rubbish': interview 21.3.94 (FW49).

Daisy Letts 'She had this … a child': to author.

Charmaine wet bed: evidence in RW trial, 9.10.95.

FW '[our] family of love … simple as that': interview 21.3.94 (FW51).

RW letter 'Darling about … Rose': RW trial evidence.

FW 'your ever worshipping husband': RW trial evidence.

Tattoos: FW's prison file, National Archives, HO 336/684.

Savage/FW 'You'd go to … protective to Rose': interview 21.3.94 (FW51).

Like a tiger: interview 21.3.94 (FW50).

RW black eye: witness Anne Knight, RW trial, 16.10.95.

RW injures herself with knife: *Out of the Shadows* (Anna Marie West) and RW trial (admissions).

FW 'anybody … trouble started': interview 21.3.94 (FW51).

FW 'We never had … with nobody': interview 22.3.94 (FW52).

FW/Savage 'Rose was not … watching them': interview 23.3.94 (FW57).

FW 'She had her own … up there': interview 26.3.94 (FW62).

SOURCE NOTES

Harrison/Savage/FW re nuns 'So what happened ... thinking, Fred': interview 23.3.24 (FW56).

FW on Partington 'I didn't want ...anybody': interview 25.3.94 (FW59).

FW '[She] said, "I've ... all happened': interview 26.3.24 (FW61) read in RW trial evidence 3.11.24.

FW 'a little fat ... the problem': interview 25.3.94 (FW60). Also, *Happy Like Murderers* (Burn).

FW/Morgan 'a poor class ... was rough ... the time is 12:54': interview 26.3.24 (FW61).

Oliver Sacks: *A Matter of Identity*, *The Man Who Mistook His Wife for a Hat* (Everyman, 2023 [first pub. 1985]).

Morgan/FW/Savage 'What we were saying ... hasn't murdered, no': 28.3.94 (FW63).

Caroline Owens' background: author's notes, RW trial evidence; also statements read at committal hearing, 8.2.95.

Owens 'The girl rolled ... After I had finished ... I looked at Anna again ... It will be our little secret ... fucking lesbians ... Rose got out ... pleasure': her book, *The Lost Girl*.

Owens 'I had always wanted to be a nanny': her trial evidence, 10.10.95.

Owens slept with Stanniland, his mate, Tony and a sailor: her evidence, RW trial, 11.10.95.

Owens 'playing with my hair ... I thought, that ... not a nice laugh ... started panicking ... bitch and that ... and they were putting tape ... a gag ... keep me down ... talking and laughing ... They told me to keep quiet ... They [then] tied my hands ... cotton wool': her RW trial evidence, 10.10.95.

FW/Owens 'It will be ... fucking lesbians ... [Fred] was being very ... Keep fucking quiet ... I could feel ... Help me! ... saying sorry': her book, *The Lost Girl*.

THE FRED WEST TAPES

Owens 'They were both ... frightened to death ... apologised ... Rose's pleasure': RW trial evidence.

Kevan Price goes to 25 Cromwell Street: his evidence in RW trial, 11.10.95.

RW 'Don't be fucking daft ... I am?': RW trial evidence, 1.11.95.

Morgan/FW/Savage 'I believe ... just too ridiculous ... vendetta ... killing instinct': interview 28.3.94 (FW63).

FW/Morgan 'put her in ... Rubbish': police interview 28.3.94, RW trial evidence.

RW 'I don't know why ... happened' and conviction: Gloucester *Citizen* 13.1.73.

Lawyer misgivings: to author.

Tony Coates hit FW: Coates to author.

FW/Morgan/Savage 'This girl at Cinderford ... I'm away [in prison]': interview 28.3.94, RW trial evidence.

Owens deal: RW trial evidence.

Steve and May West sign with *News of the World*: their book, *Inside 25 Cromwell St.*

Anna Marie signed with *Daily Star*/advance payment: her evidence in RW trial, 20.10.95.

Savage/FW 'You find things ... to disaster': interview 28.3.94, RW trial evidence.

FW/Savage 'You could pick up ... people in your cellar ... any other women ... the kids: interview 29.3.94 (FW64).

Law/FW/Savage 'cause for concern – pornographic videos': interview 29.3.94 (FW65).

Robin Holt background: author research.

Savage/FW 'What did you ... none whatsoever': interview 29.3.94 (FW66).

SOURCE NOTES

Morgan reading 'I remember ... stunned': interview 30.3.94 (FW67).

FW told father: *An Evil Love* (Wansell).

FW 'I went ... leave it': *Fred & Rose: The West Murders* (Channel 5, 2001); dmptv.co.uk.

CHAPTER 9 – THE CODE OF SILENCE

Epigraph 'We were fucking terrified ... told': author's interview with Barry West.

Alf Macklin 'If anybody ... bugger': to author.

Gill Britt 'John was a regular ... that wall': to author for *Unheard* (Somethin' Else, 2019).

Anna Marie raped by John West: indictment, Bristol Crown Court, 1996; *Daily Telegraph* 30.11.96.

May raped by John 'Without saying anything ... want to be sick ... the three of them understood': her book, *Love as Always, Mum xxx*.

FW/Morgan 'I mean ... mouth shut': interview 30.3.94 (FW67).

Barry West 'She would use that ...' and all subsequent quotes: to author.

Letts wanted to sleep with his granddaughter 'Grampy ... playing up': FW prison writings.

Children molested at parties: author's sources.

Anna Marie 'Let me say ... still a child': her book, *Out of the Shadows*.

Locked in cupboard: author's source.

'Stop it, Daddy!': Jayne Hamer RW trial evidence.

Britt 'Anne-Marie (*sic*) must ... your mum': to author for *Unheard* (Somethin' Else, 2019).

Steve West 'Her moods didn't ... the mouth': to author.

Steve 'I was covered ... fucking mad': to author.

THE FRED WEST TAPES

RW 'You fucking little ... Do you?': *Love as Always, Mum xxx* (Mae [May] West).

Contacts with hospitals: *The Bridge Child Care Consultancy Service Overview Report in respect of Charmaine and Heather West* (Part 8); also RW trial evidence, 20.10.95.

Anna Marie 'I fell over, Miss': her book, *Out of the Shadows*.

John Fitzgerald 'A paediatrician ... security': to author.

Steve 'We were never ... happy': to author.

Anna Marie's story: her book, *Out of the Shadows*; and Chris Davis to author.

FW/May 'Your mother's upset ... cry before': May's book, *Love as Always, Mum xxx*.

FW said Heather dug her grave: James McMaster evidence, RW trial, 7.11.95.

'Stop, Dad, it hurts!': *An Evil Love* (Wansell).

FW 'You mustn't say ... to prison': *Happy Like Murderers* (Burn).

Williams 'Cromwell Street is ... cables': to author.

RW 'Fuck off, you bastard': *An Evil Love* (Wansell).

RW 'Don't you dare say anything': *Happy Like Murderers* (Burn).

RW overdose: author's sources, and *The Cromwell Street Murders* (Bennett).

Steve 'Mum brought them ... you sat': to author.

CHAPTER 10 – THE DEVIL AND HIS WIFE

Epigraph 'Have you killed ... my knowledge': police interview 13.4.94 (FW70).

Rena found: RW trial evidence (Admission 17k).

FW/Morgan 'Rena was in ... India': interview 12.4.94 (FW68). Also, *An Evil Love* (Wansell).

SOURCE NOTES

Bennett 'Everything he did ... manipulate everybody': to author.

Morgan/FW 'over to you ... Right ... all of it': interview 12.4.94 (FW69).

FW 'I think that ... off my back': interview 13.4.94 (FW70).

FW 'Rena kept coming ... nightmare': interview 13.4.94 (FW71).

FW/Savage 'didn't have a lot ... at the moment': interview, 13.4.94 (FW70).

FW 'She [Rena] got nasty ... the scene': interview 13.4.94 (FW71).

885 surveillance tapes: RW trial evidence (Admission 320); also *The Cromwell Street Murders* (Bennett).

RW 'The fucking trouble ... never met him!': *Love as Always, Mum xxx* (Mae [May] West).

Witness saw RW with Charmaine: RW trial evidence of Tracey Hammond, 9.10.95.

RW 20.4.94 arrest: Gloucestershire Police; *The Cromwell Street Murders* (Bennett).

May West 'Her eyes flashed ... Look after it!'" and RW 'Fuck you, the lot of you!': her book, *Love as Always, Mum xxx*.

FW 'It's bloody ... believe it': interview 21.4.94 (FW74).

RW 'no comment ... I'm innocent': RW trial evidence (Admission 33).

Leach 'He just said ... involved': her evidence RW trial, 7.11.95.

Thérèse Siegenthaler background, including quotes from Edith Simmons and sister Marrianne: RW trial evidence, 12.10.95.

Witness claimed a Dutch hiker was staying at 25 Cromwell St: statement of Sharon Compton read at committal, 8.2.95.

Daisy Letts 'I never knew ...' etc: all interviews with author.

FW/Morgan 'gang bang ... of people': interview 21.4.94 (FW75).

Anna Marie 'Sometimes I had ... watching': her book, *Out of the Shadows*. Also, her evidence RW trial.

Barry West 'She got paid extra': to author.

Arthur Dobbs' story 'Mr West came in … undressed': his evidence at RW trial, 17.10.95.

FW 'our love children': RW evidence in court, 30.10.95.

FW 'I was their father … some reason': interview 21.4.94 (FW75).

FW 'bun in the oven': *The Lost Girl* (Caroline Roberts [aka Owens]).

Savage/FW 'Whose are they … Nothing at all': interview 21.4.94 (FW76). Also, partly in *Happy Like Murderers* (Burn).

FW 'You know, we go … suspicious of people': interview 21.4.94 (FW75).

Savage/FW 'Whose are they … in there': interview 21.4.94 (FW76).

Britt 'She never had … vile': to author, *Unheard* (Somethin' Else, 2019).

Savage/FW 'thickly stained … Nothing at all': interview 21.4.94 (FW76).

Vincent Oakes's statement: RW trial evidence, 2.11.95.

FW/Savage 'Rubbish … the other one's Anne': interview 22.4.94 (FW81).

Confessed to Leach: her 22.9.95 police statement and court evidence.

CHAPTER 11 – PLAN B

Epigraph 'I have not … matters': RW trial evidence, 3.11.95.

'moved to London': RW trial evidence, Admission 20.

Isa McNeill 'Jekyll and Hyde' and all subsequent quotes: to author.

FW 'She just made … herself': interview 2.7.94 (FW100).

John McLachlan 'Rena said, "What's … fucking pleased' and subsequent quotes and dialogue: to author.

SOURCE NOTES

FW 'Bastard! ... him': interview 11.5.94 (FW93).

Willows was a gypsy site: National Archives, D8567.

FW 'There were ... too crowded': interview 26.4.94 (FW84).

Children in a 'deplorable state': interview 11.5.94 (FW93). Also, *An Evil Love* (Wansell).

Rena's November 1966 court appearance: Gloucester *Citizen*, 30.11.66.

Clarke 'I remember one day ... would come': statement read in RW trial, 2.11.95.

FW/Savage 'I mean, Anna Marie ... that is': interview 26.4.94 (FW85).

RW 'I'm innocent': RW trial evidence (Admission 33).

FW meets legal team/Plan B: Ogden to author and RW trial evidence, 6 and 13.11.95.

FW note 'I have not ... this time': RW trial evidence, 3.11.95.

Savage/FW 'Now what on Earth ... you alone': interview 29.4.94 (FW86).

FW 'No comment on it': interview 3.5.94 (FW87).

Shirley Hubbard photo: Dr Whittaker to author.

Law/FW/Savage 'I don't [know] ...You're crying': interview 5.5.94 (FW88).

Savage/FW 'Had something awful ... she's had': interview 5.5.94 (FW89).

Charmaine's injuries and missing bones: Knight's evidence in RW trial, 24.10.95; RW trial admission 17J; and interview 10.5.94 (FW90).

FW 'I thought ... them both': interview 10.5.94 (FW92).

THE FRED WEST TAPES

CHAPTER 12 – TOUGH COPS WANT ANSWERS

Epigraph 'You are a man obsessed by sex': police interview 12.5.94 (FW98).

Law/FW 'They haven't found ... love spot': interview 11.5.94 (FW94).

Leach no longer required: *The Cromwell Street Murders* (Bennett).

Leach denies becoming emotionally involved/ says goodbye: her trial evidence 13.11.95.

Law 'surreal ... this is happening': archive interview in *Fred & Rose West: A British Horror Story* (Netflix, 2025).

FW/Savage 'When I first met ... rubbish, Fred': interview 4.3.94 used in RW trial evidence.

Stephen Harris and Tony James background: Media Pack 1.

James/FW 'And missing is ... comment on that': interview 11.5.94 (FW95). Also, RW trial admissions (missing body parts).

FW told Leach fingers were removed to foil identification: her trial evidence, 7.11.95.

James/FW 'I want to talk ... Must be': interview 12.5.94 (FW97).

Liz Agius's experience: RW trial evidence, 1995; also her statement read at committal, 8.2.95.

James/FW/Harris 'See, the whole ... angry person': interview 12.5.94 (FW98).

Anna Marie's experience: her trial evidence.

James/FW 'What do you ... No comment, sir': interview 12.5.94 (FW99).

FW 'If you see ... sort you out' and Kathryn Halliday background: Halliday court evidence, RW trial, 17.10.95.

James/FW/Harris 'She says that during ... interview now': interview 12.5.94 (FW99).

Halliday, 'It got more ... take them': her evidence, RW trial, 17.10.95.

SOURCE NOTES

Abortion kit: RW trial evidence 2.11.95.

Questions to RW 'Was [victim's name] tied up ... her body?': *Happy Like Murderers* (Burn).

FW 'I have lied ... anybody else': interview 13.5.94 read in RW trial 7.11.95.

FW admitted to HMP Winson Green: FW's prison files, National Archives, HO 336/693.

Prison doctor 'He was very polite ... lucid': to author.

Fellow inmate 'I got to know Fred ... statements about him': written statement (name redacted) 31.1.95, National Archives, HO 336/693.

FW 'Rose fucking ruled me': *An Evil Love* (Wansell).

What else FW told Ogden: Ogden to author and *Happy Like Murderers* (Burn).

John West arrested: Regina vs. John West, Bristol Crown Court, 1996.

McFall found/forensic evidence: RW trial evidence (Admissions 16 and 17).

CHAPTER 13 – ROSE DON'T WANT ME

Epigraph 'I should go to Hell ... done': *An Evil Love* (Wansell).

30.6.94 remand hearing: author's notes.

Lloyd Parry 'She dumps herself ... blanking him': to author.

Ogden 'That was a very ... turning point': to author.

Edwards 'I visited with ... thoroughly confused': read in interview 2.7.94 (FW100).

FW/Nick Barnes 'I never touched ... even a woman': interview 2.7.94 (FW100).

Daisy West's death: death certificate.

THE FRED WEST TAPES

FW 'I have not got no ... to them?': interview 2.7.94 (FW101).

FW/Barnes/Harris 'She had a glum ... at you': interview 2.7.94 (FW102).

Barnes/FW/Harris 'I shall ask ... can I?': interview 2.7.94 (FW103).

Barnes/FW 'You will not ... MO in itself': interview 3.7.94 (FW104).

Barnes/FW 'in the middle ... what happened': interview 3.7.94 (FW105).

142 interviews: RW trial evidence 2.11.95.

FW 'You know what ... interfere': *Fred & Rose West: A British Horror Story* (Netflix, 2025).

Ogden 'What is ... each other': to author.

FW telling Ogden what he claimed Rose did: *Fred & Rose: The West Murders* (Channel 5, 2001); dmptv.co.uk.

FW 'Fuck me ... done': *An Evil Love* (Wansell).

Mix-up at court: governor's letter 12.8.94, FW prison files, National Archives, HO 336/684.

Ogden 'He gave me ... in my face': to author.

FW refused to see Ogden: prison officer statement, inquest file, National Archives HO 336/693.

McMaster 'I was asked ... court case': RW trial evidence, 7.11.95.

Ogden 'I am doing what ... the deal': PA, 12.8.94.

High Court order: Bobbetts Mackan press release 12.8.94

Ogden suspended by Law Society: *Independent* 1.3.96.

Probation officer [name redacted] 'I felt ... all the murders': probation reports, National Archives, HO 336/686.

Leach visits: FW prison records, National Archives HO 336/679.

FW 'mistakes ... Rose's thing': Leach's 22.9.95 police statement, reiterated in court at RW trial (7–13.11.95); and to the *Daily Mirror*, 23.11.95.

SOURCE NOTES

Prof. Knight view: his evidence at RW trial, 25.10.95.

Probation officer (name redacted) 'He talked ... and events': probation report, National Archives, HO 336/686.

Steve West 'He is always ... started it': to author.

FW 'I was loved by an angel ... in the face': prison manuscript.

Birthday letter 'To Rose West ... his wife': RW trial evidence.

12.12.94 FW letter 'To Rose, as in life ... darling ...': *An Evil Love* (Wansell).

Leach said FW seemed 'fine': her evidence in RW trial, 7.11.95.

Anna Marie's visits/FW/last call 'finish it ... my angel': her book *Out of the Shadows*.

FW told probation officer case was a mess: probation reports, National Archives, HO 336/686.

Trouble sleeping/worried about RW: prison source.

Bennett concerns: to author.

Prison officer (name redacted) 'F. West was ... cause for concern': 3.1.95 statement in inquest file, National Archives HO 336/693.

McMaster 'He did not ... himself': RW trial evidence, 7.11.95.

FW crying Boxing Day/stayed in cell: 3.1.95 statement of fellow inmate (name redacted) inquest file, National Archives, HO 336/693.

FW appeared 'normal' on 1.1.95: 5.1.95 governor's report, inquest file, National Archives, HO 336/693.

Fellow inmate (name redacted) 'On that Sunday ... usual self': 3.1.95 statement, inquest file, National Archives, HO 336/693.

Body discovered: inquest file, National Archives, HO 336/693, quoting contemporaneous statements from prison officers and nurse (names redacted).

Items in cell: inquest file, National Archives, HO 336/693.

THE FRED WEST TAPES

New Year note 'TO ROSE WEST … EVER': RW trial evidence.

Graffiti: inquest evidence, *Guardian*, 12.7.96.

CHAPTER 14 – THE DEPTHS OF HUMAN DEPRAVITY

Epigraph 'Fred West is dead … he done': RW trial evidence 1.11.95.

Post-mortem: author's interview with Dr Peter Acland.

Bennett 'that sickeningly smug … trademark': his book, *The Cromwell Street Murders*.

Prison governor 'no cause … hanged himself': governor's report 5.1.95 (name redacted), inquest file, National Archives, HO 336/693.

Goatley 'I think there was … relief': to author.

May wept uncontrollably: her book, *Inside 25 Cromwell St*.

Anna Marie wept and overdosed: her book, *Out of the Shadows*.

Barry 'I'm completely disgusted …' and all subsequent BW quotes: to author.

Partington 'People [said] … see him [in court]': to author for my podcast series, *Unheard* (Somethin' Else, 2019).

'Welcoming the award … deserved': Gloucestershire police, 31.12.94.

DC Savage off case: *The Cromwell Street Murders* (Bennett); *Independent*, 10.1.95.

Discreditable conduct: RW trial evidence, 25.10.95.

Bennett 'a huge embarrassment': his book, *The Cromwell Street Murders*.

Bennett 'When Fred killed himself … her': to author.

Charmaine photo: RW trial evidence.

Committal: author's notes.

SOURCE NOTES

Brian Leveson 'I make it clear ...' and subsequent remarks in court: RW trial transcript.

Richard Ferguson 'speculative': opening speech, 30.10.95.

Cross worn as lucky charm: May West (*Inside 25 Cromwell St.*)

Anna Marie 'I was screaming ... my father': her trial evidence 18–20.10.95.

Ashes of Charmaine: Anna Marie in her book, *Out of the Shadows*.

Belinda Allsopp (*née* Mott) 'You listen ... why?': *Fred & Rose West: A British Horror Story* (Netflix, 2025).

RW 'He promised me ... something': her trial evidence 30–31.10.95.

RW/Leveson 'It is all ... wasn't me': RW trial 1.11.95.

FW/Savage 'I mean ... that time': interview 25.2.94 played in court.

Leach/Ferguson '[He said] he would ... No': her trial evidence 7–13.11.95.

Charles Mantell 'Let us not ... lied to you ... halfway house': his summing up, 16–20.11.95.

Leveson 'You're thinking ... convicted': *Fred & Rose West: A British Horror Story* (Netflix, 2025).

RW/Goatley 'I've decided ... oh no': to author.

John West trial/suicide: court files; *Daily Telegraph*, 30.11.96.

Mum '[Fred] was an ... peace': to author.

Dave Foreman 'He was a likeable lad ... fostering': to author.

Trace Elliott (*née* Foreman) 'and of course ... frightened': to author.

Steve West jailed: to author.

Barry West's last months and death: inquest, 13.4.21.

FW/Morgan 'Oh, he's a ... with him': interview 21.4.94 (FW75).

RW 'I don't believe ... anyone': her trial evidence 31.10.95.

THE FRED WEST TAPES

Marian Partington letter to RW and reply: her book, *If You Sit Very Still*.

FW 'That's it ... ain't no more': interview 1.3.94 (FW7).

Search of Pop-in café: *Fred and Rose West Reopened* (Blink Films for ITV, 2021).

Donna Lynn Moore: Media Pack 2; and Bennett to author.

Leveson 'We have been ... another': his closing speech, RW trial, 14.11.95.

INDEX

Acland, Dr Peter 262
Agius (*née* McCall), Elizabeth 'Liz' 228–31
Albion pub, Tewkesbury 162
Alexander Hospital, Coatbridge 67
Amis, Sir Kingsley 79
Amis, Sir Martin 79

Barnes, DC Nick 243–6
Bastholm, Denise 139–40, 282
Bastholm, Mary 139–41, 206–8, 251
Bastholm, Peter 282
the Beeches, Maidstone 279
Benji and Oscar (West dogs) 188
Bennett, Detective Superintendent John 24–6, 38, 43, 44, 46–7, 50–1, 53, 58, 74, 80, 92–3, 119, 127, 128–30, 134, 135, 136–7, 151, 191–2, 196, 197, 216, 218–19, 224, 239–40, 241–2, 256, 261–2, 264

Bible, the 284
Bickerton Cottage, Much Marcle 53–4
'Billy Boy' 67–8, 192
Birmingham 56, 125, 164–6
Bishop's Cleeve 79, 200
"Black Magic Bar" 6, 149, 157, 186
Bones (missing) 117, 127, 219–22, 225–7, 240
Brady, Ian 128
Bristol 38, 56, 229
Britt, Gill 99, 172, 177–8, 205
Britton, Paul 46–7, 53, 95, 127–9
Burn, Gordon 236
Burnside, PC Steven 187
Bus Stop film (1956) 83, 84
Butler, Chief Constable Tony 264

Canavan, Scott 33, 51–2, 73, 74–5, 92, 107, 110, 117, 191

Cardiff University 134
Carson Contractors 13, 129, 166
see also Thomson, Derek
Castle, Vince 165
Chambers, Alison 35–6, 44, 45, 47–8, 49–50, 71, 124–5, 130–2, 137, 152, 226, 239
Chambers, Dezra 131
Chambers, Robert 130
Cheltenham Police Station 11
Christie, John 87
Citizen (Gloucester newspaper) 43, 57, 214
Clarke, Margaret 66–7, 214
Coates, Tony 155, 162
Cooper, Carol Ann 89–91, 96, 106–7, 110–12, 115, 116, 132, 134, 137, 152, 165, 216
Cooper, Colin 111
Cooper, Mary 111
Copeland, Ray and Faye 128
Corbett, Raymond 69
Costello, Catherine 'Rena' *see* West (née Costello, FW's first wife), Catherine 'Rena'
Costello, Edward 66
Costello, Mary 66
Courtauld Institute of Art 79
Cowley Manor, Cheltenham 188
Cracker ITV drama series 46
Crescent School, Bristol 38
Crippen, Hawley 'Dr' 87
Cromwell Street, No. 25 3–6, 9–10, 18, 24–6, 33, 38–9, 40, 41, 43, 47, 60, 71–3, 75–6, 82–4, 92, 93, 98, 99, 101, 102–3, 113, 117, 127, 131–2, 135, 136–7, 153–4, 156, 159–60, 164, 172–3, 176–88, 198–9, 202–3, 204–5, 230–5, 244, 248, 251, 254, 266, 277, 282–3
The Cromwell Street Murders (J. Bennett) 50–1
Crown Prosecution Service (CPS) 197
Crufts 11

Dahmer, Jeffrey 127
Daily Mirror 262, 269
Daily Star 99, 163
Davies, Alan 134
Davies, Daniel 134
Davies, Enfys 131
Davis, Chris 184
Durham, HMP 271
'Dutch Girl' *see* Siegenthaler, Thérèse

East End Tavern (Gloucester) 190
Edwards, Mr 243
Evans, David 75

'the Farm' 250–1, 253
Feeney, Harry 69, 77, 211,
Feeney, Patsy 69
Feeney, Peter 69
Ferguson QC, Richard 265, 269
Fingerpost Field, Bridge Farm 56, 88–9, 103, 104, 168–9, 193, 223, 239–40, 251
Flying Machine pub, Gloucester 213
Foreman, Dave, Brenda and Trace 272
Forest of Dean 13, 154–5
Fred & Rose (H. Sounes) x–xi, 262
Fred & Rose: The West Murders Channel 5 documentary 30, 168, 247
Fred & Rose West: A British Horror Story,

INDEX

Netflix documentary xi, 131, 224, 266, 270

Goatley, Leo 11, 17, 140–1, 263, 270–1
Gloucester (city) 1, 38, 56, 59, 93, 259, 266
Gloucester, HMP 51, 87
Gloucester Central Police Station 1, 11, 43, 195
Gloucester Magistrates' Court 50–1, 162
Gloucester Royal Hospital 94–5
Gloucestershire Constabulary 41, 264
Gough, John 72, 101–2
Gough, June 72, 101–3
Gough, Lynda 71–3, 74–6, 82, 101–3, 108–10, 136, 152, 156, 165, 176, 180, 196–7, 204, 216, 248
Green Lantern café, Gloucester 48, 50, 254
Gupshill Manor pub, Tewkesbury 155, 156, 160

Halliday, Kathryn 232–4
Hamer, Jayne 177
Happy Like Murderers (G. Burn) 236
Harris, DC Stephen 225, 231, 234–5, 236, 243, 245
Harrison, DC Barbara 53, 62, 87–92, 104, 114, 136, 149, 151, 154, 159, 191, 196, 224
Hill, Brian 57
Hindley, Myra xi, 128, 271
Holt, Robin 167–8
House, Chris 86–7
Hubbard, Linda 133
Hubbard, Shirley 89–91, 96, 106–7, 133–4, 135, 165, 218, 227, 232

Hucclecote Secondary School, Gloucester 13

Incest 29–30, 62–5, 176, 178, 262
Inside 25 Cromwell St. (S & M West) 65, 119
James, DI Tony 225–35
The Jigsaw Man (P. Britton) 47, 128
Jones, Andrew 111–12
Jordan's Brook House, Gloucester 130, 131

Kempley Woods 168–9, 244
Kirby (née Corbett), Isabel 69
'Kiss an Angel Good Mornin'' (Charley Pride recording) 122
Knight, Professor Bernard 24–6, 33, 37, 44–5, 49, 91, 94, 101, 116–17, 134, 153, 219, 221–2, 240, 251
Korbi, Jean 62–3, 65, 66, 67

Lake House caravan site, Gloucestershire 214–15, 30
Law, DC Darren 11, 17, 18, 35–6, 40, 68, 78, 137, 219, 223, 224
Law Society 250
Leach, Janet 11–12, 17, 18, 49, 52, 56, 64–5, 73, 74–5, 84, 103, 137, 197, 208, 221, 224, 226, 238, 250–1, 255–6, 268–9
Ledbury 57, 64, 65–6, 67
Ledbury Secondary School 62
Letterbox Field, Stonehouse Farm 56–7, 88–9, 189–91, 194–5
Letts, Bill 29–30, 31, 176, 199–201, 250
Letts, Daisy 10, 29, 31, 145, 199–202, 254

Letts, Graham 200
Leveson QC (later Sir), Brian 265–70
Lewezki, Christa *see* Robinson, Christa
Leyhill, HMP 87
Lloyd, Glenys 133
Lombard, Miss 243
Love as Always, Mum xxx (M.West) 173
Lulu 113

McAvoy, Margaret 113–14
McAvoy, Steven 113–14
McFall, Anne (aka Anna, Annie) 103–5, 108, 113, 122–3, 132, 152, 167–8, 169, 193, 208, 210, 212, 213–15, 220, 223, 240, 242, 243–4, 245–6, 253–4
McLachlan, John 210–11, 212–13
McMaster, Dr James 249, 256
McNeill, Isabella 'Isa' 210, 212–13,
Macklin, Alf 172
The Man Who Mistook His Wife for a Hat (O. Sacks) 150–1
Manns, Pat 58
Mantell, Justice Sir Charles 269–70
Mental Health Act 272–3
Metropolitan Police 46
Midland Road, No. 25 32, 78, 87, 138, 146, 192, 195–6, 202, 209, 218–19, 228–9, 248, 267
Mirror Group Newspapers 92, 269
Monroe, Marilyn 83
Moorcourt Cottage, Much Marcle 56–7, 63, 246
Moore, Donna Lynn 282–3
Moors Murders 128

Morgan, DC Jeff 53–4, 61, 71, 87, 88, 96–7, 103, 104–5, 121, 122–3, 129, 130, 136, 151–3, 154, 159–62, 163, 174–5, 190–3, 204, 224, 280
Mott, Belinda 97–9, 263, 266
Mott, Ernest 97
Mott, Juanita 76, 82, 95, 97–9, 132, 137, 225
Much Marcle 53–7, 64, 80, 127, 138, 211–12, 257
Muir-Hill (later Winglet Ltd) 39, 139
'Mum' (Rose West's prison visitor) 271–2

National Missing Persons Helpline 121
New Inn, Ledbury 66
New Street Station, Birmingham 164
Newent Girl *see* Mott, Juanita
the *News of the World* 119, 163, 273
Niagara film (1953) 83
Nickell, Rachel 46

Ofcom 275
Ogden, Howard 10–11, 17, 22, 33–5, 39, 51, 73–4, 78, 92, 137, 151, 216–17, 227, 237, 238–9, 242–3, 246–7, 249–50, 251, 256
Oakes, Vincent 207
Onions, DS Terry 7–9, 17, 18, 22–3, 32, 40–2, 47
Out of the Shadows (A.West) 177
Owen, Owen John 133
Owens, Caroline 154–63, 167, 204, 228, 231–2, 233, 265, 283

Parry, Lloyd 242
Partington, Lucy 78–9, 80–1, 93–4,

INDEX

112, 115, 137, 140, 149–50, 152, 207, 216, 263–4, 268, 281–2
Partington, Marian 79–80, 81, 82, 94, 95, 263–4, 281–2
Partington, Margaret 79, 80–1, 95
Partington, Roger 79
Penry Facial Identification 124
Pines Children's Home, Worcester 111
Pittville Park, Cheltenham 79, 81
Pop-in café, Gloucester 139, 207, 282
Press Association 250
Price, Bob 165
Price, DC Kevan 159, 165
Prinknash Abbey 129, 206
Prison Service, HM 51

Radio Times 278
Render, Helen 79
Robinson, Christa (*née* Lewezki) 38
Robinson, Royal Baden 38
Robinson, Shirley Ann 33–6, 38–41, 43–4, 74, 105, 130, 132, 137, 152, 204, 226, 239, 254
Rock, PC John 55
'Rolf' 190

Sade, Marquis de 136
St. Bartholomew's church, Much Marcle 80, 138
St. James's Junior School, Gloucester 209
St. Paul's Primary School, Gloucester 12–13
Savage, DC Hazel 1–4, 10, 11, 16–17, 18, 26–8, 32, 33–6, 40, 44, 45, 47, 48–9, 50, 51, 54–5, 59–61, 72–3, 75, 76, 77–8, 80, 82, 105–11, 115–17,

124–6, 129, 137, 138, 139, 141, 143–5, 147, 148–9, 153–4, 160–1, 163–6, 167–8, 189, 193–5, 205–8, 211, 214, 215, 217–18, 219–21, 224–5, 264, 268, 283
Seven Year Itch film (1955) 83
Seventh-day Adventist Church, Cromwell St, Gloucester 5
Sex and the Vampire film (1970) 108
Shirley's mate *see* Chambers, Alison
Siegenthaler, Thérèse 76–7, 82, 91, 106, 135, 136, 137, 152, 197–9, 218
Simmons, Edith 198
Skulls (motorcycle gang) 122
Smurthwaite, DC Neville 42
Sounes, Howard ix–xii, 85–7, 92, 93, 119, 120, 140–1, 172, 186–7, 199–202, 262, 273–80
Stagg, Colin 46
Stanniland, Ben 75, 156
Stockholm syndrome 224
Strictly Come Dancing BBC television show 271–2
Stroud Court, Nailsworth
Sun, the 163, 229
Sunday Mirror 85, 92, 119, 262

'Teddy Bear's Picnic' (Kennedy and Bratton) 69
Thomson, Derek 123, 166, 167
Today newspaper 120
Trotter, John 212
Tyler, Glenys (*née* Letts) 30
Tyler, Jim 30

Unheard: The Fred & Rose West Tapes (podcasts) 172

Wass, Sasha (later KC) 265
Watermead Caravan Park,
    Gloucester 213, 243
West (later Anne-Marie Davis), Anna
    Marie 9, 27, 64–5, 68, 70, 146, 155,
    156, 163, 172, 173–4, 176–8, 181,
    183–4, 186, 202, 215, 222, 231–2,
    234, 243, 256, 263, 266, 271
West, Barry 3, 14, 15–16, 27, 32,
    174–6, 178, 179–80, 182–3, 185–6,
    187, 188, 203, 263, 272–80
West, Catherine 168
West (née Costello, FW's first wife),
    Catherine 'Rena' 27, 65–9, 70, 74,
    77–8, 88–9, 103, 104, 108, 112–13,
    122, 132, 138, 140, 145, 147, 148,
    152, 171, 190–5, 209–14, 215, 221,
    222, 239, 242, 243, 253, 267
West, Charmaine 27, 67–8, 70, 74,
    77–8, 87–8, 108, 112–13, 138,
    145–7, 148, 152, 188, 190, 191–4,
    195–6, 200, 209, 211–13, 214, 215,
    219–22, 242, 243, 248, 255, 264–5,
    266, 267, 283
West, Daisy (FW's mother) 54–5, 56,
    61–2, 67, 80, 168–9, 244, 283
West, Daisy (FW's sister) 54
West, Doug (FW's brother) 54, 58
West, Gwen (FW's sister) 54
West, Heather 2–4, 7–8, 10, 13–17,
    21–3, 24, 26, 27, 28, 34, 37–8,
    49–50, 77, 78, 124, 137, 138, 143–5,
    152, 155, 166, 183–6, 187, 188, 200,
    206, 221, 226–7, 239, 246, 247–8,
    255, 267, 268, 273, 277, 282
West, John (FW's brother) 54, 67,
    168–9, 171–5, 178, 208, 239, 244,
    250–1, 271
West, Kitty (FW's sister) 54, 62–4
West, Louise 27, 204
West, Lucy Anna 27
West, May 'Mae' 27, 30, 43, 65, 119–
    20, 123, 141, 143–5, 163, 172–3,
    174, 177, 178–9, 180, 184, 186, 187,
    195, 196, 231, 263, 271, 281
West (née Letts), Rose x–xi, 2, 3, 4–12,
    116–19, 22–3, 28–32, 33–4, 38—48,
    50, 52, 55, 60–1, 72, 75–9, 81,
    88–91, 96–7, 99, 102, 105, 113–14,
    119–22, 124, 125, 127–8, 132,
    135–6, 140–1, 144–9, 153–63, 165,
    167, 171, 173–88, 192–3, 195–7,
    199–206, 208, 216–18, 222, 228–9,
    232–4, 236, 238–9, 241–3, 244–45,
    246–51, 252–3, 254–5, 256, 258,
    263, 264–72, 280–2, 283–4
West, Rosemary Jnr 27
West, Stephen 'Steve' 4, 9, 27, 43, 79,
    119, 163, 179–80, 181, 182, 184,
    187, 188, 242, 251, 252–3, 274
West, Tara Jayne 27
West, Violet 55
West, Walter (FW's father) 54, 55,
    56, 168–9, 283
Whittaker, Dr David 134–5, 199, 218,
    264–5
Wilcox, DC Bob 124
Williams, Rob 186–7
Willows caravan site, Gloucester 212
Winchester Crown Court 265–71
Winget Ltd, Gloucester 39, 139
Winson Green, HMP 237–9, 246–8,
    249, 250–8
Worcester Girls see Cooper, Carol
    Ann and Hubbard, Shirley